T0399548

'This important and exquisite addition to the field of coach supervision extends the supervisor's range of possibilities, reaches into new territories and broadens our understanding of what is possible in the supervision experience. These richly varied chapters explore supervision processes ranging from the analytic to developmental, spanning the terrain of creative approaches and widening our view on several innovative modalities that will make the supervision accessible to more coaches. This contribution to the field of coaching is particularly relevant at this new stage in the field of coach supervision, when we are ready for diverse perspectives and approaches that provide new milieus for every coach's development.'

Pam McLean, *PhD, MCC, CEO, Hudson Institute of Coaching, US*

'Thank you, Jo for bringing this work together. A truly delicious text that draws the reader to enquire further, deeper, wider, taller and more wholly into themselves and their group supervision practice. The Simple Rules aptly set the stage for what follows – hearing from multiple voices in the field, refreshingly international in their tone and experience. I will savour the book's wise companionship as I navigate the complexities of my work.'

Michelle Lucas, *Lead Coach and Coach Supervisor,*
Greenfields Consulting Limited, UK

'The image of a prism or cut gem best conveys how this book enables the reader to enter an exploration of group supervision from different perspectives and angles, each quite different, though resonant, each shining a different light on practice and process. One enabled surprisingly swift deep enquiry for me into a place of stuckness with a supervisee. Others provided practical guidance, scaffolding for different processes. Some opened new horizons or took me deeper into familiar concepts. It is inspiring to learn from the learning of the very different authors who share doubts and dilemmas as well as seasoned insights.'

Carolyn Mumby, *Chair, BACP Coaching Division,*
Coach–Therapist, Supervisor and Trainer, UK

'This book has something for everyone (practitioners and participants) who engages in Group Supervision. The different perspectives the authors chose to approach this subject has connected with me from the head, heart or gut and, in some chapters, all three. You will find stimulus on developmental, ethical or good practice and heartfelt connected support on the subject after reading this collection of generous and supportive writings. The eldership of Joan Wilmot to supervision flows through in her chapter that was written with depth, experience and humility is truly inspiring.'

Felicia Lauw, *Director, Reflect4Ward Pte. Ltd., EMCC Global Accreditation*
and Supervision Workgroup, AoCS APAC Regional Co-ordinator, SINGAPORE

'A range of authors, some writing for the first time, introduce us to their personal journeys as a supervisor facilitating groups of coaches/supervisors exploring with reflective honesty the joys and intricacies of facilitating the dynamics presented in a group. Reviewing the development of coaching supervision over 50 years through to chapters on different models which enhance the group experience includes eco-therapy principles, Mirror model, peer supervision/chain and the Theory U model. Developing virtual group supervision and the digital disembodiment that can be experienced and a standard toolkit of creative approaches gently encourages you to first experience them yourself. For the new supervisee coming to group supervision there is an illuminating chapter describing what you might expect in taster group sessions. A wealth of experience is generously shared by seasoned supervisors encouraging you to be curious and explore new approaches in group supervision.'

Carole Davidson, *Accredited Executive Coach and Supervisor, EMCC Global Accreditation Volunteer and Accreditation Assessor, UK*

'This book is a compendium of approaches for those considering running supervision groups, with lots of practical exercises, insights and structural tips from 12 experienced practitioners, backed by their actual experience, theory and/or research. The book is structured in three stages: overarching principles, specific modalities and peer groups. Solid theory is explained in a jargon-free way with a lot of insightful and real experience of running groups provided. A wide range of topics awaits the reader, including psychodynamic approaches, complexity principles and practical aspects like how to set up and provide tasters for a supervision group. Working virtually is a recurring theme and some ways of overcoming barriers to online communication are identified. There are some refreshingly new topics like working in nature, creativity in groups and adapting existing theories and models for both the experienced and less experienced group leader to try. A useful addition to the coaching supervision bookshelf enabling the application of a range of techniques and practical aspects to running supervision groups.'

Peter Welch, *AoCS Co-Founder, Executive and Team Coach, Coach Supervisor and Thinking Partner, UK*

Coaching Supervision Groups

Written by experienced coaching supervisors, this book offers a kaleidoscope of wisdom drawn from a complex professional field. Theoretical concepts, practitioner research, models and techniques are brought alive here through the lived experience of the authors.

As coaching supervisors continue to develop their practice, those wishing to extend their skills into group work step into a new context which stretches and strengthens their own learning, as well as that of supervisees, in this mutual, intentional learning environment. Coaching supervisors are encouraged to begin with the inner journey, developing their own knowledge as each chapter offers a new perspective, enabling readers to gain a philosophical understanding of the process, which will guide them on their journey through the unpredictable terrain of group work.

Coaches, mentors and other practitioners looking for a Supervision Group experience will gain insights into the range of opportunities available, opening myriad possibilities for furthering personal and professional learning.

Jo Birch brings 20 years' experience providing supervision to coaches, psychotherapists and leaders. She is a passionate member of several international professional, research and practice communities. As Director of Crucial Difference, she leads an international team providing cutting-edge supervision training for coaches around the world.

Coaching Supervision Groups

Resourcing Practitioners

Edited by Jo Birch

Routledge
Taylor & Francis Group

LONDON AND NEW YORK

First published 2022
by Routledge
2 Park Square, Milton Park, Abingdon, Oxon OX14 4RN

and by Routledge
605 Third Avenue, New York, NY 10158

Routledge is an imprint of the Taylor & Francis Group, an informa business

British Library Cataloguing-in-Publication Data
A catalogue record for this book is available from the British Library

Library of Congress Cataloging-in-Publication Data
Names: Birch, Jo, 1957– editor.
Title: Coaching supervision groups : resourcing in practitioners / edited by Jo Birch.
Description: Abingdon, Oxon ; New York, NY : Routledge, 2022. | Includes bibliographical references and index.
Identifiers: LCCN 2021025455 (print) | LCCN 2021025456 (ebook) | ISBN 9780367698300 (hardback) | ISBN 9780367698355 (paperback) | ISBN 9781003143451 (ebook)
Subjects: LCSH: Personal coaching. | Counselors—Supervision of.
Classification: LCC BF637.P36 C637 2022 (print) | LCC BF637.P36 (ebook) | DDC 158.3—dc23
LC record available at https://lccn.loc.gov/2021025455
LC ebook record available at https://lccn.loc.gov/2021025456

ISBN: 978-0-367-69830-0 (hbk)
ISBN: 978-0-367-69835-5 (pbk)
ISBN: 978-1-003-14345-1 (ebk)

DOI: 10.4324/9781003143451

Typeset in Times New Roman
by Apex CoVantage, LLC

To my daughter, Anni.

Contents

Contributors

Jo Birch, MA, FRSA Supervisor, executive coach and psychotherapist Jo brings people together in global learning communities. As Director of Crucial Difference & International Centre for Reflective Practice, Jo leads an international team providing cutting-edge training for coaches to become supervisors and to continue developing as leaders in the profession. She brings two decades of experience as an accredited supervisor, together with her commitment to influence and extend the growth of supervision across the professional field – previously Chair of BACP Coaching, board member of Association of Coaching Supervisors (AOCS) and European Association of Supervision and Coaching (EASC). Jo is co-editor of the European Mentoring and Coaching Council (EMCC) Mastery Series publication *Coaching Supervision: Advancing Practice, Changing Landscapes* and was series editor of *Thinking Global in Coaching Today*. Jo lives in Edinburgh and loves exploring – kayaking the Scottish coast, mountain biking and having adventures with family.

Dr. Kathryn M Downing, D.Prof., J.D., PCC Kathryn is a coaching supervisor, executive coach, author and speaker. She has a joyous commitment to life-long learning and belief in the value and rewards of regular reflective practice. Her expertise and passion are in virtual coaching supervision. In 2021, she was awarded the Professional Doctorate (D.Prof.) in Coaching Supervision at Middlesex University, London. She is Co-Programme Leader, and Co-Creator of CSA's Certificate in Developing Self as Group Coaching Supervisor. She is Co-Lead of the ICF Community of Practice for Coaching Supervision. She is a member of the Faculty Team at Hudson Institute of Coaching and faculty for Coaching Supervision Academy – UK and Asia Pacific. She lives in Santa Barbara, California where she enjoys mountain hiking, beach walks, hosting friends and family for gatherings with food and wine and living with gratitude and joy.

Louie J N Gardiner, BA (hons), MBA, FRSA Doctoral researcher, Accredited Master Coach and Supervisor, Change Consultant, facilitator/trainer Louie has been passionately involved in liberating human potential for 25-plus years. Her pioneering approaches are born of an enduring commitment to act for the well-being of all and to safeguard her own trustworthiness in whatever she does.

Her body of work represents the fusion of real-world practice and academic research. Presence in action and symmathesic agency are at the heart what she offers. This integrating body of work – underpinned by principles of natural inclusion, complexity thinking and primal animation – brings together radically different approaches to catalysing and nurturing personal and collective capacities for generative change – consciously, creatively, playfully. Louie's past roles include CEO, Board Trustee, Head of Corporate Performance & Development, lecturer to undergraduate degrees and post-graduate. She has contributed to both academic and practice-based journals; for example, *Human Arenas*, *Cybernetics and Human Knowing*, *e-O&P Journal*, *Coaching Today*, *the3rdi magazine*, and book chapters in *The Collaboratory* and *Coaching Supervision: Advancing Practice, Changing Landscapes*.

Catherine Gorham Catherine Gorham is an independent EMCC accredited coach and supervisor and leadership consultant. Her practice extends from high performance through to mental health conversations, offering space for individuals to explore their vulnerability and possibilities for change. She is accredited in the Psychological Safety Index, supporting teams to benchmark their journey towards deeper trust and richer dialogue. Catherine's grandfather modelled the uniqueness of outdoor conversations which stayed with her beyond childhood. Her training in ecotherapy was a spiritual experience as nature's offer to be her co-partner felt profound. She now shares her passion with other practitioners through master classes and specialist supervision.

Leanne Lowish Leanne Lowish works as a leadership and team coach, consultant, facilitator and coaching supervisor in organisation and culture transformation. She has a deep professional and spiritual alignment with the journey of Theory U. In writing this chapter she draws on two decades of meditation, sensing and inquiry practices, and a commitment to a spiritual path (The Diamond Approach), as well as her knowledge, training and practice of Internal Family Systems, psychosynthesis, trauma, adult development and embodiment practice (including yoga and dance practices). Originally from New Zealand, she lived for 25 years in the UK, and now lives in the US. She attended Coaching Supervision Academy's first Diploma in Coaching Supervision in 2005–2006 and now leads the Diploma in Asia Pacific and North America.

Jeannette Marshall Jeannette Marshall is CEO of Marshall Vere Associates, an Accredited Master Executive Coach and the Association for Coaching's (AC's) Director of Accreditation, responsible for the delivery of AC Accreditation Schemes. She is a member of the Global Coaching and Mentoring Alliance (GCMA) and the working party for the Global Code of Ethics for Coaches, Mentors and Supervisors. Jeannette has contributed to *The Trainee Coach Handbook* and the Association for Coaching's *Excellence in Coaching: The Industry Guide 4th Edition*.

Ana Pliopas, PhD Ana was born in Brazil, and she received her coaching and coaching supervision training in the United States. She firmly believes coaching supervision is central for coaching practice and coach development. Ana has experienced coaching supervision from a very diverse range of supervisors, perspectives and formats: individual and group supervision, supervision of supervision and supervision triads. Ana held leadership positions for more than 20 years in such organisations as Goldman Sachs, ING, and JPMorgan, among others. She holds a PhD degree in Organizational Studies from Fundação Getulio Vargas, Brazil, where she is part of the faculty.

David Rothauser, MA, MS, PCC David brings expertise in applied psychoanalysis and interpersonal dynamics to his work as a coach supervisor and executive coach. He began his career as a schoolteacher and went into non-profit leadership before starting his independent coaching practice. David provides both individual and group supervision and has honed his craft by working closely with his own supervisors for over a decade. He studied coaching supervision at Oxford Brookes University, executive coaching at Columbia University, psychodynamic group leadership at the Center for Group Studies and Modern Psychoanalysis at the Center for Modern Psychoanalytic Studies.

Brenda Routt, MS, PCC, RN Brenda Routt has entered the realm of coach supervision as a pinnacle to a career in executive leadership, business development, coaching and consulting. She is known for her enthusiasm to learn and her support of those who care for others, whether patients, leaders or coaches in any industry. Supervision has been an integral aspect of her continuous growth since she became a certified coach, exploring the myriad of themes and styles of supervision. Currently, she is involved in peer supervision chains, a participant in supervision groups and coordinator of supervisors serving coaches in 28 countries. Brenda blends passion for learning, creativity and commitment to supporting others.

Olga Rybina, PhD, MCC, ICF Olga is a Psychological Sciences graduate, entrepreneur and co-founder of the international coaching academy, 5 Prism, in St. Petersburg, Russia. She was born and lives in Russia, entering the coaching profession through studying mathematics and clinical psychology. Mathematics taught Olga to think structurally and critically and her experience as a clinical psychologist showed her the value of each person. In 2002, she became involved in the study of stress prevention methods for professionals in the helping professions. She has been studying coaching for over a decade and has been influential in developing the coaching community in Russia – undertaking roles within the International Coaching Federation (ICF) Russia Chapter. In 2015, in collaboration with Anna Ovdienko Vidova, she created Russia's first supervisor training program for coaches. She is the creator of the "Mirror" model of group supervision for coaches and co-author of a unique method,

'5 prisms,' which helps coaches to use psychological theories in their coaching practice.

Barb Udale Barb Udale has over 35 years' experience as a leadership and executive coach, group facilitator and, more recently, as a coach supervisor. Her interest and expertise are in creating the right environment and relationship for people to reflect, grow and develop. Barb particularly enjoys working in a group setting where individual development can be enhanced by the learning and reflections of others. She is currently involved in running a successful peer supervision chain, supervising groups of coaches involved in supporting international aid workers, and of course is regularly in supervision herself.

Joan Wilmot Shohet Joan Wilmot Shohet co-founded Centre for Supervision and Team Development (CSTD) in London in 1979, and works as a trainer, supervisor, psychotherapist and mediator. Her particular interest is in working with systems using organisational and family constellation work. She has been running supervision trainings and working with teams for over 40 years. Her passion is for enabling people to find the work they love and love the work they do. She is married with four sons, is a member of a theatre company in Findhorn and is learning the accordion and Greek very slowly!

Acknowledgements

My heartfelt gratitude to the authors who have provided the substance and soul of this book. I have been honoured to be alongside each person as they moved in different ways towards completion of their chapters, together creating a diverse collection, resourcing our coaching and supervision communities.

Our work was enhanced by the keen eye of Diane Parker and invaluable support from my friend and colleague, Sam Fremantle.

My deep appreciation for June Karenina, my supervisor and mentor, who walked alongside me for over two decades.

Foreword

Having spent many years reading about various models and tools on supervision, I welcome the writing here in this book that is grounded in the supervision space, while holding the models and tools lightly. Many of these chapters enable us as readers to meet the authors and sit alongside them, learning with our colleagues as the writing unfolds.

This book on group supervision in coaching is a welcome addition to the literature both on group work *per se* and on the distinct practice of group supervision, about which Joan Wilmot Shohet writes in her closing chapter. All contributors bring to our attention the very rich and diverse range of group work being practised by supervisors in the UK, US, New Zealand, Brazil and in Russia today.

It is a very practical book for those who are either venturing into group supervision for the first time, or for experienced supervisors who are open to learning new ways of working. Contributors give valuable and detailed steps, from the beginning stage of contracting to the co-creation of the process with which they are engaged. Case studies of memorable learning experiences are threaded throughout the book and bring such approaches to life. I found myself reflecting on my own approach to contracting and learning new ways of thinking about how I engage with individuals and groups to co-create a learning space that fits our particular purpose.

Group supervision with coaches has developed from a variety of sources and here there is no hesitation in some authors' acknowledgment of our debt to psychodynamic ideas that help us understand and work with group dynamics, knowledge of which is so vital in group work of all kinds. David Rothauser gives a detailed account of the psychodynamic approach to group supervision, sharing his hard-earned and painful lessons about group dynamics as a novice teacher in the chaos of the classroom. Olga Rybina works with a model derived from the psychoanalyst Michael Balint's group work (1957), which brought psychodynamic understanding to doctor–patient relationships in the 1950s.

Some of the material is research-based, as in the chapters by Kathryn M Downing and Louie J N Gardiner (in Chapter 3); while others, Leanne Lowish, Catherine Gorham, and Louie J N Gardiner (in Chapter 9), write from their own lived experience, via autoethnography, drawing on case studies and client stories.

Each writer shares their own experience of group supervision both as leader and participant. We feel we are with them in their open spaces or in their rooms together.

Themes of co-creation and emergent learning feature strongly in approaches to the practices described in many chapters, such as that of Barb Udale and Brenda Routt, describing how they set up and facilitates a peer supervision chain with a group of colleagues who had trained together. Brenda Routt finds the words which sum up for her the importance of setting up a peer learning chain as the '*joy of learning, the messiness of practice and the heart of collegiality*.' Her words resonate with my own experience of learning and developing as a supervisor myself. Ana Pliopas writes about a peer triad set up from those which had already formed during their training. With a social constructionist perspective, she charts their transformation over time as the triad becomes a meaning-making space. I also resonated with Ana Pliopas' writing about the result of the triads development as '*a subtle, unpredictable transformation in each of us, as we drank the content of the cauldron: the new meanings we made*.'

Reading Jeannette Marshall's chapter on taster group supervision sessions and both the chain supervision experience and peer triad reminds us that there are various stages involved as we develop our knowledge about this practice and begin development of ourselves as coach supervisors. These chapters describe the different kinds of support and structure that facilitate and provide experience of reflective practice that can lead to our beginning to make meaning of supervision in wider social and personal contexts.

Jo Birch opens her chapter on creative approaches with the unexpected image she showed to participants as she opened her webinar. I felt a sudden rush of tenderness for her and her '*not quite flawlessly formed*' raspberry jelly. This set the tone for me of this chapter on using creative approaches in group supervision practice that she describes as deeply personal as well as playful and lighthearted. I loved the invitation to immerse myself into the creative process and accompany her as the chapter unfolded. The first image I had was of a piece of clay waiting to be thrown onto a potter's wheel and was aware that I was missing my own time to make art. There is rich learning here should you too decide to accompany Jo. The thread of love in supervision practice is woven throughout much of this book and Jo describes that for her '*the heart symbolises the essence that holds this work*.'

The invitational tenor of this collection invites us to step into the process of engaging with self and others in the different groups described here. Rather than following the sequence of the chapters from start to finish, notice what you are drawn to. I went straight to Catherine Gorham's chapter first as I was intrigued by the title of her chapter on working with nature. It is a beautifully clear invitation to group supervisors and supervisees to work with nature as co-partner. Taking this position, she explains, '*Prompts a softer tread on the earth as we enter as guests in the space*.' Each stage of the process of setting up the group is described in detail, and she gives some moving examples of the many gifts that this way of working offers her, her supervisees and their clients. The richness of her accounts of group learning and development of both leaders and participants is such that it feels as if we are present with the group in nature.

The idea that we enter as guests into the supervision space resonates strongly with me. Michael Paterson, director of a Pastoral Supervision course, defines the emerging discipline as '*a safe, boundaried and hospitable place*' (Paterson, 2020). What might it mean for us and our colleagues if we included in our approach to group supervision the idea of hospitality?

In many of these chapters I saw that, wherever and however the writers have arranged their group gatherings, they are attending to what being hospitable asks of them, to prepare themselves to be present and to serve their colleagues readily with the process that they have co-created and to share who they are, with humanity, in a contained and emergent learning space.

In addition to the key role of hospitality I was also struck by Kathryn M Downing's use of the term '*guardian of the reflective space.*' I think this is a valuable addition to the ideas of hosting and of containing, as each describes leadership roles within supervision groups. Leadership of the kind written about in many of these chapters is enriched by another key ingredient, compassion for our common humanity, a common theme throughout the book.

While learning, either in facilitated or peer-led groups, we will each meet ourselves, with both our current awareness and the yet-to-be-known parts of ourselves. A recurring theme here is that we all need to understand the ways in which being in groups evokes our earliest experiences of being in a group, namely, our family of origin. It was here that we developed our attachment styles that guide our ways of being in relationships, some of which may hinder our learning capacity. This means that when working with emergence and co-creation we need a safe contained space within which we can be with whatever arises in the relational field and be held and contained enough to face our vulnerabilities.

We know that relational learning is an emotional business because naturally we will meet who we really are on the way as we engage with one another. This means that vulnerability is a strong theme in many of these chapters. I think that here we have a chance to be reminded of the importance of learning to know and accept ourselves and to be at ease with our common humanity. The leader who is at ease with their own vulnerability will model this way of being and bring this into the relational field, enabling emotional co-regulation in the group and allowing the nervous systems of group members to synchronise and find ease together.

We can come to know ourselves in a variety of ways. One of the key elements of supervision is that we learn through reflective processes. One such process is that explored in Leanne Lowish's beautifully open-hearted and compassionate writing in her chapter on working through her own experience of Otto Scharmer's Theory U process. She shares movingly what it has meant to her to develop embodied consciousness and to accompany her group members into ways of being that enable all to stay present with themselves and their emergent learning. We accompany her and her groups as she brings her group members into contact with head, heart and belly, with their own embodied consciousness. I found myself drawn to journey with her and to know those places she describes for myself.

Elsewhere, Louie J N Gardiner invites us into her lived experience of conscious embodiment, what it feels like moment to moment to be in movement as a person with awareness, and with acceptance of what is unfolding. As she stays curious and open to her struggles with being in a group, she invites us to identify with her. She shares the Seven Simple Rules of coaching supervision, the essential behaviours that she weaves through her practice that include working with love, and we celebrate when love once again enters the lexicon of supervision writing (as also described in Birch & Welch, 2019).

I wholeheartedly believe that love matters in supervision. Eliat Aram of the Tavistock Institute of Human Relations describes leadership of the kind demonstrated in this book as *'that which works with – not against – not knowing, uncertainty, ambiguity, frailty. All these exist in love'* (Aram, 2015).

As I read many of the chapters, I recalled the words of one of my transpersonal psychotherapy trainers, Ian Gordon Brown, who said that the purpose of our journey in life is to *'know yourself, love yourself and be yourself.'* I find his axiom to be a thread running through many of the chapters in this book. In the kind of group supervision described here, we find rich accounts of how to work and engage with the meaning of each of these purposes for our life's journey.

I loved reading this book. It touched my heart many times and stimulated my thinking about working with groups in supervision, both as a group member and as a facilitator. At the heart of all the writers' endeavours is a firm belief that we can all be met at a deep level as we share our soul's journey with others through our personal and professional lives.

Fiona Adamson,
Executive Coach Supervisor

References

Aram, E. (2015). *Lunchtime Talk: Does Love Matter? Fear and Compassion in Organisations and Leadership*. London: Tavistock Institute of Human Relations.

Balint, M. (1957). *The Doctor, His Patient and the Illness*. London: Tavistock Publications. For Current Balint Inspired Work in the UK. https://balint.co.uk.

Birch, J., & Welch, P. (2019). *Coaching Supervision. Advancing Practice, Changing Landscapes*. London: Routledge.

Paterson, M. (2020). *Between a Rock and a Hard Place*. Fife, Scotland: Independently Published.

Introduction

Where does this book begin?

> *I'd like to run a coaching supervision group. Where do I start? What do I need to know?*

Over the last five or six years many qualified and experienced coaching supervisors have approached me with these questions.

At first, I wondered if I could design something simple . . . perhaps a 'guide' or a handbook that could easily be followed by coaches and supervisors. However, within the shortest moment, I smiled at myself. It seemed naïve, and probably impossible, to capture the complexities of the group experience in something simple. Instead, I could illustrate the complex nature of working with groups through an edited volume.

I felt excited about bringing together a group of people who could communicate a diverse yet coherent range of wisdom, experiences and skills to help coaching supervisors make informed choices as they move towards leading and participating in groups. I have included here facilitated coaching supervision groups, peer supervision groups and the asynchronous group experience of a chain supervision process.

In creating this book, I wanted to offer readers something tangible, offering different ways in which coaches can design, facilitate and participate in group experiences. Although the central task of a coaching supervision group remains that of supervision, offering and facilitating a group experience is a complex, dynamic and challenging task. I realised that supervisors wanted to *understand* more about groups, group process and individual behaviour in groups.

I looked across the range of our work as coaches. My own work, situated within an extensive psychotherapeutic background and within leadership and organisational development, reflects some of the dilemmas that exist for coaching supervisors. We find ourselves drawing from a longer embedded tradition of compulsory supervision in the psychotherapy field and yet, as coaches, we are working in different contexts with vastly different systemic influences shaping us and our work. Coaching supervisors are creating distinct bodies of knowledge as the profession moves from the pioneering stage into more maturity, embracing the emerging

DOI: 10.4324/9781003143451-1

wisdom of practitioners, supervisors, researchers, clients and the work itself. You will see this vitality and zest for expressing the diversity within the field through the work of the authors in this book.

When we turn to coaching supervision in groups, I wanted to offer theoretical insights that would stimulate you, the reader, to consider your own way of understanding the world, bringing together the paradigms in which our work is situated as the basis for your own philosophical approach to groups – and the development of the individuals within them.

Why choose group supervision?

As coaches and supervisors, we might consider ourselves a community of both supervisors and supervisees. The journey of supervision for many begins in coach training and may continue throughout our careers, including 'supervision of supervision' as some of us become supervisors and wish to continue to deepen and develop our practice. As we attend to our personal and professional development, we may find ourselves moving between individual and group supervision, at times incorporating both, serving different needs.

In my conversations with coaching supervisors, each has offered reasons for their attraction to coaching supervision in groups: to gain advanced development as a supervisor, to embed a broader range of skills, to increase theoretical understanding of people and groups and as a way to develop personally through the group environment. In locating supervision groups within a business portfolio, supervisors have spoken about responding to a need within the coaching community, with more coaches looking for group experiences, also as a potentially more lucrative business venture.

Our reasons are as varied as we are as practitioners, each being personal and valid. It is important to acknowledge our underlying motivation, which is not fixed and may change over time, as it is critical in shaping 'what comes next' as we move into the offer of a supervision group. It shapes when, how, who (and more) as we craft our invitation and communicate this to prospective participants.

In my practice, I have noticed a growth in demand for supervision groups. For those new to supervision, it can be perceived as a 'safer' starting place. For others, it is a more economically viable alternative to one-to-one work or is in addition to one-to-one supervision to get wider experience in a relational context or is an antidote to the isolation experienced by some coaches. Coaches have also expressed a desire to be part of a committed community of learning, and to understand themselves better in the group environment.

What has drawn you towards this book at this time?

Throughout my professional career as a psychotherapist, I have been prescribed, and allocated to, supervision groups as a participant. I learned through being in them what worked for me, and what did not.

When I have chosen a group supervision experience myself, I have done so by asking myself a series of reflective questions. What is drawing me towards a group? Why now? What is it that I most wish to gain? What else am I noticing? What expectations am I already holding with regard to the group?

I may look towards the facilitator. Who are you? What experiences and training do you bring? How do you describe your work? What is your theoretical or methodological understanding underpinning the work of the group? How many people are in the group and what is your rationale for choosing that number? Who are the other people in terms of their work and background? And sometimes I may ask no questions at all, simply trusting this group is 'for' me at this time. With questions – or not – I ultimately sense in my body (not in my head) whether this seems to be a fit for me at this time.

In exploring group experiences, I notice my needs change with time. Sometimes I have wanted a group where participants have a similar work focus or level of experience, addressing a need of mine at that time; at other times I have looked for a group with the greatest diversity of background and experience. Each has served a different developmental edge at particular times in my life. My first step is always that of attuning to myself.

You will notice I am using myself and my experience to illuminate more about the nature of supervision in groups. You will encounter this first-person lens many times throughout the book, and it is not by chance! Your own experiences in groups, in choosing groups, in being a participant in groups, and in leading groups, are key sources of learning in the process of becoming skilled in facilitating supervision groups.

Finding your way through the book

The aim of this book is to provide you with a range of perspectives on group supervision through which, as coaching supervisors, you can better define and evolve your own approach to group supervision; as supervisees, you might consider how to best meet your needs when choosing and engaging in a group experience.

As the authors came together, and the chapters took form, this collection of work began to find a flow. You will notice I describe the chapters as finding 'form.' This book is both a professional foundational text, *and* the result of twelve personal journeys through the process of translating knowing and experience into words. Each author voyaged through smooth waters and rough seas, culminating in the completion of their chapter. Many notice that through the process of writing they and their practice have been changed. As editor, I have been immensely honoured to accompany them and have drawn my own support from our relationships. I share this with you because the group experience touches each of us.

As you move through the book, you will notice that the inner processing of the supervisor – before, during and after the group – is critical to every group process, whether this takes place outdoors in nature or on the virtual screen, in a long-term peer group or a taster group supervision experience.

As reader you may find yourself drawn to some chapters more than others. From time to time, you may want to return and review the chapters to which you were most, or least, attracted – an opportunity to notice how your interests and needs change.

Chapters 1 to 4 offer perspectives on understanding humans, groups and systems from different paradigms and show the application of these within the Coaching Supervision field. None of these are 'the only way' – there are many theoretical perspectives through which to understand groups. See what resonates with you and your practice; follow what inspires you. These chapters are offered based on an assumption that a theoretical understanding enables supervisors to place the turbulence of 'process' in group supervision within a context and therefore become better able to embrace all that unfolds.

In Chapter 1, I begin by drawing out essential considerations when running a coaching supervision group. However, these may not be what you might expect! I invite you into a reflective process, acknowledging that what you are thinking and believing are the foundations from which the group experience will be created. Remembering that the central task remains that of supervision, I first invite you to engage with the Seven Simple Rules of coaching supervision and then pose a series of questions, carefully designed to help you to peel back layers of awareness. You may discover insights as you go, and you may find that additional questions surface. My invitation is to carry these with you as you move through the book.

In Chapter 2, David Rothauser introduces a psychodynamic approach, offering an accessible description of the foundational concepts of transference, resistance, counter-transference and parallel process. He brings these alive through vignettes and his own experience, illustrating how the concepts can be applied in practice as we seek to understand the behaviour of ourselves and others in groups.

In Chapter 3, Louie J N Gardiner interweaves personal inquiry with her unique fusion of philosophy and theory, illuminating how these come alive in group supervision practice scenarios. In doing so she offers a vivid and fascinating exploration that brings alive the essence of natural inclusion, complexity thinking and primal animation. She opens the space for us to deepen our own living-learning inquiry into the foundations of our own coaching supervision practice and how this translates into group contexts.

Ana Pliopas opens a narrative account of a peer supervision experience in Chapter 4. The group begins with a structure and form that changes over time, meeting the needs of participants as they themselves develop as supervisors. Her exploration brings us into this present turbulent time, and Ana demonstrates how the group context continues to support them. Social Constructionist theory helps Ana explore her experience and the co-created meanings that have arisen between the group members.

In the next four chapters we take a deep dive into first-person experiencing, demonstrating how our own process is essential to understanding. These chapters (5–8) offer insights into 'being' in the group, relating to self, others and context, illuminating the inner journey of the supervisor through the four lenses of the authors.

Leanne Lowish brings Theory U alive in Chapter 5 through her auto-ethnographical account of her journey through the U process with a coaching supervision group. This involves moving away from habitual thinking towards 'presencing.' Leanne demonstrates through her own experience the challenge of holding steady amidst the chorus of her inner Voices of Judgement, Criticism and Fear as she traverses the U process.

In Chapter 6 we move outdoors with Catherine Gorham, inviting nature to participate alongside us as a co-dynamic partner in the supervision group experience. Catherine's Outdoor Supervision Frame attends to psychological safety through a balance of contracting, containing and connecting. Examples drawn from Catherine's work demonstrate the power of this approach.

We move from the outdoors into online experiencing for the next two chapters.

Invited to participate in a new online group, Louie J N Gardiner shares her embodied processing with us in Chapter 7, illustrating that the dynamics playing out in a group are shaped by whatever is going on in each individual, irrespective of the role they play. She demonstrates how crucial it is to attend to others and that this capacity is sourced and enriched by attending to our inner realms. Drawing on her doctoral research, Louie links theory to moment-to-moment experiencing, illuminating parallels and connections to her practice as a supervisor.

Kathryn M Downing also shares doctoral research in Chapter 8. This study of virtual small group supervision demonstrates how the both the participants – and Kathryn, as supervisor and researcher – were changed learning and developing 'through integration of inquiry, reflection, experimentation, and action.' Small actions and gestures made a profound difference to the experience of group members, creating a 'safe and trusted space' for reflective practice.

In the next four chapters (9–12), authors offer approaches and techniques that hold the coaching supervision group through structure. The book closes with a radical new perspective, reflecting on supervision as a distinct profession.

In Chapter 9, my chapter on creative approaches in coaching supervision groups, I invite you to join me in three creative exercises through which you might explore yourself as a practitioner, within a relationship and through an example from your work. I share my own images, processing and insights as we go along. Four simple rules hold our practice. Creative approaches are playful and light-hearted *and* deeply personal.

Olga Rybina created the Mirror model from the Balint process – adapting it to better serve coaches, taking account of their skills and context. In Chapter 10, she leads us through the Mirror process demonstrating how to move between group and individual in each of the stages. Although Olga has been working with the model for over four years, using it as the basis for her own coaching supervision training courses in Russia, this is the first time the model has been published.

In Chapter 11, we enter an asynchronous group learning experience in which Barb Udale and Brenda Routt discuss the first 18 months of a peer supervision chain process – you will see it wasn't all plain sailing! They use their experience to provide guidance and tips for those embarking, as participants or as organisers, on a chain supervision experience. The chapter itself formed part of the learning experience, with the interactive process influencing and shaping how the group moved forward.

Group supervision experiences have been offered through the Association for Coaching for many years, and this learning forms the basis for Jeannette Marshall's Chapter 12. She gives guidance for those wishing to offer similar taster experiences. This seems invaluable as we seek to promote supervision to new coaches, or experienced coaches who have not yet had the opportunity to participate. Jeannette suggests Coach Training schools might find this method useful in encouraging a developmental approach to continuous learning, and an on-going reflective practice. This helpful step-by-step guide will enable supervisors to offer taster experiences as they too extend their offer within the coaching community.

In the closing chapter, Joan Wilmot Shohet reflects on her life's work as a supervisor. She takes us through her learning journey and invites us to consider the current place of supervision within the professional context. Joan encourages us to embrace supervision as an activity that could support any 'worker' or work situation; in so doing, supervision will grow as a distinct profession.

And off you go . . .

Groups are complex, dynamic, living systems in which the internal world of each group participant may be played out through external behaviour. As a supervisor, I find groups fascinating, unpredictable and the richest ground for learning. Each session offers me an opportunity to notice myself through my own lenses and also through the reflection of others: feeling the contentment of being understood and the disturbance of being misunderstood, the wave of emotion that arises with seeming acceptance and with perceived exclusion and the relationships that blossom and those that bear thorns. It is all there in the group experience – light, shade and darkness.

Enter the book, follow your own path through the chapters, noticing yourself and your process. Follow up with chapter authors if you wish; each is passionate about their work.

Chapter 1

Coaching supervision in groups

Framing the encounter

Jo Birch

In endeavouring to provide an overview and generic footprint for a coaching supervision group, I soon became acutely aware of the impossibility of the task!

As you move through the following chapters, you will notice that each group is shaped by the person opening the space, by the people in the group, the processes that play out within it and the situational context in which it takes place.

How then might I draw out the essential components of a coaching supervision group – taking account of the specific requirements of our profession, as coaches and coaching supervisors, and the contexts in which we work?

I turn first to the essence of coaching supervision, which can be found in Seven Simple Rules (Birch & Gardiner, 2019). Drawn from a small research study with 24 experienced practitioners, these systemic behaviours characterise coaching supervision at its best. They are general enough to be applied in every supervision situation and specific enough that every person can make them their own, applicable moment-to-moment in each supervision encounter. None of the Simple Rules stand alone: they are interdependent, applying to the entire system – supervisors and supervisees, equally and differently, according to their role in the encounter.

> *Simple Rules are neither simple, not rules – the two words constitute a linguistic term that describes a set of behaviours already present in a system. These are not abstract ideals to be enforced; rather they are descriptors of current practitioner behaviour (Birch and Gardiner p. 26).*

1 **Attune to self** – being present to your experiencing, self-awareness, centering.
2 **Engage with love** – bringing kindness, care and compassion to the engagement.
3 **Serve the intention** – honouring the contract and the agreed purposes in each encounter, being explicit, checking in with each other as necessary.
4 **Hold the space, work with the edges** – the quality of the reflective space. Interwoven with explicit contracting, acknowledging the boundaries as they come into view, holding and/or adapting where necessary.

DOI: 10.4324/9781003143451-2

5 **Illuminate and explore what is calling for attention** – focussing on what is present, reflecting moment-to-moment, offering wider reflections, noticing distractions.

6 **Dare to call it out** – reflecting what is present, in stories, cases, responses, relationships, dynamics and more, is not always comfortable, yet can provide the basis for fruitful exploration.

7 **Attend to the relationships, individuals and situational context** – taking a systemic approach, attending to the 'whole, part and greater whole' (Eoyang & Holladay, 2013).

It is in the Simple Rules that the quality and standards of coaching supervision are held. In both individual and group supervision we look for self-awareness; expect the engagement to be clearly defined by purpose; the container for the work held by boundaries and consideration given to ethical codes, competencies and contractual agreements. In the work of supervision, we give attention to what is present, even if we bring a case from the past; we offer different perspectives and notice newness and, finally, we attend to the multiple relationships and external factors at play influencing our work.

As we move specifically into coaching supervision in groups, the Simple Rules remain central, whether the groups are facilitated or peer-led, open or closed, short or long-term. They are illustrated in the following pages, held within a dynamic image, folding in to create a distinct space for the work of coaching supervision in groups. A dotted line symbolises the flow out of the space, taking our learning about ourselves back into our work.

Six discrete sections emerge from the frame, flowing into the space for the group experience: beginning, attuning, inviting, gathering, co-processing and closing. Each section raises questions for the prospective group supervisor. These are designed to peel back layers of awareness, searching underneath the surface for new insights, enabling the potential for more choice-ful decision-making; a quicker return to 'centre' after being triggered and, therefore, more dexterity in handling the complex dynamics at play in all groups.

The 'Beginning' section is an invitation to the supervisor to establish resonance with their existing practice through the Seven Simple Rules. These considerations remain the core purpose of a Coaching Supervision experience and serve as a point of reference as the group process unfolds.

Many of the subsequent questions reflect the balance between 'the supervisor role' and the desire for co-creation.

This exploration can be profound, touching on the supervisor's feelings and beliefs regarding power, control and collaboration. Being able to bring a clear awareness into view at different stages in the process, to hold power without harm and to hold the boundaries when necessary are essential skills of the group supervisor.

The inner reflections of the supervisor are generally offered as 'Me,' with 'We' acknowledging the collective co-created space of supervisor and group members.

In peer groups every member might hold the inner reflective and collective questions as roles move and develop.

Everything we are; our experiences with groups and the beliefs we hold about ourselves, others and groups, have the potential to affect the process that unfolds between us. Much of what we think and feel about groups lies out of our conscious awareness with no obvious need for surfacing in our everyday lives – although, I suggest, it is always influencing our behaviour. As we embark as supervisor on a group experience, it serves us to explore unconscious factors at play as those that remain out of view are potentially disruptive.

These are not the only questions you will encounter. Subsequent chapters will raise issues; later, in your supervision groups, moment-to-moment decision-making and group process manifestations will surface, calling to be addressed or taken to your own supervision.

Here, however, within the following seven pages you will find essential catalysts to help you shape your evolving personal and professional philosophy of your practice as a supervisor working, in this case, with groups. The journey of discovering 'self' in groups is likely to be a life-long commitment for the group supervisor.

Framing

Six discrete sections emerge...

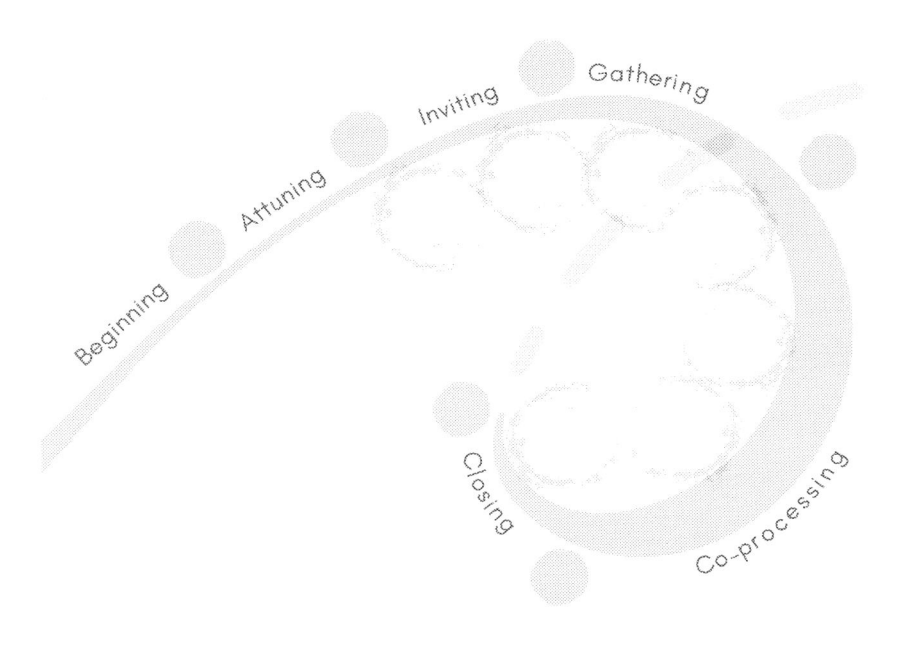

framing the space for the group experience

Figure 1.1 Coaching supervision in groups: Framing the encounter

Beginning...

Establishing resonance through Seven Simple Rules

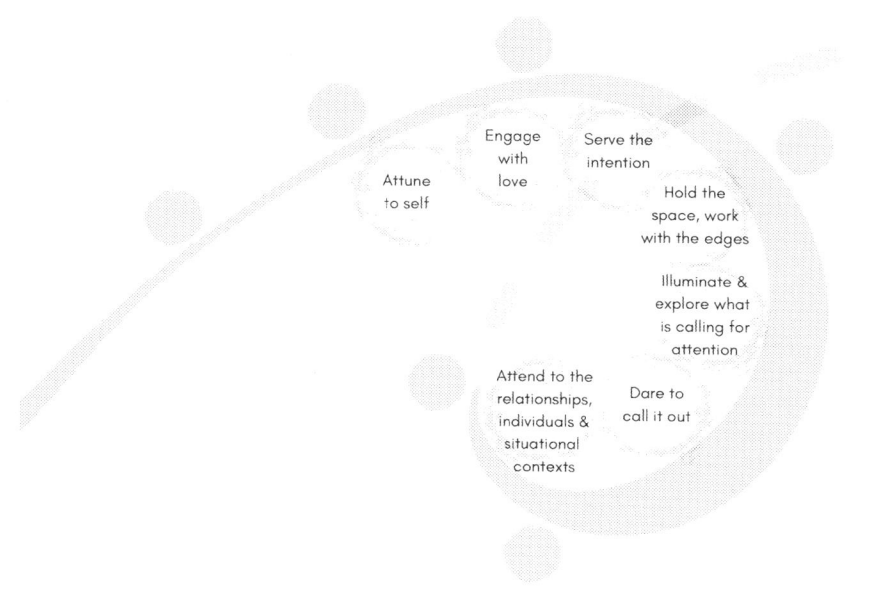

Engage with love
Serve the intention
Attune to self
Hold the space, work with the edges
Illuminate & explore what is calling for attention
Attend to the relationships, individuals & situational contexts
Dare to call it out

Coaching supervision...

Where do these behaviours show up in my supervision?
In what way does each resonate with me?
What draws my attention? Because...
What do I resist? Because...

moving into the dynamic of the group...

© Birch, J. & Gardiner, LJN. 2020

Figure 1.2 Coaching Supervision in groups: Beginning

Attuning...

Being in context

Why a supervision group (rather than individuals)?
Who, or what, is calling for a group...

        me?

        prospective supervisee?

        someone or something else?

Why now?

What is underpinning my understanding of groups, group work and human development?
What am I understanding my role as the Group Supervisor to be?
Who will establish the shape of what is to come?

Coming into Me

What experiences are informing me about myself / others in groups?
What am I believing about me...

        in groups?

        as a supervisor of groups?

What is equipping me to run supervision groups?
What supervision do I have in place to support me?
What are my (known) non-negotiables?

© Birch, J. & Gardiner, LJN. 2020

Figure 1.3 Coaching Supervision in groups: Attuning

Inviting...

Me

Who am I imagining will want to participate in this group?
What do I want to know about participants?
What is my rationale for open inclusion or membership criteria?
Is there any person or group of people that I would not accept?
    What is my rationale?
Will I interview prospective participants?
        If so, what am I looking for in the exchange?
What do I want participants to know about me? Because...
What would I prefer they didn't know? Because...

What invitation will I extend?
What are the initial parameters?

Becoming We

How many participants do I want?
        What is my rationale for this number?
What is important in establishing my initial contract with
each participant?
What do I need to do to lay foundations for us to manage
potential multiple containers and relationships?

© Birch, J. & Gardiner, LJN. 2020

Figure 1.4 Coaching Supervision in groups: Inviting

Gathering...

Me

What is my role in creating the space?

What am I believing should and shouldn't be co-created?

        What is my rationale?

What am I believing my role is in managing lateness, shared time and space, nature of contributions, conflicts, vulnerability...?

What am I noticing about...

        me?

        my skills and confidence?

        my feelings?

How will I structure the first meeting?

We

What relationships already exist between us?

What experiences are informing us about ourselves and others in groups?

In what ways are we each similar and different?

What are our individual expectations of ourselves, the supervisor, each other, the group experience?

What are our roles in co-creating the space?

What additional contracting is needed now?

© Birch, J. & Gardiner, LJN. 2020

Figure 1.5 Coaching Supervision in groups: Gathering

Co-processing...

Me

When have I felt most/least at ease in this group (so far)?
    What was I feeling?
    What was happening?

What am I keen to take to supervision?
What am I less likely, or reluctant, to explore?

What am I learning about me in groups?
What am I learning about me as the supervisor in this group?
What am I noticing about enabling others as co-supervisors?

Me in We

What am I noticing about how feelings are handled in this group?
What feelings have been present, what has not been present?
What am I noticing about contributions and in-process decision-making in this group so far?
What am I noticing about how ethical dimensions and diversity are being surfaced and explored in this group?
What do we need to consider, or put in place, if our contract is open-ended?

Figure 1.6 Coaching Supervision in groups: Co-processing

Closing.

Me

What am I noticing about my own relationship with endings?
What do I need to do to acknowledge and celebrate my work?
Where, and when, can I express my thoughts and feelings?
What am I believing about the end boundary?
What might I put in place to bring our work to a close?

We

What emotional responses am I noticing in myself and others?
What are we each believing is important about the end of our work?
What do we each need to say or express to close the container?
What might we put in place to bring our work to a close?

Figure 1.7 Coaching Supervision in groups: Closing

Acknowledgements

The author would like to acknowledge Louie J N Gardiner for creative and editorial support.

References

Birch, J., & Gardiner, L. J. N. (2019). Seven Simple Rules: An Alternative Lens. In *Coaching Supervision: Advancing Practice, Changing Landscapes* (pp. 21–34). Abingdon: Routledge.

Eoyang, G., & Holladay, R. (2013). *Adaptive Action: Leveraging Uncertainty in Your Organization*. Stanford: Stanford University Press.

Chapter 2

Group supervision with executive coaches

A psychodynamic approach

David Rothauser

My introduction to group supervision began in my early 20s, at the beginning of my career, when I worked as a science teacher. My sixth-grade classroom was an exciting place, full of 11-year-old exuberance, but it could also be devastating, as I attempted to do a good job in the face of multiple forces at play. One student, Jonathan, had a particularly powerful capacity to derail my lessons. He found marvellous ways to make himself the centre of attention, from comically falling out of his chair to surreptitiously launching projectiles. The more skilfully Jonathan inhabited a clowning role, the more rigid I became. I worked so hard to plan engaging lessons, yet he got all the attention! By January, I was exasperated. I felt I had tried everything: from rewarding Jonathan's desirable behaviours, attempting to build a personal relationship with him (he saw right through my efforts), calling his home and involving his family (he felt betrayed and less willing to cooperate), to more punitive measures like detention when all else failed. Alas, Jonathan had become my biggest challenge. I felt helpless in the face of his antics and spent my weekends ruminating about interactions we'd had and anxious about what the following week would bring.

As I became increasingly filled with the feelings of frustration that accompanied my repeated failures, I needed help discharging and making sense of what was stimulated inside of me before I could be effective with Jonathan or my class as a whole. I joined a psychodynamic supervision group where I could talk about all of this. Things began to change once the group helped me venture beyond my perspective that Jonathan was the problem. Jonathan, the class and I were caught up in a group dynamic, and Jonathan's behaviour spoke for a subset of students in the classroom. I was busy trying to get it right as a new schoolteacher, pushing the class too fast and too hard. The more outcome-focused and inflexible I was, the more the tension in the classroom increased.

Underneath Jonathan's derailing behaviours were needs for connectedness and attention, needs I also had. I learned to validate Jonathan's position while also setting behavioural limits. For instance, I would invite him to verbalise his need to pass gas and step into the hallway rather than do it spontaneously in the classroom. His verbal expressions about farting resulted in momentary, needed laughs from his classmates and were more playfully constructive than destructive. With

DOI: 10.4324/9781003143451-3

respect to the larger group of the classroom, Jonathan functioned as a barometer – his finger was on the pulse of the group's need for a pressure release, and I began to view this as a strength. I learned to intervene proactively with him and the class by asking questions like, "Jonathan, will you let me know when the class needs a break?" By recognising his emotional talents and preemptively inviting him to join the verbal dimension of our classroom, I enabled Jonathan to enjoy positive attention without acting out his impulses. Jonathan became my consultant, helping me balance my anxiety about results with attention to the unfolding group process. The more Jonathan and I learned to collaborate, the more the class functioned cooperatively.

I share this story because it is one illustration of how a psychodynamic supervision group can help a member grow through developmental issues that arise in the course of their work. My supervision group helped me experience and appreciate my own needs underneath some of my reflexively defensive positions. Through being understood in this way, I was able to identify and empathise with the needs underneath Jonathan's reflexively defensive behaviours. In the process, he got to experience an authority figure who was invested in understanding him. My initial interventions failed because I was trying to take something away from Jonathan before he or I understood its function – we were enacting something from each of our histories as I became a controlling and punishing authority figure. With the group's help, I came to see that I was as much a part of the issue as Jonathan. I had a need to "get things right" and I acted within my own historical relationship to authority when my capacity to "do a good job" felt threatened. I needed help moving beyond the sting of what Jonathan's behaviours initially represented for me in order to perceive what they communicated about his needs. Without the help of my supervision group, who knows how long Jonathan would have had to wait for me to grow up and become the teacher he needed me to be.

Working concepts that distinguish a psychodynamic approach

Psychodynamically informed group supervision is ultimately a tool for building each member's effectiveness, whether the participants are educators, coaches, or others in helping roles. This can be emotionally challenging yet rewarding work. In addition to the presentation and collaborative analysis of case material, a psychodynamically informed supervisor utilises the unfolding interpersonal group process that arises in the here-and-now to aid members' understanding of the case material and themselves. The group becomes a microcosm of the systems that coaches and their clients inhabit, and aspects of client personalities inevitably show up in the personalities of coaches in the group. This is referred to as the *parallel process*. Working with these emergent dynamics in the group is a pathway to helping coaches work with emergent dynamics with their clients. In these ways, a psychodynamically informed supervision group provides opportunities for experiential, emotional, and intellectual learning.

We must define the term *psychodynamic* to understand the heart of this approach more fully. *Psychodynamic* refers to work informed by the fundamental principles of psychoanalysis, initiated by Freud in the early 20th century and elaborated on by many others over the past 125 years. *Psyche* refers to the soul or the mind, so *psychodynamics* aims to discover the dynamics of the mind, both individually and how they are reflected in relationships and social systems. Primarily, a psychodynamic approach factors in the workings of the *unconscious* and holds that we are influenced or motivated by parts of the self that we can never see or experience directly. There are aspects of unconscious motivation that can become conscious, and since we cannot directly see the unconscious, we infer its workings through creativity, metaphor, non-sequiturs, slips of the tongue, uncanny coincidences, moments of associative thinking, and enactments or interpersonal dynamics that emerge in the coaching dyad and in the supervision group. Once we allow for these possibilities, we may begin to understand previously inexplicable, perplexing behaviour. Leadership expert and psychoanalyst Manfred Kets de Vries (2006) asserts that even the most irrational behaviour always has a rationale behind it that can be discovered. We are mystified by the unconscious. And so it is important to keep working on our ability to give good attention to everything that is happening in the group supervision environment, sensing our way through the unconscious layers.

There are three psychodynamic working concepts that enrich our exploration in the supervision group: resistance, transference, and countertransference. These concepts are useful for understanding what happens in all kinds of groups where multiple psyches collide, including supervision groups and groups in the workplace. A supervisor informed by these powerful ideas can help the group appreciate and learn from the way these concepts play out, both within the group and within the members' work lives. In the sections that follow, I will explore each of these ideas and illustrate them through a vignette of an interaction in a supervision group.

The ways we protect ourselves

Even when our clients have explicit goals, there is always a part of the self that works to counteract progress. This paradox was observed by Freud (1914), who viewed resistance as anything that interferes with the patient's ability to say everything that comes to mind. We can apply this idea to the coaching relationship and view resistance as anything that interferes with the agreed-upon task at hand. The psychodynamically informed supervisor helps coaches become intrigued by this state of affairs. We want our supervisees to appreciate the unique nature of their own and their clients' resistances. We want to understand how they operate, as we assume they serve a much-needed, protective function. Louis Ormont (1992), a pioneer of group therapy, reminds us that although resistances interfere with our clients' progress, they also provide crucial information about how they get in their own way.

Although some coaching approaches advocate for directly calling out resistances in an attempt to help clients consciously overcome them, the psychodynamically informed supervisor takes a more subtle approach, as naming resistances prematurely can have the unintended effect of either strengthening them or driving them underground where they lay dormant and untouched by our efforts. We initiate this process by creating a welcoming environment and accepting what the client brings. We want our clients to be themselves with us, allowing their resistances to flourish before our eyes. Since resistances are often held unconsciously, we tend to experience them emotionally before becoming fully cognisant of them. Once we've identified that a resistance may be at play, our next job is to contain our feelings and observe, which allows us to learn how the resistance operates. This process yields knowledge that allows the coach to make a non-confrontational communication that engenders curiosity. If the client can get interested in and talk about their need for the resistance, they are more likely to generate their own insight and make a shift. This is illustrated in the following example.

> *A senior executive was initially enthusiastic about coaching, but she employed a filibuster-like talking style in each session that left the coach feeling shut out – it was a monologue rather than a dialogue. The coach attempted to interject several times and failed to get a word in as the client raised her volume and increased her pace each time. The coach realised his approach was futile and brought the case to supervision. Bolstered by the group's exploration of his dilemma, the coach stopped attempting to intrude on the monologue and started to learn more about the client's resistance by studying his experience of feeling shut out. The coach began to see that this executive was most comfortable being right, felt uncomfortable with silence and was threatened by ideas that were not her own. Her nonstop talking was a way to protect herself from experiencing those feelings. It was a short step from here to imagining this executive's early life as the wellspring of her need for control. Eventually, towards the end of a session, the client was feeling more relaxed and revealed, "I've been talking a lot and I'm not giving you much space. I have a big personality and have a lot to say that I need to get out to make sure you get all the details of the context. Otherwise, I worry you won't understand me." Relieved by the client's awareness, the coach responded, "I can see how important it is for you to know that I get you. Does worry about not being understood appear in other relationships at work?" The client's resistance was now available for collaborative exploration.*

The supervisor helps the group identify and resolve resistances in coaching cases, as well as those that emerge in the group itself. The resolution of these group resistances aids in members' learning from the parallel process. In a coaching supervision group, the agreed-upon task is to collaboratively understand case material, including the significance of members' reactions. Resistances in the supervision group could look like showing off (a defence against vulnerability), giving advice (a resistance to feeling helpless or incompetent), talking more than listening (a resistance to learning from others), or subtly criticising (a resistance to feeling inadequate). Some resistances are overt, such as missing sessions unannounced, while others may be harder to detect, such as a patterned avoidance of a particular topic. Resistances in the group are often shared among several members or held by the entire group, including the supervisor. As coaches become familiar with studying and resolving resistances within the supervision group, they become more attuned to these phenomena in their work with clients.

The living past

Transference refers to the tendency to displace feelings from old relationships onto present-day ones. We all do this. This process can be seen as a natural mechanism the psyche uses to make our environment more familiar. *Something* from the past is transferred, across space and time, into the present. These can be wishes, feelings, aversions, expectations of an environment or a role, or an entire worldview. Some transferences emanate from the earliest, pre-verbal moments of life. Other transference reactions spring from later periods in childhood. Regardless of its source, transference involves a distorted reaction, and these out-of-sync perceptions are something we can concern ourselves with in coaching (Orenstein, 2002; Diamond & Allcorn, 2003; Allcorn, 2006; De Haan, 2011) and supervision (Searles, 1955; Spotnitz, 1976; Sandler, 2011; Hawkins & Shohet, 2012).

We often talk about transference in coded ways, such as referring to someone's "authority issues" or when we observe somebody, ourselves included, struggling with a certain category of relationship, such as peers, men, or women. Loving feelings towards an idealised mentor could include an element of transference, while envious feelings towards a fast-promoted colleague may harken back to the perceived favouriting of a sibling. An executive raised in a family in which children were meant to be seen and not heard might demand automatic deference from their direct reports and may confuse well-intentioned questions with signs of disrespect. This very same executive might be overly deferential in the relationship with their coach.

The variety and types of transference reactions are as infinite as the uniqueness of our clients' histories. Still, there are some broad categories of transference worth mentioning. Expectations of authority figures are common, sometimes referred to as *vertical* transferences, as are sibling or *lateral* transferences, displaced from early relationships with peers. Another class of transference particularly relevant to executive coaching is the *environmental* transference, which involves anachronistic expectations of the workplace or the organisation itself. Ormont (1992) describes the observable distortions that suggest transference: pervasiveness, insistence, excessiveness, and displacement. Pervasiveness indicates a blanket view is operating, wherein the client is inclined to view particular situations through a static lens. Insistence involves clinging to a thesis regardless of facts. Excessiveness refers to an outsized emotional reaction, given the context. And displacement is observed when a client actively associates a present-day relationship with a figure from their past. The out-of-sync nature of these four qualities signals that something from the past may be lurking in the present. In the next example, we see a coach deepen her understanding of her client by unearthing a transference reaction.

> *A coach suggested to her client, a senior executive, that they have a three-way meeting with the CEO. She asked her client, "Can you imagine such a meeting being helpful to you in any way?" In her supervision group, the coach described her client's knee-jerk, outsized negative response to the thought of such a meeting, explaining, "His body appeared to recoil upon hearing my question and he said, 'I was always one of the top three smartest kids in the class, but I was also one of the top three troublemakers.'" When the coach asked her client about the connection between his association and the potential meeting, he replied, "It feels like I'm being sent to the principal's office. The idea that that could be useful never, in my many years at work, ever crossed my mind." The supervision group discussed how the excessiveness of the client's reaction, as well as his displaced association of the CEO with the school principal of his youth, suggested a transference reaction was at play. The coach's new understanding allowed her to help her client reflect on his attitude towards the CEO.*

Supervision groups study ways in which transference emerges with clients and how it comes alive and is illustrated through relationships among members in the group. A group might observe how a member who grew up in a permissive family bristles in the face of perceived rules or group norms. Or one member's slight, yet chronic, lateness might stimulate outrage on the part of another member whose sibling was never punished for their transgressions. Through tuning into these easily overlooked dynamics in the supervision group, coaches learn about their own transference and also about how this ubiquitous phenomenon plays out in their coaching engagements. Developing an appreciation for the power and pervasiveness of transference enhances coaches' self-knowledge and ability to tune into and work with their clients' relational struggles.

What the coach feels

We just discussed how the client inevitably projects onto the coach, termed *transference*. *Countertransference* refers to the feelings aroused in the coach in response to these projections. These feelings were originally seen as an obstacle (Freud, 1910). Countertransference is now viewed as utterly fascinating and of immense utility in coaching (Orenstein, 2002; Diamond & Allcorn, 2003; Allcorn, 2006; De Haan, 2011) and supervision (Searles, 1955; Spotnitz, 1976; Sandler, 2011; Hawkins & Shohet, 2012). These feelings and reactions are personal data that the coach can put to use. We may become increasingly irritated in the face of a client's complaining, intimidated in anticipation of a client session, or compelled to rescue a client who is facing a challenge. Some countertransference feelings may be pleasant, like delight, affection, and hopefulness. Some may be feelings we don't particularly want to have, like boredom, anger, impatience, or sadness. Our emotional experience might mirror the client's, such as feeling sad along with them. Alternatively, we might have a complementary reaction. A client may feel helpless and we find ourselves enraged, or they might feel enraged and we find ourselves feeling sad. In this next example, we see how the coach's countertransference shines light on the client's experience.

> *A coach reported to his supervision group that he repeatedly feels inadequate in relation to a client who brags incessantly. By exploring his emotional experience of the case, the group helped the coach become more tolerant of and curious about these feelings. He left the group wondering, "Where else in the client's system does this feeling live?" In a later supervision session, the coach reported back to the group that he'd interviewed the client's stakeholders as part of a 360 assessment and discovered an emotional theme of inadequacy among the client's direct reports. They discussed not feeling good enough about their work around their boss. Debriefing the assessment with his client led to a rich exploration of the client's own inner conflict between perfectionism and praising his employees. The client feared that providing recognition or praise would be demotivating for his direct reports and revealed that his own father was impossible to please. The supervision group's hunch that the coach's countertransference feelings of inadequacy were valuable data about the case was further confirmed when the coach learned that his client is constantly haunted by these same feelings.*

Rather than push countertransference feelings aside or take them personally, we can use them as data in service of the client's growth. Exploring our reactions in supervision can reveal clues about our clients' inner lives and the emotional landscapes with which they contend. The ability to observe and thoughtfully consider the nature and meaning of our reactions makes it possible to use ourselves as instruments in the coaching relationship. Using one's self as an instrument involves listening closely to the more subtly felt layers of experience in order to perceive what is not communicated directly with words. To tune our instrument, we must become intimately familiar with our own histories, characteristic vulnerabilities, and blind spots. Professor of coaching psychology Tatiana Bachkirova (2015) observes that we usually need others to help us with this difficult work as self-deception abounds. The coaching supervision group provides the multiplicity of perspectives needed to see ourselves and our countertransference more fully.

We begin to make sense of our countertransference by distinguishing between two main types of reactions: *subjective* and *objective*. This distinction comes from Modern Countertransference Theory, outlined by psychoanalyst Hyman Spotnitz (1985), and helps us parse the source of our reactions to our clients.

Subjective countertransference, roughly "the coach's stuff," refers to the coach's reactions that emanate from their personal history. On the other hand, objective countertransference refers to the emotional reaction that any reasonably mature observer would have in the same situation. The objective countertransference helps us understand our clients and their effect on others. Knowing that countertransference can present in these various ways gives us pathways for conceptualising the client's inner world and responding in ways that lower tension and promote curiosity and learning. Some of the most challenging moments for coaches occur when something about their own history, their subjective countertransference, makes it difficult to perceive their client clearly. It is the supervision group's task to help one another sort out these emotional knots. The vignette that follows exemplifies such a tangle.

A supervision group explores a puzzling dynamic

The following vignette comes from a coaching supervision group I lead that had been meeting every other week for six months at the time the following interaction occurred. The members of the group are experienced coaches who are new to a psychodynamic approach to supervision. The vignette illustrates how exploration of the emotional dynamics between supervision group members can help resolve the coach's resistance in the face of the client's stuckness.

Janet, a mid-career coach, presents a client she's worked with for over a year. She tells the supervision group that her client, a senior executive in a professional services firm, insisted on showing her yet another email exchange with the CEO, a long back-and-forth that left the executive feeling unsuccessful. Janet reports that the client felt helpless about not being able to get her boss to listen to her. I notice that Janet's voice lacks her usual enthusiasm, and she seems almost bored. She tells us, "I'm presenting this client today because David said we should present clients who stay on our minds in between sessions, and there's something that keeps bothering me about this case. I'm just not sure what it is. In our last session, she showed me more emails, and I explored the situation yet *again* with her. I'm not sure why I keep thinking about this client, and I'm afraid I may not be doing a very good job."

I scan the group as Janet speaks, looking to see or sense nonverbal or emotional reactions in any of the members. I see that Margot, a particularly expressive member of the group, is looking away, and I feel a momentary flutter in my chest that registers as trepidation. I investigate by asking, "Margot, what reactions are you having as Janet talks about her case?"

"I'm embarrassed to say this, but I'm a little checked out," Margot reveals. "I don't know what I'm feeling, so I guess I'm dissociating."

I reassure Margot that her reaction is interesting and valuable and then ask Janet, "Does Margot's dissociation appear anywhere in your case?"

To Margot's surprise, Janet reports, "Actually, I'm a little checked out too. I'm bored with myself for presenting such an uninteresting case, again." Margot appears relieved by Janet's openness to her and sits a little taller in her chair, now leaning forward towards Janet.

I turn to Brian, who appears to have been paying close attention to the exchange, and ask, "Brian, what do you observe happening between Janet and Margot?"

Brian pauses and looks thoughtfully back and forth between the two women before responding, "Margot's feeling just like Janet. She's holding back because she doesn't want to hurt Janet's feelings. It's just like how something was bothering Janet about her client, but she kept it in." I am pleased to hear the way Brian is thinking about parallels between what is happening in the here-and-now of the group and between Janet and her client. Knowing that dissociation is a retreat from feeling rather than a feeling itself, I wonder to myself what feelings Margot and Janet might be avoiding. My reverie is suddenly interrupted.

"Actually, I'm feeling a little bit pissed off!" Margot declares with more energy in her voice.

"Can you say more?" I inquire.

Margot goes on, "I'm just beside myself! I feel angry and hopeless when I hear Janet talk about herself like that! How can a highly competent, experienced coach like Janet still be dealing with self-doubt after all these years?"

"Where do you hear Janet doubting herself?" I ask.

"When she said she's bored with herself and that her case is uninteresting. I'm just pissed that women our age, at our level of experience and having done so much self-development, can lose our confidence at this stage in the game," Margot explains. I suspect that Margot's personal history is enlivened by the case, and at the same time, her emotional reaction is likely a clue to understanding the dynamics between Janet and her client. I also notice that Margot has stepped back from the here-and-now of the interaction with Janet by expressing a generalised lament about senior women coaches, which leaves me curious about her more specific feelings towards Janet.

I modulate the intensity of Margot's feeling by reflecting her outrage a few decibels lower, "It *is* a travesty! And while it's both sad and true, do you know what you might be feeling in this moment towards Janet?"

Margot pauses, takes a breath and turns towards Janet, "Frankly, I'm reluctant to say this, but I'm actually a little pissed off at you." I momentarily ponder whether the trepidation I felt earlier was Margot's own fear in the face of her unexpressed anger.

A grin spreads across Janet's face, and she chuckles a little bit as she responds to Margot, "You know, I think I'm understanding something about what's going on, with your help. I'm also pissed off at me! And I'm pissed off at my client! But I didn't know what I was feeling until I could see it in you."

I note to Janet, "You're smiling." Janet goes on to help the group know something about her personal history with anger and how she learned to inhibit herself in her family of origin. In the face of uncontained parental expressions of emotion, Janet adapted by numbing herself so as not to inflame their destructive dynamic. I feel the tension dissipate inside of me as Janet gives voice to feelings that had previously been mysterious and obscured by her boredom.

Now that Janet has identified a relevant piece of her personal history, I concern myself with helping her and the group connect this with her client dilemma. I turn to the group and ask, "Is Janet's reaction to her client particular only to her own history? How are others reacting to what you've heard of Janet's client?" Group members share a range of reactions to Janet's client, from annoyance with her repetitiveness to identifying with her feelings of frustration and powerlessness.

Janet's shoulders relax as she listens to their words, and she says, "It's so relieving to hear your reactions and I feel those ways too. I didn't allow myself to consciously know about all of those feelings because I guess I was scared to have them. I became a little girl again in the face of my parents' unpredictable emotionality. Now I can think a little more clearly and see that I share the same feelings as my client – she feels like she can't get her boss to listen to her, and I feel like I can't get her to listen to me. Considering things in this way, I can actually empathise with her. It *is* really painful to not be listened to by your boss, or by your coaching client for that matter. But why have I been so unsuccessful at helping her get out of this repetitive cycle?"

At this point, I can see Janet and the group have moved into a more reflective space. Janet is exhibiting curiosity, and I share her question with the group, "Group, why has Janet been stuck in a rut with her client?"

Patrick says, "I think of Janet as such a polished professional. And it looks like she might have become extra polished in the face of her client's messiness by avoiding her feelings. Given what she's told us about her history, that seems to be how she protects herself."

Ben suggests, "What if you just empathise with your client's feelings and tell her directly that she's been making you feel powerless and angry too because she hasn't been letting you help her?"

Renata, identifying with the client, chimes in, "Well, I think Ben's idea is on the right track, but I worry that saying it in that way could leave the client feeling attacked or shamed or blamed."

With a growing understanding of the client's and the coach's psychodynamics (transferences, countertransferences, and resistances), the group is now in a problem-solving mode, thinking together about how to communicate with the client in a new way that could possibly shift the repetitive cycle of complaining. Janet is on her way.

In the next supervision session, Janet updates the group on developments in her case. When the client brought up the emails again, Janet supported her in feeling and outlook by saying, "Not only is your boss terribly unresponsive to you, but I must be too! How come I haven't helped you resolve this by now?" Janet tells us she really felt what she said and that it sparked her client to verbalise her frustrations with the way Janet had been working with her. Janet's experience with Margot's anger in the supervision group was fortifying, in that it allowed her to better tolerate hearing her client's negative feelings. Janet proudly reports that once the client expressed her irritation aloud, she was finally able to reflect on her own role in the dynamic, wondering, "Perhaps there's something I'm contributing to this situation?" Janet was impressed with the seeming simplicity and ease of her intervention.

I remind Janet and the group about the emotional complexity beneath the surface of her communication, saying, "The way this group helped Janet explore the feelings she was containing about her client freed her up to feel something new in the session. By accepting her client's negative feelings and inviting the client to express her frustration directly, the client was free to have a new thought about herself, which had the potential to interrupt the repetitive cycle." Janet's case gave way to a generative conversation in the group about other clients who stimulate feelings that group members struggle to tolerate.

* * *

Ultimately, this is an example of a supervision group helping a coach build her awareness, tolerance, and understanding of her *countertransference* feelings, which enables her to communicate in a new, more effective way with her client. Janet's client was caught in a repetitive dynamic that she attributed to the CEO when, in fact, she was unaware of her own role in maintaining that dynamic. The client's pervasive and insistent view of the situation suggests an element of *transference* that limits her ability to see herself in the situation more clearly. In parallel, Janet finds herself caught up in a repetitive dynamic with her client – resigning herself to discussing the emails session after session – that leaves her filled with hard-to-tolerate countertransference feelings. After consulting the supervision group, Janet is able to resonate with her client's underlying attitude that everyone else is to blame when she says, "Not only is your boss terribly unresponsive to you, but I must be too! How come I haven't helped you resolve this by now?" This helps the client feel understood, which lowers her anxiety and frees her up to have the new thought that she is partially responsible for the dynamic with the CEO. The numbness Janet reported at the start of the group session can be seen as a *countertransference resistance*, a resistance to experiencing the countertransference feelings. Resolving this resistance, with the group's help, was the key to making progress.

The supervision group played a key role in Janet's learning by feeling and giving voice to what she did not yet feel. While Janet's numbness obscured her emotional reactions to her client, Margot was free enough to feel and express her own emotional reactions, in this case feeling "pissed off" at Janet. Margot's constructive expression of anger resonated with Janet on some level – "a large grin spreads across Janet's face" – and stood in contrast with Janet's historical expectation of anger as dangerous. This new experience was a relief to Janet, and prompted her to remember and describe her history of suppressing anger in her family of origin. Thus, Janet became aware of how her personal history influenced her reaction to her client, her *subjective countertransference*. When multiple group members shared their reactions to Janet's client, Janet became even more confident that her newly uncovered emotional reaction was on target. In other words, the group helped Janet appropriately identify the *objective countertransference*, the feelings that any reasonably mature observer would have in the same situation. By exploring the underlying and unexpressed feelings within and between members, the group discovered the emotional core of the issue.

As the group leader, I hold in mind the principle that the group is the agent of change, not the leader, and I facilitate a learning process wherein group members explore their reactions to cases and to one another. In the previous example, I launch this process by scanning the group for nonverbal and emotional reactions as Janet presents her case. When I do this, I notice each member and imagine what they might be feeling, a way of taking each member and the group's emotional temperature. I'm paying attention to my own countertransference: feelings, associations, and sensations in my body. The trepidation I felt when attending to Margot was a clue that she might be resonating on an emotional level with Janet's case. I followed this clue and elicited Margot's response by asking her, "What reactions are you having as Janet talks about her case?" Encouraging Margot and Janet to talk directly to one another kicks off the here-and-now, interpersonal process that surfaces the in-the-moment transferences and resistances needed to understand the case. The goal is to expand understanding and develop each coach's capacity to use themselves as instruments. Each case exploration becomes an opportunity for everyone in the group to learn something crucial about themselves and each other, which they can carry forth into their work. As the reader can see, while facilitating the group, I mirror the language of the members. It's the lived experience of the transference, countertransference and resistance, not the language of psychodynamic theory, that touches the soul.

Because the psychodynamic lens invites emotion, it's important that the group supervisor is well-trained and equipped to regulate the level of stimulation in themselves and in the group. If a member appears to be going too deeply for their own and the group's well-being, I help them change course. I guide the group to work at a depth that's appropriate for each member and the group's purpose, which is to help members become more effective coaches. To be able to hold the complexity that comes along with inviting history, emotion, and interpersonal processing into group supervision, it is recommended that the supervisor seek experiential training tailored to this approach.

Conclusion

When we work with others, our own unresolved developmental needs rise to the surface, much as mine did with Jonathan in my sixth-grade classroom and much as Janet's did with her coaching client. Supervision groups across the theoretical spectrum provide space for shared insight, reflection, and professional community. The psychodynamic lens can be integrated with other theoretical approaches, as it aids in peering beneath the surface, making sense of what is known but not yet comprehended and strengthening the developmental focus of supervision. We slow down and begin to listen more closely to the subtle layers of our clients' communications. We learn to tolerate and understand our reactions. With these expanded capabilities, we use our reactions constructively to help our clients perceive themselves and their obstacles more clearly. Group members come to know one another's unique strengths and blind spots. As members internalise one another and also the group's process, they take the learning into their coaching and their lives in both direct and unexpected ways. This intimate work takes courage and requires supervisors to grow alongside their supervisees as they grow alongside their clients.

References

Allcorn, S. (2006). Psychoanalytically Informed Executive Coaching. In D. R. Stober & A. M. Grant (Eds.), *Evidence Based Coaching Handbook* (pp. 129–149). Hoboken, NJ: John Wiley & Sons, Inc.

Bachkirova, T. (2015). Self-deception in Coaches: An Issue in Principle and a Challenge for Supervision. *Coaching: An International Journal of Theory, Research and Practice*, 8(1) 4–19.

De Haan, E. (2011). Back to Basics: How the Discovery of Transference Is Relevant for Coaches and Consultants Today. *International Coaching Psychology Review*, 6(2), 180–193.

Diamond, M., & Allcorn, S. (2003). The Cornerstone of Psychoanalytic Organizational Analysis: Psychological Reality, Transference and Counter-Transference in the Workplace. *Human Relations*, 56(4), 491–514.

Freud, S. (1910). The Future Prospects of Psycho-Analytic Therapy. In J. Strachey (Ed. & Trans.), *The Standard Edition of the Complete Psychological Works of Sigmund Freud* (Vol. 11, pp. 139–152). London: Hogarth Press.

Freud, S. (1914). Remembering, Repeating and Working-Through (Further Recommendations on the Technique of Psycho-Analysis II). In J. Strachey (Ed. & Trans.), *The Standard Edition of the Complete Psychological Works of Sigmund Freud* (Vol. 12, pp. 145–156). London: Hogarth Press.

Hawkins, P., & Shohet, R. (2012). The Seven-Eyed Model of Supervision. In *Supervision in the Helping Professions* (4th ed., pp. 85–111). Maidenhead: McGraw-Hill.

Kets De Vries, M. F. (2006). *The Leader on the Couch: A Clinical Approach to Changing People and Organizations*. San Francisco, CA: Jossey-Bass.

Orenstein, R. L. (2002). Executive Coaching: It's Not Just About the Executive. *The Journal of Applied Behavioral Science*, 38(3), 355–374.

Ormont, L. (1992). *The Group Therapy Experience: From Theory to Practice*. New York, NY: St. Martin's Press.

Sandler, C. (2011). The Use of Psychodynamic Theory in Coaching Supervision. In T. Bachkirova, P. Jackson, & D. Clutterbuck (Eds.), *Coaching & Mentoring Supervision: Theory and Practice* (pp. 107–120). Maidenhead: McGraw-Hill.

Searles, H. F. (1955). The Informational Value of the Supervisor's Emotional Experience. *Psychiatry*, 18, 135–146.

Spotnitz, H. (1976). Trends in Modern Psychoanalytic Supervision. *Modern Psychoanalysis*, 1(2), 201–217.

Spotnitz, H. (1985). *Modern Psychoanalysis of the Schizophrenic Patient* (2nd ed.). New York, NY: YBK Publishers.

Chapter 3

No way is the only way

Louie J N Gardiner

Setting the scene

▶ Ahead of the read . . .

. . . take heed, as I invite you to enter into an experience of 'Attending, Responding, Becoming' by engaging with the strange and familiar in the pages that follow. As you proceed, hold this in mind:

> ♫◆ *No element, whatever form, alone conveys what's held by all.*
> *No wordy tomes do knowledge state, 'til human beings assimilate.*
> *All knowing flows through interchange as Beings engage with what's in range.*
> *Such knowing cannot be maintained – for each who learns is always changed.*
> *What's been has gone; there's more to come –*
> *yet none can know what will Become.*
> *I open up, welcome you in.*
> ▶≈ If you respond . . . our dance begins . . .

(Gardiner, 2021a: p. 13)

I imagine you might be thinking that this is a strange way to open a chapter about group supervision and its theoretical underpinnings! This poetic excerpt certainly sets a particular tone. Think of it as one of four ways (*statewaves*[1]) of expressing knowing that arises from within – me, in this instance, as the author. ♫**Aesthetic–Poetic** carries her message in emotional, artistic and poetic forms. ▶**Navigator–Narrator** is speaking right now, offering you information about what is showing up now and what is coming. ≈**Visual–Kinaesthetic** uses visual and verbal concepts and metaphors to leverage bodily senses of seeing, feeling and moving. There is little space for her in a textbook such as this, but she comes out to play when we engage in ways of working and processing that invite us to move and notice what is manifesting through our bodies. You will get a sense of her in the scenarios I share later.

The fourth *statewave* is the one you might be expecting. If I were writing from the perspective that dominates academic convention (based on assumptions deeply embedded in the philosophy of science), then ◆**Intellectual–Theoretic**

DOI: 10.4324/9781003143451-4

would dominate, drawing upon prior knowledge from other sources. In communicating through third-person forms of expression, she would absent her personhood as if there were no person there (e.g. using 'it', 'there is'); and she might be inclined to tip into strident assertions suggesting knowledge from books represents (the) truth, rather than simply recognising those contributions as different people's explanations for what they encounter in the world.

Now, if I were to only give space for ♦Intellectual–Theoretic, I would diminish or negate all other dimensions of what it is, for me, to be a human being, being human with all of my being. This, I believe, would not serve you as a supervisor working with coaches individually and in groups, and it would not serve our developing profession.

The burgeoning of the coaching industry[2] calls on us as supervisors to resource ourselves so we may better nurture its practitioners. Something in me shifted when my supervisees (mostly practising coaches) asked me to share what, why and how I was doing what I did. I realised I had knowing (which they wanted to access), but at the time I could not clearly express my philosophical and theoretical grounding. I wanted to be able to pass on what I was doing, and that meant being able to comprehend and talk about what has been *en*forming[3] my ever-emerging, integrating praxis. Eventually, the discomfort of the tension building in me tipped me into undertaking a doctorate.

I now find myself better equipped to manifest, represent and articulate what is mine to pass on.[4] Yet I say this humbly. If I know one thing for sure, it is this: '*No way is the only way*'. Our worldviews/paradigms (assumptions about the world, life, people, etc.) affect the way we see, understand and engage with all we encounter. We resonate with those whose worldview is similar to our own. Discordance arises when different worldviews collide, as well as when we bump up against day-to-day differences such as 'how to chop the carrots' or 'which way to hang the toilet roll – with the loose end coming over the top or round the back?' Being able to recognise our own assumptions, as well as those of others, is essential to our work as supervisors, helping us navigate our relationships wherever we are. So, when we meet the unfamiliar, engaging with curiosity and love releases generative potential and learning. This, to me, is when the power of group supervision really comes alive.

Although my praxis has been subject to myriad influences, in the next section I refer to those with which I have found greatest resonance and coherence: the philosophy of Natural Inclusionality,[5] theory lenses informing complexity thinking[6] and my living expression through primal animation.[7] In the following pages, I hope to illustrate ways in which these shape my interventions in the context of group supervision so that, perhaps, you can begin to appreciate your own praxis from different angles.

Bringing praxis alive

Serve the intention

In the poem that begins the chapter, the line beginning: '*No element, whatever form*' establishes a crucial imperative for what follows.

It lays the philosophical and theoretical ground on which all you are about to encounter stands. I am implicated in every encounter, so I use all of my being, as a living–learning[8] presence and resource, to navigate what unfolds. I do this, to honour my intention for this chapter: to serve you, as readers, and to those whose lives you will touch in the future.

Allied to this, you will notice shaded text boxes. These introduce the Seven Simple Rules of Supervision, which afford a holding frame for my practice. These are drawn from theory related to swarm behaviours in complex living systems, explained in Chapters Two and Seven of *Coaching supervision: Advancing Practice; Changing Landscapes*.[9] I use these in this first section to illustrate that Simple Rules **non-consciously manifest** and **can be used consciously** to guide individual/group behaviours across scales and situations within any given context, for example, coaching supervision. Here, I am illuminating how these showed up in and informed my writing of this chapter. In the three scenarios I share later, I invite you to see if you can spot when/where these simple rules show up!

> **Hold the space, work with the edges**

In undertaking my doctorate,[10] as a mature practitioner–researcher with 30-plus years of working in the realm of people development, I found myself called to hold the space for my inquiry and to work with the edges that were characterising it and me. I attuned to what had a bearing on what I experience, feel, think, know and do. This was not about a 'doctorate'. It was about the integrity of my living–learning, emerging praxis, so I needed to be clear about what I was willing to relinquish and unwilling to set aside. This became a hugely creative and productive undertaking, exploring my resistance, receptivity and responsivity. ♦**Intellectual–Theoretic** wanted to know more; yet all other aspects of myself were showing up with something to offer that had yet to find visual and verbal expression. So, when my *state-waves* showed up, I listened. I attended to what they were bringing. I **admitted**[11] and gave diligent attention to them. In return, they gave of their unique capacities, in ways I could neither have foreseen nor demanded.[12]

> **Engage with love**

I invite you to see this experience of mine as an analogy for the generative potential that can be invoked when we invite differences to show up each time we open a shared supervision space. In each gathering of individuals, the possibility for mutual contextual learning – a key condition of living, learning systems or 'symmathesies'[13] – comes alive through everyone's differences, not their similarities. There is no guarantee that this learning potential will be released, but we can become better at establishing conditions to enhance the likelihood. Its release begins with unconditional acceptance – love of self and other.

> **Illuminate and explore what is calling for attention**

Trusting whatever was showing up in me signalled something latent, something ready to be surfaced and **admitted**. I had no idea what was coming and so had no attachment to a specified outcome. This meant all of my being came out to 'play' freely, without being attached to pre-determined outcomes nor trying to prove or protect[14] myself. I wanted to meet not-knowing with not-knowing. I wanted to enter each encounter with the playful spirit of childlike curiosity and to invite others to join me, accepting all that showed up between us. In so doing, I found myself aligning to my deeply held commitment to safeguard my own trustworthiness.[15] Allowing my different *statewaves* to express freely opened the space for me to experience and recognise first-hand the essence and living expression of Natural Inclusionality.[16]

> **Attend to the individuals, relationships and situational context**

Later, I came to appreciate how opening receptive spaces, **admitting** differences, responding to invitations and working with not-knowing were already playing out in my relationships with others, in my supervision groups and in other group-work. Along the way, I found myself drawing upon other disciplines. Amidst well-known names and familiar models, approaches and theories, I delighted in discovering relatively unknown figures whose work somehow resonated far more strongly than many conventional sources. I cannot begin to do justice to the terrain I have covered. Neither can I present the entirety of the fruits of my research here.[17] Instead, I introduce you to some that serve the work of supervision in group contexts. Each draws upon the synthesis of my personal knowing (first-person), relational (second-person) and theoretical (third-person) explorations.

> **Dare to call it out**

In taking this naturally inclusional approach, I am tickling at the bedrock of the philosophy of science, which advocates taking a singular epistemological[18] stance in relation to what may be accepted as valid 'knowledge', that is, objective **or** subjective **or** inter-subjective/constructionist. There are times when the dominance of one of these is fit-for-purpose.[19] However, in my undertaking, I realised that all three are necessary and interdependent. None can 'be' without the others. My *statewaves* cut across these false divisions, bringing alive the inseparability of these philosophical stances. All *statewaves* flow through this chapter, sometimes as discrete streams, as in the poetic piece at the outset. Mostly they ebb, flow and mingle together in varying concentrations, tumbling forth and then receding, when each unique voice is called to be stronger.

Moreover, I have been confronted with something that, when caught in my most reactive states, I find hard to admit – my partiality. When activated, I access and act upon only that which finds its way through me. This confronts me starkly with what is my responsibility. When I engage as a supervisor accompanying others, I need to leverage all that I can in service to them, their clients, our profession, the wider world and, indeed, myself. This means accessing all sources of knowing and knowledge that are within my range, using 'all of my being' when process(ing). Yet subjectivity – first-person sense-making – is often judged pejoratively. Because it is unverifiable by others, its validity is considered unreliable and therefore inadmissible. Being unverifiable by another is not what makes subjectivity unreliable. It is our inherent partiality – being unaware of what and how much we are not noticing. The challenge, therefore, is not to ditch subjectivity but to enrich it with what else is available and to hone it by developing our reflective–reflexive[20] capacities.

| Attune to self | We are the instruments of our work. As with any instrument, it takes practice to develop our art and artistry. Every time we play an instrument, we need to tune it. As an aspiring manager in the mid- |

1980s, I confronted myself. I was an 'emotional mess', and, one day writing in my journal, I found myself asking: '*How can you presume to manage another, when you cannot even manage yourself?*' The tone of my question was accusatory, yet it did galvanise me to step up to becoming 'the manager I wanted but never had'. Attuning to myself came to be about safeguarding my trustworthiness in all I do, as a practitioner serving others and in trying to be a better human being. *Everywhere I am, I am*, which means, before I attend to you, I must attend to what in *me* might get in the way of *us*.

Folding in before stretching out

Before proceeding, I invite you to pause to check in with yourself.

- *What are you feeling?*
- *What are you thinking, imagining, remembering?*
- *What are you learning about your philosophical leanings?*
- *How do these show up in your life and your supervision practice with individuals and within groups . . . when you are activated . . . and when you are grounded?*

Write down everything that comes up for you . . . and then return here.

What to expect, amidst the unexpected

First, I lay the groundwork by clarifying my use of particular terminology and how this explicitly reflects my philosophical stance (worldview). In setting out mine, I hope to help you clarify yours. This will help you make sense of what you do and why you do it, in contrast to what I do and why.

In embarking on this exchange, I offer due warning. Though I hope you find this fascinating, it may not always be comfortable! So much of what goes on within us occurs outside of our awareness – none more so than the fundamental assumptions about what we believe 'is' or 'should' be; and about 'how things (should) work'. Such assumptions shape what we notice and the meanings we make of that. Becoming ever-more attuned to ourselves helps us surface what is non-consciously activating us.

I bring attention to some assumptions that routinely pervade and disrupt our potential for generative inquiry: 'either/or' polarities and beliefs that we can predict and control desired outcomes. These are tied to 'objectivity' and the scientific method of invoking linear causality through traditional experimentation[21] (e.g., if I do X then Y will happen). This is not fit-for-purpose in complex living systems.[22] Early coaching tools like GROW are infused by this mechanistic type of thinking which persists in the profession. Certainly we can increase the chances of reaching some goals if we remove or reduce variables over which we have some control. But as complex living beings, in complex community and organisational systems within our wider world, effecting change is neither predictable nor controllable. If it were, arguably many more of us might be living happily and productively flourishing!

In contrast, systems and complexity sciences help us recognise a different kind of causality that is nonlinear – where an infinite number of unknown and unknowable variables affect all known variables in unpredictable ways. This means we cannot predict outcomes with any degree of certainty because we simply do not know most of what is actually affecting us. Principles have been extrapolated from these newer sciences (e.g., quantum mechanics, thermodynamics, complex adaptive systems, swarm behaviour, bijective physics) which seem to apply from the quantum to human to cosmic scales. I became fascinated how such principles reflected my day-to-day experiences of living and engaging at this human scale; over time, I found my praxis transforming in light of my insights.

Recognising our assumptions and relinquishing those that are outdated or no longer fit-for-purpose brings agility. Acuity of this order liberates us in compelling, creative and joyful ways. Many of us have found ways of doing this without necessarily being able to verbally articulate what is in play when we do what we do. If this chapter helps you make your own tacit knowing explicit, that would be a wonderful outcome indeed!

Making distinctions: 3Fs

I continue by sharing where I have arrived in my own supervision praxis[23] as a way to bring your own into relief. In sharing aspects of my living theories,[24] I reflect on practical examples drawing upon the bodies of knowledge that inform how I respond.

Three simple words – *Facts, Feelings, Fictions* – are core to the praxis of Presence in Action,[25] held by the P6 Constellation framework.[26] These three words link directly to the philosophical distinctions mentioned earlier: *Facts* – objectivity; *Feelings* – subjectivity; *Fictions* – subjectivity and inter-subjectivity.

I offer descriptions of the 3Fs (Gardiner, 2021b, PhD pending publication: p. 123) before considering some group supervision examples:

> *Facts*: The presence of a thing or person (material objects) that can be named; events/happenings; what someone says or does (transient happenings) that

Figure 3.1 3Fs within the P6 constellation

can/may be recorded, noted or measured, such as that which is considered to be 'objectively' available to all, though not necessarily accessible by all, by virtue of personal perspective/position, proximity/scale or perceptual filtering.

Feelings: Physical/physiological bodily sensations are experienced in our bodies and are usually located 'somewhere', for example, e.g. 'my skin is tingling', 'my lips are dry', 'my hands are shaking'. Other outwardly imperceptible sensations are also accepted as empirical if they can be measured, for example heartbeat, sweating and liver function. 'Unmeasurable' affective states are considered 'subjective' (which means that an outsider cannot know what goes on inside another), emotions such as anger, disappointment, frustration, delight and so on. In the midst of experiencing, we simply need to recognise all the feelings we are feeling – and often there are several to many, rarely just one!

Fictions: '*What my mind does with*', in other words, the meanings we make of all that we consciously and non-consciously encounter and experience. We make assumptions, interpretations, judgements, conclusions, myths, stories, metaphors, imaginings and so on. Meanings do not exist outside a relational and wider-world context. They are constructed and shared 'inter-subjectively' through language and symbols. However, my meaning-making is mine, accessed through me; yours is yours through you. Sometimes our meaning-making coincides and sometimes it collides.

The *3Fs* are distinct data types[27] which show up together in dynamical (nonlinear) interplay within each of us. In recognising this interdependency, I found myself sitting comfortably with the philosophy of Natural Inclusionality rather than being cognitively split apart by the assumptions embedded within the philosophy of science, which would have had me separate and elevate one above all others. *Everything is interrelating, tangibly or intangibly.*

Favouring any one of the *3Fs* and disregarding the others will have us non-consciously slide towards one or other of the philosophical positions. For example, if you were to draw upon approaches anchored in storytelling/narrative and metaphor, you would be amplifying the *Fictions* portal. If your meaning-making is not at some point grounded in the context of what has been and is now (*Facts*) and the *Feelings* showing up in you in relation to those stories/narratives, then your sense-making could turn out to be 'non-sense'. Even though you may be unaware of the *Facts* and *Feelings* implicated in your approach, **they will be there**. I have found that surfacing all three brings about surprising and rapid transformational shifts and insights.

To illustrate this, I might suddenly become aware that I am feeling something but may struggle to access what is going on. I reach for my Emotions Palette© – a set of colourful cards that help me discern the variety of feelings I am experiencing right now as I write:

Tense, irritated, excited, earnest, anxious, hope, weary.

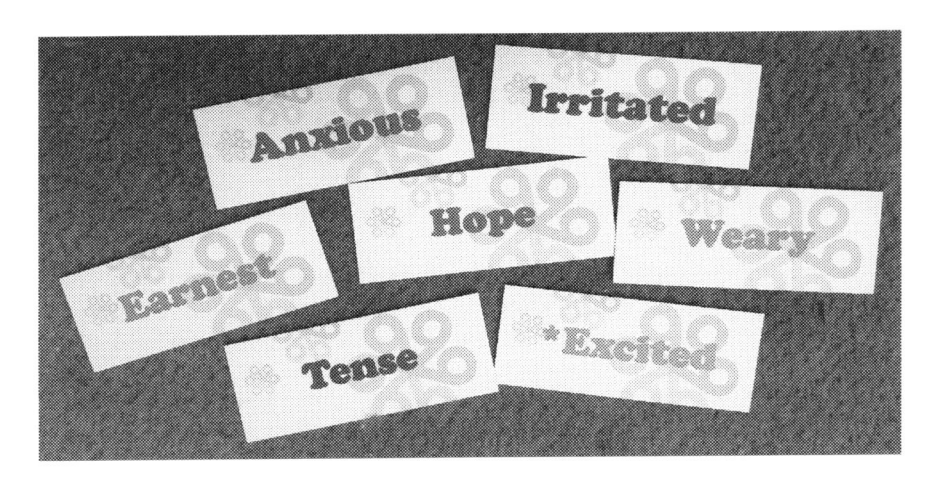

Figure 3.2 What I am feeling right now

Notice these are single words. What happens in you when you read my list of current *Feelings*? Where has your focus of attention moved to? Have you gone to you and lost awareness of me? What are you feeling? What are you thinking and remembering? Are you wondering if I have experienced what you experienced?

With very little context about me and my life, you may start trying to fill the gaps. You may start imagining what might be going on for me. You may try to put *Facts* in place. You might even recognise that by the time you read these words, many months will have passed – so are you wondering what I am feeling now? Which feelings were to do with this chapter? What else might have been going on in my life that might be related to these feelings? Of course, beyond what I actually shared, everything you are imagining about me that is showing up in you, will be created by you. Without any *Facts* as back-up, your *Fictions* may be running riot, signalling what, **in you**, has been activated. Groundless *Fictions* serve no one, other than indicating to the person generating them, that they may have something to attend to!

Our *Feelings* are related to exterior and interior happenings, affected by past memories and future imaginings, collapsing into our present-moment sensing and processing. Only the person experiencing their feelings, knows what it is like for them to feel those feelings. Added to which, without context, they 'mean' nothing. They just are. *Facts* and *Fictions*, when dismembered from context and from the person in whom they originated, are similarly devoid of meaning.

Crucially, this means that no one can know what another person feels, what they are thinking or what they could or should do in any given situation. What goes on within each of us is inaccessible to, and unverifiable by, anyone outside of us. On at least two counts, the import of this cannot be overstated: firstly, as one human impacting and being impacted by others in the world and, secondly, as a professional supervisor supporting others in supporting others. Being both of these means I cannot in all conscience proceed under the delusion that I know what goes on for others, nor can I reliably serve them without robustly, boldly and compassionately attending to myself.

The responsibility for attending to my interior realm, and how this tips me out into the exterior realms we share, lies entirely with me. When I was unclear about the *3F* distinctions and how they play out in me, I found that my sense-making (and therefore action-taking) was frequently flawed – sometimes disastrously so. Recovering from the deep shame I felt about things I had done that had damaged several precious relationships brought alive a deep resolve in me to resource and equip myself to become more aware of what was activating me.

My passionate, lifelong quest delivered the P6 Constellation (in which the *3Fs* find their place) – scaffolding[28] my personal and professional praxis. Noticing all that is roiling within me, and being able to recognise the distinct 'data-types' and patterns arising from their interplay, has transformed my pain-ridden struggling into journeying and generative encounters fuelled by presence-ful, childlike curiosity and creativity.

The difference that makes a difference in all this is the stunningly simple *Acuity Practice* that sits at the heart of it, which opens with, and iterates around, this single question:

What am I/are you noticing?

Presence holds a space open in me, for **admitting** (acknowledging, accepting, letting in) all without judgment – including all feelings, all fictions, all facts, 'imaginings' and 'rememberings' that come 'alive' or are 'current' for me in that moment. This is what Natural Inclusionality means in practice: admitting tangibles and intangibles, recognising that all are implicated in whatever dynamics play out within, between and beyond us. When I remember the fact of my Dad dying in 2018, my eyes fill with tears. I feel grief rise in me instantly . . . and then huge relief and gratitude as I return to this present moment. He is not here to suffer from the impact that COVID-19 would inevitably have had on him. He was a fun-loving, gregarious, social being with countless friends he saw every day of the week. Being forced into isolation would have been extremely difficult for him. If all I had said to you was: 'My Dad is dead and I feel gratitude' . . . I wonder what might have become activated in you?

In embracing a naturally inclusional paradigm, I hold that *Facts*, *Feelings* and *Fictions* are neither good nor bad, right nor wrong. This might appear to challenge our usual ways of thinking about ethics and morality which rely heavily on *Fictions* – the judgements/meanings we make. In actuality, seeing the *3Fs* as distinct 'data-types' enables a more discerning, self-centering and stretching, ethical inquiry. It becomes clear that ethics cannot be treated from a singularly objectivist, subjectivist nor inter-subjectivist position. Bringing what is showing up alongside what else is running or 'current' within us and in the actual situation we are in delivers us to a state of coherence: bringing insight and personal knowing about what is ours and what is ours to do something about.

Self-centering is paradoxically expansive. In discovering more about what is going on within us, different options for action are revealed. Whereas denying or disregarding what is current means getting caught in old repeating patterns of thinking and doing, which generally reap unwanted consequences.

With all this brewing within you, let's launch into a few scenarios!

Playing with scenarios

The rest of this chapter is offered as a series of mini-scenarios from group supervision sessions.[29] I recount an incident. On reading it, I invite you to notice what happens within you and to note your immediate reactions.

I then share what I did, illuminating the worldview and theoretical perspectives manifesting through my actions. As you read, I encourage you to reflect more deeply and expansively on the nature of the micro and macro assumptions affecting what you do and how you do it and also what lenses you draw upon that inform your own sense-making. Notice where we coincide and collide.

Box 3.1: I just want to lie down

Two of the group are in their seats, ready to start. Sarah opens the door, takes a step over the threshold of the doorway. Stops. Looks at the rug in the middle of the room and says:
> *'I just want to lie down there and close my eyes'.*

What are you noticing within you?

- *What are you thinking/imagining/remembering?*
- *What are you feeling?*
- *What are you imagining you would have done if you had been faced with the same scenario?*
- *What is your rationale for this?*

What actually happened next?

I witnessed Sarah's entry into the cabin. I visually met the eyes of each of the others in the room then turned to her and said, 'Well, Sarah, you best lie down then!' She dropped her bag and coat on the floor, took off her shoes and lay down on her back in the centre of the rug with her eyes closed. She lay in silence whilst the rest of us in the room held her in our gaze, quietly witnessing her being and breathing. In the time she lay on the rug, her breathing settled. At some point, she opened her eyes, thanked us, stood up and went to sit in a chair. She did not tell us what had transpired for her.

In complex adaptive systems (e.g., the weather, human beings), it helps to understand 'tension' as concentrating energy generated, either by an accumulation of differences (e.g., ideas, people) flooding into a 'system' or by the constraints around a system tightening. Tension-building signals a system moving towards a threshold of changing. One tiny addition can catalyse that tension to tip one way or another, outwards or inwards. When it tips outward, the system might disintegrate/explode or empty itself, experiencing a temporary relief before tension begins to build again. Tipping inwards means the energy has a chance to convert to something more sophisticated and complex. This is made possible if/when we as human beings hold our internal tension long enough for a more generative conversion to occur.

Tension-tipping outwards includes: the process triggering a bomb exploding; water bursting through a crack in a reservoir wall; a young man setting himself alight in a public square; a woman erupting into laughter; a child bursting into tears; a verbal tirade from the manager of a sports team; a person shoplifting; a toddler hitting another; a teenager cutting themselves on their body, where no one else will see; an executive coach telling another coach about a difficult interaction with a client.

With Sarah, I noticed her entrance and saw it as a sign that she was carrying a lot of internal tension and was on the edge of tipping. Her *being~doing* body had expressed what it wanted, and I invited her to 'go there'. As a group, we held the space long enough for her to hold and meet the tension she was experiencing within herself. Whatever was spinning reconfigured and found resolution, enabling her to settle and join the circle when she was ready. We played our part as silent, receptive witnesses. What matters in this scenario is recognising that her process was hers, not ours. For us to serve her well, none of us needed to know what was going on for her. If we had asked her what had happened, that would have served our own curiosity, not any need of hers.

There are some 'things' I rarely do in supervision sessions. I rarely open a space with a pre-determined schedule – not even a formal check-in. I am cognisant that the moment I open my mouth, I start shaping the space. Instead, I wait for signals that enter/open the encounter (e.g., someone speaking first and others reacting). This presenting data attunes me to what is alive in each person, giving clues about what is calling for attention, what, when or whom to follow.

One exception to this is when commencing a new group or training. In those first encounters, I briefly set the stage for participants to anchor the difference between linear and nonlinear engagement. I help them attune to their experiences of both and to reflect on how these ways of perceiving the world show up in their lives, relationships and work. In exploring this, I illuminate a crucial principle – even though, initially, this is deeply uncomfortable for some: we cannot learn about working with not-knowing by following a fixed schedule that sets out what we are going to learn! Having a repeating format for how to run sessions is entirely fit-for-purpose in many group encounters, but we need to discern when to plan and organise with precision and when not to. But if we only ever do something one way, that is a clear sign we may be serving some non-conscious need or fear of our own. We need to experience not-knowing to be able to notice what goes on for us, what shows up in others and what happens between us. Being it and being in it establishes conditions for developing our capacities from the inside, to engage with it, with acuity and agility.

> ## Box 3.2: Emotions she did not want
>
> *The group sits in a circle around the floor mat which is encircled by Emotions cards. Each member is taking their turn to bring something to work on.*
>
> *Billie steps into the space. She stands silently on the mat with her eyes closed, facing downwards. I ask her, 'What brought you to the mat?' She shakes her head. I recall something about what happened to her in the past and wonder if this is what she is bringing. I know she has not told*

anyone else. Hmmm. I am not sure this is for this context, but I can see she has already 'gone there'. I choose to trust her, me and the group. I ask, 'Which emotions do you wish you could avoid ever feeling again?' I invite her to walk within the circle choosing emotions that come up. She walks clockwise, looking at each emotion in turn. Using her foot, she slides one, then another, and another into the circle. When she is done, I ask her to walk round, reading out loud what she has selected ...
   'Awe, wonder, joy, delight, passion, love, excitement, hope'.

What are you noticing within you?

* *What are you thinking/imagining/remembering?*
* *What are you feeling?*
* *What are you imagining you would have done, if you had been faced with the same scenario?*
* *What is your rationale for this?*

What actually happened next?

When I saw the emotions cards Billie had selected, I felt surprise and shock. I also felt irritated with myself about my question. Which question? I had made a bunch of assumptions. Clocking myself, I brought my attention back to her. She had actually responded to something that had meaning for her, even if it did not seem to fit with my question.

I said that she did not have to tell us what happened to her, then asked what it was about those emotions that had her 'never want to experience them again'.

She replied, 'Because when I have those kinds of feelings, really bad things happen to me'.

I reflected her words back: 'So when you have those kinds of feelings, really bad things happen to you?'

'Yes'.

I said 'Now you don't have to say what happened, but can you say **when** the really bad things happened?'

'Two years ago'.

'How long did they last?'

'About 4 days'.

'In your whole life, you only ever felt those particular feelings two years ago?'

For the first time in the session, she looked up at me, with her brow slightly furrowed, and said 'No!'

'No?' I reflected back. Then she smiled . . . and I smiled back.

Billie did not speak when I asked what had brought her to the mat. I assumed that something big from her past had been activated in the session, which I knew about, but others in the room did not. I noticed suddenly feeling hyper-vigilant. Was this mine or hers? I reminded myself that she had taken that step onto the mat and that she was in charge of anything she disclosed. I trusted Billie. This process was hers, and my role was to support her in a way that also served the group.

Even though Billie had moved herself onto the mat, her silence signalled she was not quite ready to speak. She was able to move and to engage with her feelings.[30] Through my own living–learning inquiry, I recognise this in myself – that my feelings and body move me, long before my mind comprehends what is happening and why, and certainly ahead of my ability to talk about it. This played out in Billie's process. She moved onto the mat. She walked through her emotions; she used her feet to slide the emotions clearly into view. Only then was she able to speak them out loud and to engage with my questions.

In this short encounter, she accessed crucial factual 'data' that had previously been out of reach. The moment she said 'No!' and then smiled, was the moment her *Fiction* lost its grip. She did not need to talk about the details of what happened to her in the past, because her meaning-making had become 'stuck' on a false causal link that disintegrated in light of her irrefutable lived experience: she had felt 'those *Feelings*' many, many times in her life without other 'really bad things' occurring as a consequence. My odd question brought this locked-in causal relationship into view. This provided a clue to seeking out other 'data' – *Facts*, in this instance – which, in turn, disrupted what was stuck, enabling a new meaning-making pattern to arise.

As a group, we later explored what I had done, as well as what went on for the other's witnessing. Here I offer what I shared of my process, to illuminate some of the underpinning dynamics playing out in the approach. I spoke of being slightly thrown when Billie shook her head in response to my first question, and how my prior knowledge had me jump to assumptions. I fell into *Fictions* about what Billie would be *Feeling*; and *Fictions* about what she would 'want to feel' and 'not feel'. Whatever was going on in me came out in my asking her a somewhat 'odd' question about her feelings . . . and yet, I noted that it had actually opened up something for Billie. I reminded myself that in working with not-knowing, *interventions are simply experiments with uncertain consequences.* And, because she was slowly moving around the circle in silence with me accompanying her, I had time to process what was going in me, without disrupting her. Irrespective of my question, she was actually processing something, and my task was simple: attune to her and follow her lead! My early intervention was imperfect, yet because I did not get caught by *Fictions* about myself, I was able to stay in the present and work with each unfolding, until her moment of release.

Complexity thinking and primal animation,[31] were alive in what played out for her and me as well as for the group. Working with such complex entanglements in this group supervision space is made possible because everyone engaged (host/ supervisor, person on the mat, witnesses) is held by the same self-centering, motion-oriented praxis. So, although all our processing dynamics are nonlinear and unpredictable, the P6 Constellation provides a universal framework that brings constancy to the holding space, with a place for everything that shows up. Everyone is doing their own personal work, whether or not the group focus and supervisor's attention is explicitly on them.

Natural Inclusionality comes alive in drawing upon all of our being when processing, that is, through our sensing and sense-making faculties. However, we can become confused if everything roils around within us in an undifferentiated muddle. The scenario with Billie reminds me how easy it is to slide into pervasive ways of referring to feelings, for example, when someone asks us 'how' we feel, we may say 'good or fine or bad!' These are not feelings, they are *Fictions*. And notice this: I am **not** saying *Fictions* are bad! I am saying *Fictions* are *Fictions* (meaning-making is meaning-making, and it is essential to life). *Feelings* are *Feelings*. They are not 'good/bad', 'right/wrong' or 'light/shadow'; they are essential to life. Knowing this to be so, I still slid into assuming (*Fictions*) that Billie would not want to feel feelings she might judge as 'bad' like shame, guilt, fear, panic, rage, resentment, and so on.

She went somewhere I did not expect. I could have tipped into a cascade of *Fictions*/self-accusations about myself: 'I got that so wrong', 'I feel like I messed up with Billie', 'I feel like I made a fool of myself in front of the group', 'I feel really stupid!' Thankfully, I didn't. But in offering these possible examples, you can see that none of them mentions a single *Feeling* nor indeed any *Facts*. Our common vernacular is often imprecise. These two data types are tightly coupled in our interior processing and, when trying to express *Feelings*, our phrasing commonly collapses into *Fictions*. Our imprecision can precipitate confusion, misunderstanding and sometimes even conflict.

A presence-ful inquiry invites a naturally inclusional stance, which means accepting whatever is showing up so we may attend to it. Noticing **that** we are making judgements is not the same as believing those judgements! Noticing and **admitting** our *Fictions*, *Feelings* and the *Facts* of a situation is key to accessing the insights that free us into more generative patterns of being~doing in the world. So, for example, when I feel shame or embarrassment, rather than suppressing or trying to run from them, I turn to meet them. I have become intensely curious about what might be revealed to me. What have I done or am I believing I have done? What else is in the mix? These questions open me up to discovery.

I have come to realise that the only pro-active thing we can do to support ourselves is to embark on making conscious what has been non-conscious. Accessing and leveraging all of our faculties helps us to notice what we notice, and the more we do this, the more we develop our capacities to notice more than we did before. All else that transpires – insights, learning, transformational shifts – becomes more coherent and generative as we become more adept at supporting our natural living–learning, nonlinear processing dynamics. Doing this solo takes practice and initially is challenging because it is harder to catch our blind spots. Group supervision, with those who are committed to self-inquiry, holds the potential for accelerated, personal and relational learning.

Box 3.3: Not enough time

We are one hour and 40 minutes into a two-hour group supervision with three people. I invited Susan first, then Mary. We focused on what was coming up for the two of them. We spent 40 minutes with Susan and the last hour with Mary. With 20 minutes left, I turned to Fliss and asked her what she was bringing. She fidgeted in her chair, looked up at the clock and said:

    'There's only 20 minutes left, we're not going to have enough time!'

What are you noticing within you?

- *What are you thinking/imagining/remembering?*
- *What are you feeling?*
- *What are you imagining you would have done if you had been faced with the same scenario?*
- *What is your rationale for this?*

What actually happened next?

Fliss stood up and started talking quickly about all the things that were going on and going wrong. I asked her to pause, and she kept going. I spoke a bit louder, asking her to take a breath. She kept going. On the third time, I said even more loudly, 'Fliss, stop. Of everything that is going on, what is common to them all that is bothering you most?' She stopped talking, eyes wide open. Blinked at me, then burst into tears. . . . Out tumbled the accusations she was believing about herself. . . . And within minutes, she realised that she could remember nothing in her life that substantiated those accusations. The grip of another *Fiction* was broken, and having been released from it, Fliss sat back down in her chair. We all looked at the clock. Fifteen minutes had passed. Susan leaned forward to Fliss, saying, 'So there wasn't enough time to work on your stuff then?' We all erupted into hysterical laughter.

In this last scenario, I was attuning to the levels of tension present in Fliss. This was a repeating pattern of hers. Usually, she would speak first – to get whatever was going on in her out, as soon as possible. Mary had a tendency to hold back 'so there would not be time for her'. On this day, sensing that this pattern was about to play out again, I intervened by inviting the others in the group to bring their issues first. In so doing, I created the conditions for her to experience holding her tension longer than usual and for Mary to tip out sooner. Systemically, I was attending to both of their patterns in a single intervention.

The mechanistic (linear causality) worldview infusing Fliss' comment would have us believe that change requires 'lots of time', and this was no longer available. Added to this, you can imagine a tumble of possible *Fictions* that might have surfaced for Fliss. Rather than me speculating on what they might have been, I invite you to imagine being in her position and to tune in to your *Fictions*. Or perhaps you find yourself resonating with Mary. What gets activated in you?

What happened for Fliss is a wonderful example of nonlinear processing. *Emergence emerges beyond reason or control.* When conditions align, an internal reconfiguration happens incredibly quickly, literally from one moment to the next. Witnessing a person's shift is quite something to behold. That moment when a person's state changes from deep distress to calm serenity or unbridled laughter is breath-taking, awe-inspiring. This encounter surfaced the patterns playing out in the individuals and within the group. It proved a turning point in catalysing new levels of acuity, intimacy and daring amongst them. Yet none of us can predict what will catalyse such shifts, nor when or how. The only active contribution we can make when hosting ourselves or others, is to open and scaffold the space, and to facilitate noticing what is current. That. Is. It.

How else does this fit with my theoretical grounding? Firstly, the fundamental principle of natural inclusion expressed succinctly is that *receptive space invokes the in-flow of responsive energy.* So, in supervision, I am creating a receptive space into which others can flow; in a group, we hold this space together. This quality of receptivity is everything and it turns typical mechanistic notions of power, agency, leadership and proactivity upside down and back to front. In nature, receptive space is far from passive; it is a potent presence into and through which all energy flows. Without it there can be no motion. The heart, when it relaxes, draws in blood; the lungs, when the surrounding muscles relax, draw in air; the female egg opens up and admits a sperm cell – the sperm does not and cannot force its way in! Our human-made conceptions of 'leading' are contrary to nature's way. To re-align ourselves with nature, we simply need to recognise this receptive–responsive dance and to follow and flow when and where receptive space opens up for us.

So, when I invited Fliss, she flowed in, ready and full of her own latent transformative potential. I and the group held the space for her being–doing body to show up and literally move/walk through what was roiling within her. The P6 Constellation served as an external framing of her interior realm. The power of metaphorically stepping inside our Selves and literally experiencing our bodies walking from portal to portal in attunement with what comes out of our mouths or shows up in our beings un-spoken is where the theory of primal animation comes alive in this way of working. We find our emotions moving through us as they move us to move, and we find ourselves thinking in movement, which

> Means that a particular situation is unfolding as it is being created by a mindful body; a kinetic energy is forging its way in the world, shaping and being shaped by the developing patterns surrounding it.[32]

Having a shared framework as a resource makes an incredibly complex processing dynamic seem so very simple. How does it do that? Because it reduces one-dimensional cognitive overload by bringing all of our being~doing moving bodies into the inquiry. It opens us up to using our aesthetic, affective, auditory, kinaesthetic, kinetic, spatial, verbal and visual faculties, as well as our rational thinking, past recall and imaginations.

Closing comments

I am keenly aware that what you have encountered in these pages may be unfamiliar, surprising – and perhaps, at times, perturbing. In these pages, I have opened a window into how my worldview and theoretical grounding shows up in my praxis. My deepest hope is that in this account you may have found something that affirms, excites, aerates, inspires and enriches your own practice and, ultimately, our evolving profession – remembering that

No way is the only way!

Notes

1   In my thesis I use four icons (▶ ♫ ◆ ≈) to represent these four statewaves (Gardiner, 2021, PhD pending publication)
2   (Birch & Gardiner, 2019).
3   Enform means to form, shape or fashion.
4   (Gardiner, 2019, 2021b, PhD pending publication).
5   Natural Inclusionality (Rayner, 2017: pp. 55–59) is comprehensible only through modes of inquiry that attend to our actual experiences of natural phenomena: 'combine intimate (first person) with distanced (third person) modes of perception, to enable relational/empathetic (second person) perception . . . Intuitive, aesthetic, imaginative, empathetic, poetic modes of enquiry and expression are all valid, so long as these are experience-based' (Rayner, 2020: online).
6   In referring to 'complexity thinking', I bring together complexity science ('objective') and systems thinking (including meaning-making and perspectives typical in inter-subjective domains).
7   Animation is 'the fundamental, essential, and properly descriptive concept to understanding animal life' (Sheets-Johnstone, 2009: p. 375).
8   Living Theory Action Research (Whitehead, 1985, 2000, 2010).
9   These chapters offer more in-depth explanation of swarm behaviour, complex adaptive systems and natural inclusionality (Birch & Gardiner, 2019).
10   In the School of Systems Sciences in Hull University Business School.
11   I use **'admit'** in a very particular way. When I **embolden** the word, I invoke the complex of its meanings: '**Admit**: acknowledge/recognise; allow/take in, allow the possibility/validity of; accept as valid/possible' (Gardiner, 2021b, PhD pending publication: Appendix, p. 133).
12   Aesthetic–Poetic gave birth to 34 poems during my doctoral inquiry. Additionally, I have created several approaches, frameworks and models (Gardiner, 2021b, PhD pending publication).
13   (Bateson, 2016: p. 169).
14   Self-protection is one of two primal purposes I see playing out repeatedly in myself and others. This shows up, often inappropriately – not when I am **actually** under threat, but

when I am **believing** I am; that is, when something from my past that is not grounded in present actualities becomes activated and begins to play out through me, often precipitating outcomes I am trying to avert (Gardiner, 2021b, PhD pending publication).

15 This behaviour sits at the heart of my praxis, keeping me alert to my ethical commitment to act for the well-being of myself, others and the wider world (Gardiner, 2019).

16 (Rayner, 2017, 2018).

17 My composite doctoral submission will be in the public domain 2021/2022.

18 Epistemology refers to how knowledge is 'created' and what is knowable. Simplistically, this is delineated in three ways: objective (that which exists independent of an individual; factual, tangible, quantifiable); subjective (personal: meaning a person makes of something, unverifiable by anyone except the individual whose meaning it is); inter-subjective/constructionist (that which arises between subject–object where the object can also be other persons; meaning-making conveyed in and through language/symbols and taken to be real, amongst those who agree it to be so).

19 (Crotty, 1998; Evely et al., 2008; Moon & Blackman, 2014).

20 By 'reflective', I mean looking back to the past to better understand what we did, how and why and referring to other knowledge sources to see if/how they may illuminate what we experienced. It also means reflecting back 'mirror-like', with nothing added, and nothing taken away. 'Reflexive' refers to in-the-moment **noticing** and **attending** to what is happening in the here and now (Gardiner, 2019, 2021b, PhD pending publication).

21 Scientific experiments rely on creating stable experimental conditions, for example, by introducing fixed protocols (not possible in 'real life'), attempting to remove variables (that are inextricably linked in 'real life' so cannot actually be removed) and then assuming that if we do the **exact** same thing over and over again we will get guaranteed results (which, in real life, we know rarely happens, because everything is always changing and we are adapting accordingly).

22 In complex living systems, there are infinite, entangled interdependencies. When we 'remove' variables to try to make a situation more 'stable'(i.e., more predictable and manageable), we may inadvertently introduce far greater instability. This is why many change programmes fail.

23 Praxis: the generative fusion of practice and theory informing and enhancing each other.

24 (Whitehead, 1985).

25 The praxis of Presence in Action is scaffolded by a framework called the P6 Constellation, a practice called the Acuity Practice; and set of paradigm-attuned behaviours through which our embodied knowing is expressed. These are called Symmathesic Agency Behaviours (Gardiner, 2019, 2021b, PhD pending publication).

26 See Chapter 7 herein; and also Gardiner (2014, 2019, 2021b, PhD pending publication).

27 In using this term 'data', I am expanding its meaning to include intangible as well as tangible data.

28 (Andersson, 2018).

29 All names are made up and some details are brought together from different cases to safeguard anonymity.

30 (Sheets-Johnstone, 1999).

31 See Chapter 7 herein (Sheets-Johnstone, 1999, 2009, 2011).

32 (Sheets-Johnstone, 1981: p. 405).

References

Andersson, P. (2018). *Making Room for Complexity in Group Collaborations: The Roles of Scaffolding and Facilitation*. Doctor of Philosophy Doctoral Thesis. University of Gothenburg, 9 November. http://hdl.handle.net/2077/57854.

Bateson, N. (2016). *Small Arcs of Larger Circles – Framing Through Other Patterns*. Triarchy Press.

Birch, J., & Gardiner, L. J. N. (2019). Seven Simple Rules: An Alternative Lens. In J. Birch & P. Welch (Eds.), *Coaching Supervision: Advancing Practice, Changing Landscapes* (pp. 21–34). London: Routledge.

Crotty, M. (1998). *The Foundations of Social Research: Meaning and Perspective in the Research Process.* London: Sage.

Evely, A. C., Fazey, I., Pinard, M., & Lambin, X. (2008). The Influence of Philosophical Perspectives in Integrative Research: A Conservation Case Study in the Cairngorms National Park. *Ecology and Society*, 13(2).

Gardiner, L. J. N. (2014). Changing the Game of Change-making. *Coaching Today*, 12, 6–11.

Gardiner, L. J. N. (2019). Attending, Daring, Becoming: Making Boundary-Play Conscious. In J. Birch & P. Welch (Eds.), *Coaching Supervision: Advancing Practice, Changing Landscapes* (1st ed., pp. 103–125). London: Routledge.

Gardiner, L. J. N. (2021a). *Attending, Responding, Becoming: An Anthology of Surprises Beyond Intention or Design.* Edinburgh: Flora George Publishing.

Gardiner, L. J. N. (2021b). *Attending, Responding, Becoming: A Living~Learning Inquiry in a Naturally Inclusional Playspace.* PhD University of Hull, PhD pending publication.

Moon, K., & Blackman, D. (2014). A Guide to Understanding Social Science Research for Natural Scientists. *Conservation Biology*, 28(5), 1167–1177.

Rayner, A. D. M. (2017). *The Origin of Life Patterns: In the Natural Inclusion of Space in Flux.* Cham, Switzerland: Springer Nature.

Rayner, A. D. M. (2018). The Vitality of the Intangible: Crossing the Threshold from Abstract Materialism to Natural Reality. *Human Arenas*, 1, 9–20.

Rayner, A. D. M. (2020). The (New) Natural Evolutionary Science & Philosophy of Inclusive Flow: Natural Inclusionality. https://admrayner.medium.com/the-new-natural-evolutionary-science-philosophy-of-inclusive-flow-natural-inclusionality-3ecd19ad7657 [Accessed: 23 June 2020].

Sheets-Johnstone, M. (1981). Thinking in Movement. *The Journal of Aesthetics and Art Criticism*, 39(4), 399–407.

Sheets-Johnstone, M. (1999). Emotion and Movement. A Beginning Empirical-Phenomenological Analysis of Their Relationship. *Journal of Consciousness Studies*, 6(11–12), 259–277.

Sheets-Johnstone, M. (2009). Animation: The Fundamental, Essential, and Properly Descriptive Concept. *Continental Philosophy Review*, 42(3), 375–400.

Sheets-Johnstone, M. (2011). Embodied Minds or Mindful Bodies? A Question of Fundamental, Inherently Inter-Related Aspects of Animation. *Subjectivity*, 4(4), 451–466.

Whitehead, J. (1985). An Analysis of an Individual's Educational Development: The Basis for Personally Oriented Action Research. *Educational Research: Principles, Policies and Practice*, 97–108.

Whitehead, J. (2000). How Do I Improve My Practice? Creating and Legitimating an Epistemology of Practice. *Reflective Practice*, 1(1), 91–104.

Whitehead, J. (2010). Creating an Educational Epistemology in the Multi-Media Narratives of Living Educational Theories and Living Theory Methodologies. *Action Researcher in Education*, 1(1), 89–109.

Chapter 4

Meaning-making encounters
The strength of peer supervision

Ana Pliopas

The calendar reminded me that the following day, the three of us – Rick, Sally[1] and I – would have a 90-minute virtual call, our monthly triad supervision meeting: Sally and Rick calling from Santa Barbara, California, and I from São Paulo, Brazil. We would greet each other with warmth, then one of us would bring a topic to the group. Without following any rigid format or order, we would be curious about the topic, look at it from different angles and feel it from our hearts and bodies. This would not be a trivial conversation between friends nor a learning session about supervision. Our peer supervision meetings were meaning-making encounters, and I always left the calls a changed person.

As the world becomes more complex, traditional approaches to coach development must go beyond skill-based competencies; alongside mastery of asking powerful questions, coaches need to be very familiar with systems thinking[2] and be able to explore complex issues (McLean, 2019). Coaching supervision is one of the means coaches may rely on to continue to learn, develop and confront continually transforming and complex issues. Research shows that coaching supervision outcomes for coaches include increased self-awareness, confidence, objectivity, resourcefulness and capability (Tkach & DiGirolamo, 2017). In 2013, a coaching school based in the United States decided to offer its students coaching supervision services and part of the faculty was invited to join a supervision program to become coach supervisors. Following completion of the 10-month-long training, we engaged in monthly group supervision to reflect on our supervision practices, a supervision of supervision (SoS) group. Nine faculty members had monthly group supervision together to reflect on, and learn from, our own interventions as supervisors. Participants of this group were also divided into practice triads, to strengthen our supervision skills and to deepen the reflection and the learning. These practice triads met outside the larger group. This is how our peer supervision group was born: three supervisors who supervised coaches, mainly in group settings. We have continued to meet for almost four years now, and in that time our triad has changed in format and content.

Since our first peer supervision session, in January 2017, the three of us have had an average of 10 peer supervision meetings per year, and each call has lasted 90 minutes. In this chapter, I share how our peer supervision encounters transformed

DOI: 10.4324/978100314345-5

over time, divided in three phases: the educational phase, the meta-supervision phase, and the phase when we made sense of senseless contexts. I then share some concepts about social constructionism, to provide context for my description of our peer supervision triad as a 'meaning-making space'. As Kenneth Gergen (2009) suggests, by playing at the edges of common sense, people may cross the threshold into new worlds of meaning. In our triads, by speaking together, listening to alternatives and going beyond the obvious, we have been able to create new meanings. We are able to make sense of our worlds.

The three phases of our peer supervision group

During the almost four years of peer supervision, our journey together transformed as our lives changed and as we brought ourselves to each supervision session. During the first phase, we followed a traditional triad practice format very common in coaching and in supervision training courses. During the second phase, we reflected together about coaching supervision itself: what it was and how it affected our practice and our views towards supervision. In the current phase, we have grappled with how the world is changing and the intertwined effects of this on each of us, our labour and personal aspects of our lives.

The educational phase

The traditional triad setup is commonly used in coaching and supervision training programs in which people enroll to become certified coaches or certified coaching supervisors. Participants are divided into groups of three and meet to practice, and therefore develop, their coaching or supervision skills. The roles of supervisor, supervisee and observer rotate at every meeting of the triad members. In our case, as explained earlier, triads were formed to deepen the reflection and learning from a larger SoS group.

During this first phase of our peer supervision group, we followed the conventional triad format: Rick, for example, would volunteer to play the role of a supervisor, Sally would be the supervisee, sharing a case she would be willing to learn from, and I would play the observer role. Our focus during the educational phase was mainly to strengthen our capacity as supervisors. This phase clearly mirrored the triad supervision structure some of us had experienced in supervision training programs we had attended.

Throughout this phase, the negotiated reality of our practice had the following outline: we were in our triad to improve our coaching supervision skills. The roles of supervisor, observer and supervisee would rotate among us. We trusted everything we said would be kept private within our little group, so information shared would be treated as confidential. We were in the business of becoming better coaching supervisors, and the meaning we attributed to this was "supervisors with superior skills." When I use the term "superior skills", I mean not so much related to external standards that might have been imposed on us but skills improvement according to our own desires and expectations. Although we never made such aspects explicit, the experiences we had had – like being part of a larger supervision group, having been through coaching and supervision training programs and also being coaching trainers – created the dynamics of how our triad worked.

The term "negotiated reality" deserves a closer look: in social constructionism, what is considered *real* depends on people agreeing with this truth: reality depends on interactions between people. It is in interpersonal communication processes by which the world gains meaning (Gergen et al., 2009). What we take for granted in the world depends on the social relationships that we are a part of, and nothing is real until people agree that it is real. The realities in which we live are the result of the interactions in which we engage. We deal with the world through the construction of meanings, and it is in this sense that we build our world (Potter, 1990), our reality. What effectively happened in the meetings, our reality, was negotiated, implicitly or explicitly. For example, the meaning of "supervision skills" took on different dimensions as the three of us continued to rotate as supervisors, supervisees and observers.

Each of us brought to the triads the different selves from the other aspects of our lives. For example, during the first phase of our triad, I was writing my doctoral thesis and seeing the world through very critical eyes. I felt that all aspects of my research could be questioned and was mainly concerned in building solid arguments for my thesis. Because I was making sense of what being an academic meant, as well as having imaginary conversations with academic authors and experiencing actual talks with my advisor, different professors and many colleagues, I brought my tentative academic self to our triad conversations.

At the same time, Sally was collecting the data for her doctoral program and seemed fascinated with the meanings people attributed to their own development. Her research was about supervision of coaching groups, and she was particularly moved by a supervisee who was one of her research participants. This supervisee was extremely uncomfortable with having her coaching skills recognised, acknowledged and appreciated by her supervisor or other members of the supervision group. She would only accept comments that highlighted aspects she needed to improve. Sally saw how the participant was so critical about herself and her coaching skills. Sally brought her researcher self to our peer supervision calls.

Another perspective of social constructionism relates to the concept of being a person: as we relate to one another, we bring to the interaction the traces of former relationships and all of us are involved in continuous processes of negotiation in interpersonal spaces. Social constructionists call this way of defining a person the "relational self". I brought my tentative academic self, and Sally brought her researcher self to our triad conversations: she could see the self-critic in me as she had seen the self-critic in one of her research participants. We both brought the experiences we were having in other areas of our lives to make sense of the cases we were bringing to our triad practices.

Also, as an academic in the making during the first phase of our triad, I was trying to understand social constructionism from an epistemological perspective.

I remember attempting to explain to Sally and Rick what this way of seeing the world and supervision processes meant to me. After what was probably a collage of ideas without many connections among them, Rick asked me to move from *The New York Times* version of what I meant to the *USA Today*[3] description of social constructionism.

Once again, I brought my exploratory academic self and Rick brought his American newspaper reader to our triad. After he offered his metaphor for what I was saying, we entered in a dialogue in which the three of us grappled with the meaning of social constructionism in the coaching and supervision setting.

The meta-supervision phase

Without conscious decision, we moved from the educational phase in which we rotated the roles of supervisor, supervisee and observer to a thoughtful space where we mainly reflected on coaching supervision. As I write and reflect on the phases our peer supervision group went through, my guess is that the main change that moved our triad to the second phase was Rick enrolling in a year-long coaching supervision program. Although he had already been trained as a coaching supervisor, he decided to take a deeper dive into coaching supervision and off to training he went.

The three of us started reflecting on how the supervisor in our SoS group conducted the sessions, learning from our interpretations of her supervision interventions, making meaning of how we showed up in the SoS group and in the groups we supervised. For example, we reflected on how the supervisor in our larger group was able to create a resonance chamber for the group members: creating a safe space where the supervisee could show their vulnerability and holding the space for reflection to happen. As we experienced our SoS group supervisor and made meaning about what we had seen and mainly felt in our larger supervision group, we realised that supervision was more about holding the space for the reflective work to happen than demonstrating a set of skills.

During the second phase of our triad, we overcame our concerns with the format, interventions, and structure of coaching supervision sessions, probably because these aspects had already been incorporated in our regular supervision practices and triad meetings. As we transitioned to phase two, our triad calls started and we checked in and offered themes for reflection and meaning-making in a natural and organic way.

During the meta-supervision phase, I moved from feelings of fear of being incompetent to admitting to and sharing how I judge others, for example. As an illustration, it was fascinating to see how Rick was able to draw on aspects of his life in order to make meaning about his interactions with two different groups of coaches he was supervising. During one of our meetings, he brought differ-ent aspects of his relational self: the coaching instructor, the man who chose his high school friends according to a certain logic and the brave vulnerable supervi-sor willing to own his feelings. By bringing the different and interrelating lenses through which he was seeing his two supervision groups, and by inviting me and Sally to make sense of what "judging" meant for Rick, the three of us were able to reflect on, and to make sense of, what "judging" meant in group coaching supervision contexts. We were not solving Rick's case; we were grappling, playing with ideas, perspectives and contexts. Without a final solution, verdict or truth, the three of us ended the call transformed as supervisors, having made sense of what the word "judgmental" meant to each of us.

The way I make sense about my own way of showing up in our triad meetings was that by this time I had already completed and defended my thesis and a heavy weight had been lifted from my shoulders. For the four years of my doctoral journey, I had felt like I was walking inside a big grey cloud filled with thoughts of deadlines, bibliographies, categories and methodologies. In phase two of our triads, I was lighter, freer to make meanings and further from the critical tentative academic self I had brought to our triads in the first phase.

The second phase was also much more fun and interesting compared with the educational one. Seeing the triad call in my calendar instilled feelings of happiness and excitement because we had moved from "let's learn how to be better supervisors" to "let's make sense of what being a supervisor means". The three of us were willing to show up and to be changed by our life experiences. Rick was being changed by becoming a student again, I was a lighter, freer person, and Sally was being transformed by making sense of the data on her research; on top of that, she had gone through a radical personal change.

Making sense of senseless contexts

With the advent of the coronavirus pandemic in late 2019, the context changed dramatically. One frequent characteristic of our conversations in this new phase was the ambiguity of the feelings we experienced. On the one hand, there were feelings of fear about the pandemic and, on the other, glimpses of joy when we were able to connect with loved ones and for trivial pleasures, like cooking a tasty meal.

Our triad calls could have become conversations between three friends: the context we were living in was so bizarre that we could have used our time together just to chat, and that certainly would have been satisfying. But that was not what happened: we continued to come to our calls to reflect and to make sense of what was happening in the world in general, in our particular worlds and in our worlds as supervisors.

The reason we were able to make meaning of our three selves who were being transformed by dramatic changes in our context was the invisible, delicate structure that guided our conversations. This gentle structure had been built during the two previous phases and was supported by the underlying truth that everything we said in the triad would continue to be kept confidential. Also, as a natural coordinated dance, we would do a gentle check-in, in which we each shared how we were arriving to the conversation. After the check-in, or sometimes encapsulated in it, we identified what we would offer as a reflection theme. The tacit question was "where will we go today?", and off to meaning-making we went.

Another feature of the gentle structure that permeated our triads was welcoming silence and emotions. As experienced coaches and supervisors, we were used to sustaining silence or, as Pam McLean (2019) says, letting the silence do the work. Also, we were skilled in welcoming emotions with curiosity and warmth, and, because we were experienced in dealing with both silence and emotions, there was a gift of knowing what we were doing and simultaneously experiencing the benefit of the interaction of silence and emotions.

One example of this phase was our reflection on how the word "presence" gained a whole new meaning during the pandemic. As coaching supervisors, it was habitual for us to invite coaches to perceive their roles not as experts whose mission was to fix the client and tell her what to do. In one of our triad sessions during this phase, we reflected on the importance of *presence* for our supervisees: in a context where nobody knew how reality would unfold, it was impossible to tell what people should do, based on the simple fact that nobody knew what the world would look like after the pandemic. So, the temptation for the coach to add value by providing advice was not there anymore: what advice might be given if nobody knew what the future would bring? The unprecedent context provided coaches with the opportunity to experience *presence* as a powerful intervention.

Coming to our triads while in quarantine helped us to understand who we were becoming during this time and how we were being transformed and affected by this stretch. The significance of human touch took on a whole new dimension for us. When Sally, who had been living alone, shared how much she missed physical contact with other people, I immediately remembered the strong and cadenced hug from my father and how much I missed that. Rick also told us how much he missed being with his two-year-old granddaughter. We agreed that being able to connect virtually was a blessing and at the same time there were precious, very precious, aspects of human connection that we had taken for granted before being isolated and that gained new meaning under quarantine.

The gentle structure which permeated the third phase of our triad allowed our triad meetings to be more than warm conversations between friends. Meaning-making in the triad setting was not a debate of ideas but a genuine disposition to bring who we were to the conversation; to listen with our entire selves, head, heart and souls; and a willingness to produce new meanings about what was going on with us, in the world, with our practice and our clients.

In the previous two phases of our triad, we were used to making sense of supervision interventions, of coaching supervision and the meanings we attributed to our practices. Time together during the triads and continuing the peer supervision group encounters for almost four years provided us with the subtle structure that allowed us to make sense of the many changes and challenges we are currently facing.

Explaining the lenses through which I chose to look at our triad journey

Although I introduced the concepts of relational self and negotiated reality previously, it is relevant to share briefly where such concepts came from. Social constructionism is a theoretical perspective influenced by different intellectual traditions such as Sociology, Social Philosophy and Sociology of Knowledge (Cunliffe, 2008). One fundamental idea about social constructionism is that reality, the world as we understand it and take for granted, is shaped by the meanings we attribute to it. Such meanings are derived from cultural, social and historical aspects and are mediated by language (Philp et al., 2007).

Scholars have different interests in and approaches to social construction-ism. Some authors take a macro-level approach and are concerned with cul-tural, institutional and ideological aspects of the world. For example, some social constructionists researchers ponder how socially constructed categories such as gender or race are discursively produced and enacted within broader his-torical contexts (Cunliffe, 2008). This has not been the path we have chosen to suggest the different phases of our triad. I prefer to take the perspective of authors who are concerned about how people create meaning and realities with others in spontaneous, responsive ways, via relational encounters, such as McNamee and Gergen (1992), for example, who explore psychotherapy through social constructionist lenses.

Considering relational encounters, which are the basis of psychotherapy, therapists who are influenced by realist models tend to seek therapy supervision aiming to uncover "the truth" about their clients and expect authority prescrip-tions from their supervisors. Distinct from realist perspectives, supervision as social construction implies the deconstruction not only of the supervisees, but also of supervisors' ways of working. This approach involves more than a supervisor approving or correcting a technique; it requires a supervisor's pre-disposition and willingness to examine her own beliefs. It is not surprising that psychotherapists who conduct their practice from a social constructionist perspec-tive also seek therapy supervision with the same approach. Social constructionist therapy supervision views supervision not as a conclusive or absolute model, a pursuit for objective diagnosis or the finding of corrective, fitting interventions. From the social constructionist view, therapy supervision is an opportunity for development and cocreation of new meanings (Philp et al., 2007: p. 52).

It is not only psychotherapy and supervision psychotherapy that have adopted social constructionists' perspectives. In the coaching space, there are authors who adopt the social constructionist approach in their practices. Constructionists consider coaching sessions as privileged opportunities for the elaboration of meanings and view coaching as a special form of conversation in which new realities and new narratives are elaborated by the coachee in the conversational process with the coach (Stelter, 2007, 2019; Pliopas, 2018). Although construc-tionism clarifies that people create reality all the time by elaborating meanings in relational processes (Gergen, 2009; Burr, 2015), coaching authors with a constructionist perspective propose that during coaching sessions, coachee and coach may challenge "taken for granted" narratives and build new ones. For constructionist coaches, a coachee's description of a situation does not correspond to the picture of the world but rather to a selectively edited *representation* of the world (Barner & Higgins, 2007).

Du Toit (2007, 2014), for example, presents coaching as highly appropriate to support the elaboration of meanings because coaching deals with people's beliefs and values. Social constructionist authors on coaching emphasise the importance of language in the construction of reality and the elaboration of meanings in relationships (Barner & Higgins, 2005, 2007; Stelter, 2007, 2009, 2014, 2015, 2019; Du Toit & Sim, 2010; Reissner & Du Toit, 2011; Du Toit, 2014).

Choosing the ontological lens that guided scientific research was an important step in my doctoral journey, and social constructionism has turned out to be a congruent view that incorporates not only academic instances but also my practice as a coach and coaching supervisor. I have been embedded in social constructionism since 2004. It is therefore not surprising that I see our peer supervision group as a meaning-making space, where the three of us were not in pursuit of a conclusive, objective answer to a question or the discovery of the best intervention for a supervision case or a technical doubt. In this space, our triad call, we were not fencing with ideas or debating with the objective of convincing one another. We looked at each other's perspectives with genuine curiosity and passion; we contributed our own feelings and ideas, and, in an imaginary cauldron where the three of us added new ingredients, our perspectives and ideas, we cocreated new meanings: meanings that none of us would have created by ourselves. For example, one theme that we looked at in some of our supervision sessions was what "judgment" meant for us, our reactions to and experiences of the word, the different lenses through which we looked at the concept, and mainly, how the meaning of the word "judgment" was transformed for us due to our interaction.

The other concept mentioned earlier, and which deserves a closer look, is the understanding of relational self. Social constructionism places special importance on interactions and relationships we develop with each other in understanding what it means to be a person. In order to compare the constructionist perspective with other views in a very simplified way, the personal identity, or self (Sampson, 1993), can traditionally be perceived in an individualised way on one side, or a communal way, on the other extreme of an imaginary spectrum (Gergen et al., 2009). In the trait tradition, in which a person is perceived as individualised, people are seen as a sum of their traits, and their behaviour is determined by the sum of such characteristics. People are perceived as solid agents, and the person is understood to have only one identity: his or her personality (Whetherell & Potter, 1989). Also in a simplified way, on the opposite side of the continuum, roles theorists argue that the self is a social product, and people have different parts to play in society, which require different manifestations of self, or different personalities (Whetherell & Potter, 1989).

Unlike the two poles (people taken as individualised in one extreme or communal in the other), in the constructionist perspective, personal identity is constantly emerging in conversational and continuous socially rooted processes (Sampson, 1993). The self is a manifestation of relationships (Gergen, 2000), and the person is not seen as isolated but as a complex phenomenon of our past and present relationships. Selves are built and negotiated in relationships and each new relationship in which we interact has the mark of other previous relationships.

From the social constructionist view, the person we are depends on other people (Burr, 2015). People are not, therefore, immutable entities in themselves and they owe their stability, constancy and uniqueness to the stability of their activities and practices with other people (Shotter, 1989). In this way, the self is created and maintained via social interactions, and some individual self is subjectively preserved (Back, 1989). Each person is embroiled in a constant process of negotiation in an interpersonal space (Spink & Medrado, 2000). In this process of constant elaboration of the relational self, it is through language and in relationships that we become who we are and that the world becomes rational or irrational, good or bad (Gergen et al., 2009).

For example, the three of us brought different relational selves to our meetings. Sally may be portrayed as a researcher, Rick can be seen as a coaching instructor and I show myself as an academic in the making. Also, in another part, Rick is perceived as a supervisor student, Sally as a supervisor instructor and me as an adjunct professor. Many other relational selves were also present in our peer supervision group, and we transformed ourselves during our journey with the group.

Final words

It is worth looking deeper at the components of the "cauldron" metaphor of our peer supervision group. In each meeting, it was as if we had a cauldron in front of us, with each of us offering ingredients and stirring the content to represent the reflection process during our triad. First, there is a strong container to hold the process, the cauldron itself, that represents the safety we felt with each other to bring our entire selves to the calls. The structure of the calls, with some sort of predictable framework, was also a component of our meaning-making cauldron. The ideas we shared and the new ways to look at realities represent the ingredients we brought to the cauldron. Our ways of interacting with each other, bringing emotion, different paces and silence, may be seen as a big spoon used to stir the meanings in the making. The result was a subtle, unpredictable transformation in each of us, as we drank the content of the cauldron: the new meanings we made.

We not only created new meanings via reflection in our peer supervision groups but, by bringing our relational selves to the calls, the meetings also changed as our contexts, our lives and ourselves changed. The three phases of our triad journey illustrate how I have made sense of the changes in our journey so far.

I identify four aspects that have been key to the continuity and development of our peer supervision group: safety, structure, consistency and care. These aspects are intertwined and feed each other. Our peer supervision group has been a safe space, and this has allowed us to bring our entire selves to the meetings. We showed up with curiosity, with full dedication to our time together. Besides being present, we came with openness to reflect and to be changed by the interactions with one another. I felt safe, not only because the content of the call would be kept confidential, but also because I knew what would happen in terms of the meeting configuration and that both reflection partners would be there with me.

The educational phase of our triad was key to provide us with structure for the calls because it gave us an idea of what was going to happen in the encounters. It was the structure built in the educational phase and transformed in the meta supervision phase that differentiated our calls from loose conversations with friends. Consistency is another component for the unfolding of our triad: in almost four years we have attended every single call. It was this regularity of attendance that allowed us to move from phase one, to phase two and now phase three. If we had not showed up, there would not have been a journey. There has been transformation in our triad journey, internal and external. As contexts have changed, so have the three of us. And such transformation has been possible because we have not only arrived at each call, we have showed up and been part of the meaning-making in our peer supervision group.

Finally, care matters. Sally has been the glue in our peer supervision group: she reminds us when there are no further calls booked in our calendars and proposes we take five minutes to schedule future ones, and she sends the meeting link two days in advance. Without Sally's kindness our peer supervision group would not have come this far. All my gratitude to you, Sally.

Notes

1 Names have been changed for purposes of confidentiality.
2 The term "system thinking" refers to considering broader contexts: organizational, social, political or economic, for example.
3 My American friends share that, in terms of easiness of reading, *The New York Times* is perceived as high-school level and *USA Today* is seen as elementary-school level.

References

Back, K. W. (1989). Triller: The Self in Modern Society. In J. Shotter & K. J. Gergen (Eds.), *Texts of Identity* (pp. 220–236). London: Sage.

Barner, R., & Higgins, J. (2005). A Social Constructionist Approach to Leadership Coaching. *OD Practitioner*, 37(4), 37–41.

Barner, R., & Higgins, J. (2007). Understanding Implicit Models That Guide the Coaching Process. *Journal of Management Development*, 26(2), pp. 148–158. doi: 10.1108/02621710710726053.

Burr, V. (2015). *Social Constructionism* (3rd ed.). Hove: Routledge.

Cunliffe, A. L. (2008). Orientations to Social Constructionism: Relationally Responsive Social Constructionism. *Management Learning*, 39(2), 123–139. doi: 10.1177/1350507607087578.

Du Toit, A. (2007). Making Sense Through Coaching. *Journal of Management Development*, 26(3), 282–291. doi: 10.1108/02621710710732164.

Du Toit, A. (2014). *Making Sense of Coaching*. London: Sage.

Du Toit, A., & Sim, S. (2010). *Rethinking Coaching: Critical Theory and the Economic Crisis*. London: Palgrave Macmillan.

Gergen, K. J. (2000). *The Saturated Self: Dilemmas of Identity in Contemporary Life*. New York: Basic Books.

Gergen, K. J. (2009). *An Invitation to Social Construction* (2nd ed.). London: Sage.

Gergen, K. J., Schrader, S. M., & Gergen, M. (2009). *Constructing Worlds Together: Interpersonal Communication as Relational Process*. Boston: Pearson Education.

McLean, P. (2019). *Self as Coach, Self as Leader: Developing the Best in You to Develop the Best in Others*. Hoboken, NJ: Wiley.

Mcnamee, S., & Gergen, K. J. (1992). *Therapy as Social Construction*. London: Sage.

Philp, K., Guy, G., & Lowe, R. (2007). Social Constructionist Supervision or Supervision as Social Construction? Some Dilemmas. *Journal of Systemic Therapies*, 26(1), 51–62. doi: 10.1521/jsyt.2007.26.1.51.

Pliopas, A. (2018). *Coaching Executivo: Dinâmicas das relações entre o coachee, o coach e a organização*. EAESP-FGV. file:///C:/Users/Claudemir/Desktop/TESES_GT/010_PLIOPAS (FGV, 2018).pdf.

Potter, J. (1990). Discourse : Noun, Verb or Social Practice ? *Philosophical Psychology*, 3(2), 205–217.

Reissner, S. C., & Du Toit, A. (2011). Power and the Tale: Coaching as Storyselling. *The Journal of Management Development*, 30(3), 247–259. doi: 10.1108/02621711111116171.

Sampson, E. E. (1993). *Celebrating the Other: A Dialogic Account of Human Nature*. Boulder: Simon & Schuster International.

Shotter, J. (1989). Social Accountability and the Social Construction of "You". In J. Shotter & K. J. Gergen (Eds.), *Texts of Identity* (pp. 133–150). London: Sage.

Spink, M.-J. P., & Medrado, B. (2000). Produção de sentidos no cotidiano: uma abordagem teórico-metodológica para análise das práticas discursivas. In M.-J. P. Spink (Ed.), *Práticas discursivas e produção de sentidos no cotidiano: aproximações teóricas e metodológicas* (2nd ed., pp. 41–61). Sao Paulo: Cortez Editora.

Stelter, R. (2007). Coaching: A Process of Personal and Social Meaning Making. *International Coaching Psychology Review*, 2(2), 191–201.

Stelter, R. (2009). Coaching as a Reflective Space in a Society of Growing Diversity – Towards a Narrative, Postmodern Paradigm. *International Coaching Psychology Review*, 4(2), 207–217.

Stelter, R. (2014). *A Guide to Third Generation Coaching*. Dordrecht: Springer Netherlands. doi: 10.1007/978-94-007-7186-4.

Stelter, R. (2015). "I Tried So Many Diets, Now I Want to Do It Differently" – A Single Case Study on Coaching for Weight Loss. *International Journal of Qualitative Studies on Health and Well-Being*, 10(1), 26925. doi: 10.3402/qhw.v10.26925.

Stelter, R. (2019). *The Art of Dialogue in Coaching: Towards Transformative Exchange*. Abingdon, Oxon: Routledge.

Tkach, T. J., & DiGirolamo, J. A. (2017). The State and Future of Coaching Supervision. *International Coaching Psychology Review*, 12(December), 49–63.

Whetherell, M., & Potter, J. (1989). Narrative Characters and Accounting for Violence. In J, Shotter & K. J. Gergen (Eds.), *Texts of Identity* (pp. 206–219). London: Sage.

Chapter 5

The terror and transformation of coaching supervision groups

Leanne Lowish

What are some of the struggles you are facing in your world right now?
What about your clients and client organisations – what is on their minds?
What about your community and your clients' communities?
What are the big challenges we are facing in the world, in the planet now and in the future?

These are big questions with which to start a chapter. In my experience, our concerns – about our clients, our family, our communities, our organisations, our planet – sit uncomfortably with us as we go about our day, either in our consciousness or slightly out of it; maybe appearing in our dreams; maybe we react more quickly or startle more easily; maybe we notice an aching shoulder or stiff neck. I believe our concerns and worries live in our psyche, and our bodies and stop us from fully relaxing and opening to our collective and embodied wisdom. And yet, I would argue it is in our collective and embodied wisdom that we find solace for our concerns.

One way of finding this comfort with our concerns is to come together in community (Huebl, 2020). We meet as humans from different fields, countries, cultures, races and ages to inquire together into what is happening *within* us and *around* us, to sense into our interconnectedness, to drop into 'not knowing', to feel into the mystery and to allow our collective embodied wisdom to emerge.

This chapter seeks to explore group coaching supervision as a place of community, a place where coaches can come together in service of our coaching and supervision practices, our clients and the communities and systems within which they operate; a place where we can inquire and dig deep to discover insights that reveal the future that is waiting to emerge and be lived.

I have centred this chapter around my own personal inquiry into the process of creating and running a coaching supervision group, using the key concepts from Theory U (Scharmer, 2007) to illustrate the process of working with emergence in this setting. I use an autoethnographic approach to describe my own journey and to seek to reveal what is under the surface. Autoethnography calls for an increasingly deeper inquiry into the embodied experience (Birch, 2020) 'asking over and over if we have penetrated as many layers of our own defences, fears and

DOI: 10.4324/978100314345-6

insecurities as our project requires' (Ellis, 2019: p. 10). As I introduce you to the process of the U, I will make explicit some of the voices of judgement, cynicism and fear that arose in me as I descended the U and comment on the techniques I used to help me stay in a place of 'not knowing', allowing the dynamism and alive-ness that is inherent in our human nature to arise within me and guide me.

The autoethnographical process can be enhanced by including the experiences of others in the system to give additional perspective. So, I have engaged the participants from a coaching supervision group in dialogue about our collective process, and their voices are included throughout this piece. I also include reflective prompts for you, the reader, and invite you to join in this inquiry by noticing your own responses, feelings and thoughts.

What is Theory U?

Theory U focuses on 'how individuals and groups and organisations can sense and actualize their highest future potential' (Scharmer, 2018: p. 16). I encountered Theory U 13 years ago and have simultaneously followed its development while experimenting with and adapting it to my own working situations, in this case, coaching supervision. For me, it outlines a process that I have witnessed and experienced in myself and my clients over the 20 years I have been working in the field of organisational transformation.

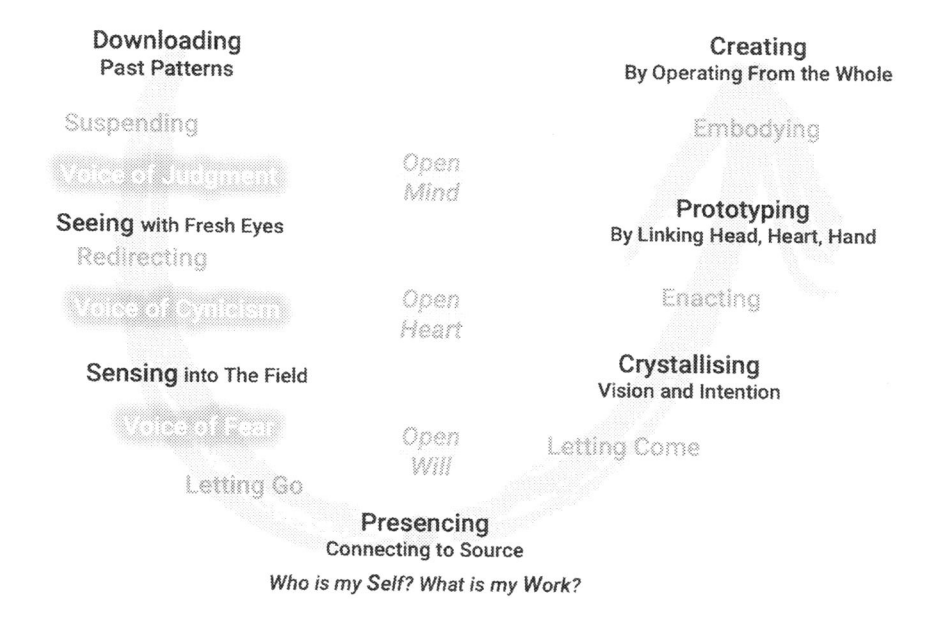

Figure 5.1 (This work is licensed by the Presencing Institute – Otto Scharmer – www.presencing.org/resource/permission)

The process begins at the top left side of the U shape, with a complex issue, question, concern or situation that indicates a future we want to bring forth. We want to get to the other side, the top right-hand side of the U, to where this future is being created, by operating in a new way from the integrated whole! We may be tempted to jump across the top, believing that our thinking mind, using our past thoughts, experiences and habitual behaviour patterns, can generate the outcome we desire in the future.

However, if we are to truly get the best outcomes in complex issues and situations, we might be better served by travelling down the left-hand side of the U. This involves *suspending* our *downloading* from past experiences and instead getting curious, thereby *opening our 'minds'* to new ways of thinking and our eyes to *new ways of seeing*. We take a deep dive into *sensing* what is in us and around us, activating our compassion and *opening our 'hearts'* to new perspectives. We use our courage to *open our 'will'* to *let go* of everything we know, or think we know. We surrender to the bottom of the U, where we can *connect to a deeper source* of wisdom beyond our customary knowing, the world that is emerging from within, which is concerned with the fundamental questions of our soul: '*Who is my Self?*' and '*What is my Work?*' Scharmer (2007) calls this central feature of Theory U '*Presencing*': the integration of 'presence' and 'sensing'.

In this place of '*presencing*', we let go of our ego self and open to our deeper source of knowing, *letting come a vision and intention* from our highest future possibility: our 'Self' rather than our ego. We are then moving up the right side of the U and exploring future possibilities. These possibilities start to *crystallise* into practical applications *(prototyping)* and we learning through doing thereby *embodying* these new ways of *creating by operating from the whole*. This process "intentionally reintegrates the intelligence of the head, the heart, and the hand in the context of practical application" (Scharmer, 2007: p. 11): the *Open Mind, Open Heart* and *Open Will*.

The descent down the U is not an easy journey. The Hero's (Shero's/Theiro's) journey as described in the work of Campbell (1949) comes immediately to mind – as we let go and move into the unknown, we might expect to meet challenges and trials along the way.

Scharmer (2009) introduces the pivotal points along the journey down the U and the qualities that enable the passage through each stage: *curiosity to access Open Mind, compassion to access Open Heart* and *courage to access Open Will*. As we move down the U, we meet resistance in the form of the *Voice of Judgment*, which attempts to shut our mind; the *Voice of Cynicism*, which tries to close our heart and the *Voice of Fear*, which tries to keep us from using our will to let go (Scharmer, 2018).

Our journey is enabled by changing the quality of our way of listening and attending. We move through four levels of listening – from *downloading* ('I've heard this before, I know what will happen') to 'open mind' through *factual listening* (looking to learn new facts) to 'open heart' through *empathic listening* (tuning into another's point of view) to 'open will' through *generative listening* in which 'we listen for the highest future possibility to show up while holding a space for something new to be born' (Scharmer, 2018: p. 27).

Our challenge is in holding steady on the journey amid the voices that call us back to our habitual ways of being and to the ease of following that well-trodden pathway. However, in order to hold the complexity of issues we now face, and to support our clients and their communities and systems, we need new thinking and that cannot be born from old patterns. We need to take the journey around the U.

Writing this chapter by journeying the U

The description presented here might suggest a linear process; however, in practice, descending the U is a complex, multidimensional process that involves at its heart a deep dive into the unknown where we *let go* of all we know, *sense* into the field (the relationships, communities and systems that have an impact on us) and *connect to a deeper source*, from which an emerging future arises. For example, when asked to write this chapter, I noticed an immediate sense of emerging possibility and my curiosity was activated: 'What if we explore what is emerging in one of my supervision groups?' and 'what if we include the group members in the inquiry?' I could feel a call to explore and was intrigued by what would emerge in the inquiry with myself and with members of the group.

I immediately encountered the familiar Voice of Judgment:

> *'No, you can't do that, you won't be attending to psychological safety'.*
> *'What about the 'rules' around group work?'*
> *'What about professional boundaries?'*
> *'This will not be ethical!'*

In Campbell's (1949) hero's journey, this is the first threshold: do I take the risk and allow myself to feel the vulnerability of opening to the unknown, or do I turn around and go back to what is known/familiar?

> *Do you know this place? Do you recognise moments of choice: to turn back to the comfort of familiar habitual ways of being or to let go of the known and embrace what is arising in you?*

As I got curious about the Voice of Judgment and engaged my mind, I recognised that these are parts of me that want me to stay safe; they are protectors of my vulnerability and the parts of me that have been hurt by being unprotected in the unknown (Schwarz, 2000). I found my heart opening and compassion arising. I turned towards myself with openheartedness and kindness, asking, 'What is it I need to see, to attend to, to sense into?'

As I progressed in my writing, I encountered the Voice of Cynicism:

> *'This does not make sense, you're not clever enough to write this!'*
> *'No one will want to read it, who are you to write this?'*
> *'It's already been said, no one will be interested!'*

As I continued to meet these voices with compassion and curiosity and continued to dive deep into the writing of this chapter, I encountered the Voice of Fear. This voice was so strong that I was paralysed with shame as I recalled my school days! My amygdala was activated, sending me into my 'fight, flight, freeze' response, shutting down my cognitive thinking abilities. In these times, Scharmer (2007) asks us to call forth our will and our courage. I know deep down that my desire to inquire into the truth of the moment and my direct experience is greater than my desire to shrink back. Time and again I have found the courage to dig deep. I experience this as an embodied knowing from deep within my belly that I can trust. And when I connect with this, my courage arises, and I know that I can face my fear and let go and truly inquire into *Who is my Self* and *What is my Work?*

When I truly surrendered and was able to *let go* and sit in not knowing, the ideas, thoughts and images arose from somewhere beyond my ego; they arose from my deeper Self, from a wisdom beyond my ordinary knowing. As I further aligned my heart, head and hand the paragraphs started to *crystalize*, and the first *prototype* emerged, eventually developing into what you read here. However, it does not stop here; there is no end, we are a living system and as such constantly evolving into our emerging future. I will continue to develop and embody this emergent wisdom and you may take this on your own journey around the U if you choose to do so.

In order to surrender and *let go* to *let come* I draw on more than two decades of meditation, sensing and inquiry practices, and a commitment to a spiritual path (The Diamond Approach, 1976). I also draw on my knowledge and practice of Internal Family Systems (Schwarz, 2000), my trauma knowledge and practices (Van Der Kolk, 2014; Psychosynthesis Trust, 1989), my embodiment knowledge and practices (Palmer & Crawford, 2013) and my yoga and dance practices. This professional and spiritual alignment with the journey of Theory U gives me an embodied wisdom and strength on which to draw when the Voices of Judgment, Cynicism and Fear are at their strongest. Without these practices I would not be cultivating the curiosity, compassion and courage to stay in these difficult places. In my darkest hour, the child's pose from yoga is all I can muster!

How do you work with your Voices of Judgment, Cynicism and Fear when they arise to protect you from the vulnerability of not knowing?

Applying Theory U to group supervision

As a coaching supervisor, I aim to co-create a safe enough space for coaches to connect to themselves, their clients and the organisational, cultural, economic, ecological, social and political systems in which they and their clients live and work. I encourage, facilitate and support them to listen deeply for what is present; to inquire into what is arising and to sense what is emerging in them, their clients and their client systems. In this process they often meet their own and others' Voices of Judgment, Cynicism, and Fear. If they can bear their discomfort of *letting go* and not knowing for the sake of what is emerging for them and their work, we might travel down the U and sit at the bottom, inquiring into *Who is my Self* (connecting to their bigger Self) and *What is my Work?* (connecting them to what their future work is that is emerging). The challenge is to hold that place open to the *letting come* process in which vision and intention enable a way forward to *crystallise*. A *prototype* emerges through aligning the mind, heart and will, the *embodying* of which leads to a new way of *creating* by operating from the whole.

To guide this process, I use my first-person experience. The use of 'self' in service of the work seems to originate from the psychotherapeutic field (Rowan & Jacobs, 2002). Some coaching schools teach that the coach keep themselves out of the process, and yet others believe using the coach's in the moment experience is essential. In coaching supervision, using the 'self' as a source of information is critical. The Coaching Supervision Academy highlights the importance of 'self' in their teaching around 'Who you are, is how you coach, supervise, lead', asserting it is a key determining factor in successful outcomes for the client (Murdoch & Arnold, 2013). Modes (or Eyes) 5 and 6 of the Seven-Eyed Model (Hawkins & Shohet, 1989; Hawkins & Smith, 2006) require the supervisor to use themselves as the instrument – tracking moment-to-moment inner experiencing to provide essential data and perspective.

When I tune into my immediate experiencing and notice myself staying in my head 'thinking or solutioning', feeling the endorphin rush of being in control and solving the 'problem', then I hypothesise we have not entered into the U, and I am trying to zip across the top to the answer.

I stay very close to noticing what is arising in my head, heart and gut/belly (Mode 6) and what is happening between me and my client (Mode 5) and how that might give me information about what is happening for my client, their clients and their systems. I have found this way of using 'self as an instrument' to be profoundly helpful in accessing more collective and embodied wisdom and working in a more emergent way. I use it in group work, encouraging the group members to do the same, enabling access to a different type of knowing, an embodied knowing, a felt sense (Gendlin, 1978) that we are able to describe and share with each other.

> Imagine a world where we intentionally access our head, heart and gut/belly wisdom and offer that as information for what might be happening in us, in our connections and in our environment. How do you think you could offer that wisdom when you are in your next group?

Moving from downloading past patterns to seeing with fresh eyes

When we are in the process of *downloading from past patterns*, we come out of the immediate, present situation and place emphasis on knowledge we already know. Many of us come to supervision to explore what we do not yet know, a spark of an emerging future that calls us. We want to explore the unknown and yet our Voices of Judgment, Cynicism and Fear beckon us back to the familiar comfort and the perceived certainty of knowing what will happen. We like certainty! However, we also know when new thinking is needed.

How do you let go of downloading from past patterns and move to seeing with fresh eyes?

Groups can be uncomfortable places, especially if a person has had previous experience of being harmed in a group (either physically and/or psychologically) and more so if that group was their family of origin. When we have had traumatic experiences, Huebl (2020) offers the perspective that we split off the traumatised parts of ourselves – those disconnected parts then become stuck in the past with the potential to be re-activated in a new group setting in the present. When something happens in a session, it can resurface all that unprocessed emotion from the past and bring it rushing forward into the present. It can be overwhelming. Palmer and Crawford (2013) describe this process in neuroscience and evolutionary biology terms as a part of our brain, the amygdala, sending a signal to activate our survival responses, more commonly known as the 'fight, flight, freeze' response. When this survival response is activated, the cognitive rational brain shuts down and we are at the mercy of our more primitive reptilian brain.

Knowing how our past history in and around groups impacts us is essential for group supervisors and can often be the content of supervision sessions. We need to understand what will activate our amygdala to set off our survival instinct and how to calm our nervous system and deactivate our survival instincts. When we know how to do this for ourselves, we can understand how to do that for others (Porges, 2011). This knowledge is important so that people feel safe enough to be able to move out of the past, suspend their old ways of thinking and doing and descend the U. The safer people feel, the greater their likelihood of letting go and 'being' with the not knowing and emergence and not being caught by their fear response. If the group feels 'safe enough' participants will be able to enter into '*presencing*' at the bottom of the U and able to inquire into the questions of '*Who is my Self?*' and '*What is my Work?*'

Have you noticed how your past impacts the way you interact in a group? Perhaps the way you join, contribute, allow vulnerability, take risks? Think of the last group you attended. How did any resistance to being vulnerable show up? If you allowed yourself to be vulnerable, what made it possible?

Creating safety and building trust to journey the U

One of the practices I have found valuable for creating safety and enabling people to come into a group and open to *seeing with fresh eyes* is contracting. Contracting conversations can unveil unconscious expectations, assumptions and meanings that people are holding about the group, the people and the work. Many of these come from the past. If we can make these explicit and discuss and agree on the ways we want to be with each other going forward, this often creates more safety and allows people to enter more fully into the present. I explicitly speak about what happens if someone is activated into a survival response and how we work together with it. A contract is not static; it's a living agreement that defines the way we work together and is continually reviewed and recreated together. We use our Open Mind for this conversation, and we bring our listening for new information to *suspend* our Voice of Judgment and our *downloading from past patterns*.

To illustrate the process of creating the conditions for safety and trust to arise, I turn to the supervision group I mentioned at the beginning of this chapter. We created our initial contract in the first session. We spoke about what work we would be doing together, what we were expecting of ourselves and each other, how we imagined we would be together when difficulties arose, and how each participant would want to respond to the work of the others and what each group member expected of me, as supervisor.

Every member of the group was a coaching supervisor, and three members ran their own supervision groups, so there was already a level of experience and maturity with contracting and group process. They were also aware of Theory U and the concept of working emergently. In more structured groups, the supervisor may contract with more detail regarding how the time is allocated and how the feedback process will be managed. This is particularly useful for coaches new to supervision and group work.

My desire to hold a more emergent process arose out of my own experience in a group run by Louie Gardiner based on her research into complexity and systems. This inspired me to bring more emergence into my own work and to use Theory U as a holding framework.

For this supervision group, our contract centred around the following principles:

- Everything is welcome here.
- Everything can be held and explored and wondered about, including 'less welcome' emotions such as anger, judgment, envy and hatred.
- Everything is something.

'One of the ways-of-working that has helped me to be open and more vulnerable is the very clear understanding that "absolutely everything and anything is made welcome in the group"'. *(Group Participant)*

'In one session I was very fidgety and clearly not present. In naming and inviting my irritation, it allowed a deepening to the bottom of the "U" to acknowledge the disappointment at how this was taking me away from my presence in the group.' *(Group Participant)*

How do you set up your contracts with your coaching or supervising clients? How do you consider the multitude of factors that affect whether we feel safe to trust and be vulnerable?

Another way I create the conditions for safety and trust to arise is by starting each session with everyone checking in with 'how I am arriving'. The check-in helps with transitioning from the past to the present moment and gives us all valuable information about the physical and emotional state of how the group members are arriving: 'I am feeling anxious as my partner might be losing his job' or 'I am here and ready to go'. Sometimes the check-in is brief and sometimes it requires more time.

In this place of emergence, sometimes the Voice of Judgment arises in me:

> *'This is taking too much time; people will be wanting me to get onto the real work'.*

However, in my experience, this time helps us all to arrive, to open our minds, to listen for new information and to start to *see with fresh eyes* both ourselves and each other in the group.

For this group it was especially important, as we were meeting during the COVID-19 pandemic when people had been in lockdown for several months and were being impacted in difficult ways. The simple process of checking in was experienced as 'grounding' and profound.

> 'Sometimes, the quality of being heard in this group has been so luxurious it has made me tearful'. *(Group Participant)*

> *How do you create the space to arrive for yourself and others? What voices get in the way of your listening to what is needed?*

In all my groups I use centering practices (Palmer, 2012) to *suspend* habitual processing and thinking patterns and to invite our hearts, our minds and our gut/belly wisdom into the space. In my experience this assists group members in *letting go* of their ideas, beliefs, and assumptions about what they 'think' will happen. It helps them to settle, to slow their thinking and to breathe more slowly and deeply, which precipitates calming the nervous system (Lyon, 2019). This relaxation activates a different quality of awareness and changes the way we view things. When we open our eyes at the end of the centering exercise, we often *see with fresh eyes*.

In this group I led a different centering practice every time. I didn't prepare; I just allowed whatever I was *sensing* from the space we had created to direct me in my guiding of the centering.

In this place of emergence, sometimes the Voice of Judgment might arise:

> *'You should be using the same guiding every time, people need structure!'*

Or the Voice of Cynicism:

> *'You are not sensing anything; you are just making it up!'*

However, I noticed over time how often the response from the group members was that this was exactly what they needed. I noticed after the centering practice that the energy of the group was different: more spacious, slow and calm.

> 'The centering exercise is something that I recently brought to one of my own supervision groups. The group arrived, they didn't have a clear case study or discussion topic. Previously this would have caused some agitation for me. I would have tried to think about what we could do, feeling the expectation of needing to have answers. Instead, I brought in the centering exercise and then explored with the group about what was emerging now. This brought much deeper reflection'. *(Group Participant)*

> *How do you help your clients to arrive and become present in your sessions and to see with fresh eyes? Do you have a practice?*

Moving from seeing with fresh eyes to sensing into the field

We now redirect our attention from *seeing with fresh eyes* to *sensing into what is happening within us, and around us, in the field,* which I take to mean the relationships, communities and systems by which we are impacted. This requires a movement from our Open Mind to our Open Heart and engaging our empathic listening.

After centering, I invited the group members to begin with a round of sharing what was on their minds with regards to their work and what they wanted to explore. This was a place of listening and *sensing into the field* for what was emerging. We contracted right at the beginning that we would not have a structure of equal time for each member; rather, to allow emergence and, as a group, we would *sense into the field* for what was needed. I listened, waiting for a theme to emerge, made a suggestion, invited the group to build on the theme and we began. Sometimes there was no theme, yet we found a beginning as we listened to the topics that were arising.

> 'My experience of the start is that sometimes a theme emerged at the beginning and sometimes it became clear only part way through, or even wasn't apparent until the end. This really didn't seem to matter. Even when there wasn't a clear theme at the beginning'. *(Group Participant)*

> 'My experience in the group has been that it didn't matter which thread was pulled, there was always some new insight to take away, even if entirely unexpected'. *(Group Participant)*

In this place of emergence, I found the familiar Voice of Judgment might arise:

> *'You can't just start, you need to wait for the right theme!'*
> *'That is not the right theme, you missed it!'*

Or maybe the Voice of Cynicism:

> *'This way of being unstructured is not going to work'.*
> *'You can't trust your intuition!'*

Or maybe the Voice of Fear:

> *'If each person does not have equal time, they will get upset and leave the group'.*
> *'If it is the wrong theme, they will think you are not a good facilitator'.*

What helped me to stay present and to exercise compassion towards these Voices was applying the group contract to myself – everything is welcome here – and inviting all the parts of me, even the distressed parts, to be present, as well as inviting my wiser Self to enable me to *see with fresh eyes.* (Schwarz, 2000). One of my ways of connecting with my wiser Self comes from a Chinese Taoist parable:

An old Chinese farmer lost his best stallion one day. His neighbour came around to express his regrets, but the farmer just said, 'Who knows what is good and what is bad?' The next day the stallion returned, bringing with him three wild mares. The neighbour rushed back to celebrate with the farmer, but the old farmer simply said, 'Who knows what is good and what is bad?' The following day, the farmer's son fell from one of the wild mares while trying to break her in. He broke his arm and injured his leg. The neighbour came by to check on the son and offer his condolences, but the old farmer just said, 'Who knows what is good and what is bad?' The next day, the army came to the farm to conscript the farmer's son for the war, but found him invalid and left him with his father. The neighbour thought to himself, 'Who knows what is good and what is bad?'

> 'I have felt that each of us has been prepared to be vulnerable, to share something that has challenged us significantly. The group has felt "equal" in that sense, in a way that other groups have not always felt to me. The group process is also relatively less structured, less "turn-taking" perhaps. Somehow, it hasn't mattered how often which of us has had an issue that received focused attention. I did worry in the early sessions that I was getting "more than my fair share" of time. However, I have learned since how powerful the learning can be from others' experience. It has felt like freedom within a loose framework, like there is scaffolding and that scaffolding primarily comprises trust and respect, and therefore psychological safety'. *(Group Participant)*

One way I *sense into what is emerging in the field* is to ask the members what they are feeling and noticing in their bodies as they speak or listen: 'What's happening in your body as you say that or hear that?' or 'What are you noticing as you are speaking or listening?' This also develops their ability to use 'self as instrument', their Mode 6 (Seven-Eyed Model, Hawkins & Shohet, 1989; Hawkins & Smith, 2006).

> 'When asked what was happening in my body, I was able to access a particular emotion more keenly, and to make additional associations to that emotion (thoughts, memories, etc.) that deepened my understanding'. *(Group Participant)*

When one person described their 'in the moment' experiencing, and I asked others to respond by noticing what was occurring in them, this often created a spiral of deepening connection to themselves and each other. I felt my heart open, my compassion arose and I felt a wider connection to all beings. Through this process I accessed a different kind of wisdom: the wisdom of the heart. This had a warm, allowing, connecting quality that was different from the curiosity flavour of my Open Mind.

> 'We are often encouraged to stay with the body, to sense and notice, to explore our experience. It takes us away from just thinking, away from the cognitive. I remember one of our group saying "let their hearts find the wisdom"'. *(Group Participant)*

Often in a session, one of the members touched a place inside them that held a lot of emotion. I asked myself and the other members to sense into that place in ourselves as we listened. In that moment, I experienced our separateness fall away and a feeling of oneness emerge. Yalom and Leszcz (2005) refer to this experience as universality. It is the way in which the members who take the risk to be vulnerable in group realise that they are not alone in their suffering and that others are willing to support them. Upon realising this, they often access an inner strength that connects them to source and to presencing (Almaas, 2008).

Another way of *sensing into the field* is through parallel process. Dynamics happening in the session between the supervisor and group members might be mirroring or paralleling that which is happening for the client and/or the client system (Searles, 1955 in Sumerel, 1994). Working with parallel process can be transformational when a group member brings a client system into a session, and we allow ourselves to fully connect in ourselves to the feelings and difficulties potentially arising in the system. If we can bear the tension and stay with the process until it shifts and transforms in the session, we might open the possibility for the group member to change the way they are currently holding the issue. If that occurs, when they go back into the client system, they may bring a different energy, and the client system can be changed through their changed presence.

I make a correlation here with Tonglen meditation taught by Chodron (2009), in which the practice is to breathe in (receive and acknowledge) the suffering of others and then breathe out (sending out) joy, harmony, peace of mind to others.

> *How do you use your body/feelings/parallel process to sense into what is happening in you and your clients and their systems?*

Moving from sensing into the field to the bottom of the U into Presencing

'At the bottom of the U, individuals or groups on the U journey come to a threshold that requires a "letting go" of everything that is not essential. . . . At the same time that we drop the non-essential aspects of the self ("letting go"), we also open ourselves to new aspects of our highest possible future self ("letting come"). The essence of presencing is the integration of presence and sensing, enabling the experience of the coming in of the new, and the transformation of the old' (Scharmer, 2007: p. 7).

For me this is liminal space – we wait silently in stillness, like a trapeze artist having let go of one rope before picking up another, hanging, waiting for the next rope to appear.

This is where we need our courage and Our Will to let go of our identity and certainty, to enter into deep inquiry around '*Who is my Self?*' and '*What is my Work?*' and be willing to be transformed.

This can be a place of deep discomfort rife with the Voice of Fear.

My deepest fear is that:

> '*I am not enough as I am, I need to do/say/be something different*'.

I hear this in myself and with many of the coaches and supervisors I train, supervise and work alongside.

In the face of the Voice of Fear, I need to evoke my courage to access my Open Will. One of the ways I do this is by inviting the wisdom of Gendlin (1990: p. 1):

> 'The essence of working with another person is to be present as a living being. And that is lucky, because if we had to be smart, or good, or mature, or wise, then we would probably be in trouble . . . . Then I am just here, with my eyes, and there is this other being. If they happen to look into my eyes, they will see that I am just a shaky being. I have to tolerate that. They may not look. But if they do, they will see that. They will see the slightly shy, slightly withdrawing, insecure existence that I am. I have learnt that that is OK. I do not need to be emotionally secure and firmly present. I just need to be present. There are no qualifications for the kind of person I must be'.

> 'The vulnerability when being the supervisor is whether I know everything, that I'm an expert in everything. I learn that this responsibility I impose on myself creates a load and heaviness that impedes my ability to supervise. Being a participant in our supervision group allows me to experience how Leanne and my fellow participants display honesty, openness, vulnerability, with no hint of trying to be expert. Simply having an experience of this helps me to remember that when I'm a supervisor, I'm not required to be the know-it-all, to be in control. What I learn instead is the craft of supervision'. *(Group Participant)*

When finally, often after much internal struggle, I surrender to the process and *let go*, I can loosely hold all the threads that are emerging in the conversation without needing them to come together in a tidy bow. I can be there, holding them untied and trusting that, as we sit together, a deeper collective wisdom will emerge and guide the way. It is a place of sweetness and stillness and silence, and I have learnt how to hold and wait. This has taken 25 years of spiritual practice and I still have much to learn!

> 'I have noticed that the quality of presence I have experienced with this group is something that has impacted my own presence and confidence just "to be", when doing my own group supervision work. I feel less need to "prepare", more trusting of my ability to "know" what is "right" as I tune in to what my supervisees are bringing. In turn, this has made my work as a supervisor more enjoyable, fulfilling, and – I believe – impactful'. *(Group Participant)*

> *What is your process around letting go and allowing yourself just to be? What are the Voices of Fear that emerge?*

We, as individuals, journey through many Us, often at the same time, especially as we are confronted with an increasing number of complex issues in our lives. We are also as a collective confronting many complex situations – planetary, social and restorative justice, COVID-19, health, economic, homelessness and many more crises. We need a new way to come together and envision a future.

As a supervision group, we were also going through our collective U and navigating working in an emergent way. Scharmer (2018) presents his work as a 'method for consciousness-based systems change'. He writes: 'Once a group crosses this threshold, nothing remains the same. Individual members and the group as a whole begin to operate with a heightened level of energy and sense of future possibility. Often they then begin to function as an intentional vehicle for the future that they feel wants to emerge' (Scharmer, 2007: p. 7).

> 'In this group supervision experience I have often felt like I was being supported individually to travel to the bottom of the U, but then we emerged as a group up the other side, because of the collective "presencing" that took place at the bottom of the U. We "met" one another at the bottom of the U'. *(Group Participant)*

In the final session of the contracted six sessions with this supervision group, a shift happened.

One member of the group responded to another, spontaneously picking up the inquiry, taking the role of leader and directing the inquiry. Realising what she had done, she then paused and, in a moment of self-consciousness, asked for a response from the group.

It felt as if her contribution had arisen from the bottom of the U, from what was wanting to emerge. We were individually, and collectively, sitting at the bottom of the U, and the member who was moved to speak, spoke.

> 'We talked about co-creation of the process, there was full engagement and willing contribution from all, yet I was curious that no-one in this group of

skilled and experienced supervisors was venturing beyond the parameters that we had tacitly adopted. By session 6 my experience of the group was that we had bedded down the psychological safety required for some risk taking. I was gaining some great learnings, and I was bursting to become more active and involved in the supervision process of this group. I didn't want to BE supervised, I wanted us to supervise with each other. So, when the moment arose, I ventured, with some trepidation, to break the rules and ask a question'. *(Group Participant)*

Even in a contracted emergent process, we look for the rules to follow; our ego wants certainty, consistency, predictability (Almaas, 2008). In the journey down the U the invitation is to use our curiosity, compassion, courage and generative listening to activate 'Our Will', to allow the *letting come* of what is wanting to happen.

Moving up the right-hand side of the U

Once we have surrendered to the stillness, dropped to the bottom of the U and *let go* of all that we know, we are open to allowing ourselves to be called into action from a place beyond ego, from the future wanting to emerge. Vision and intention *crystallise*, a *prototype* is created, the experimenting begins and we find ourselves *creating, by operating from the whole*, from the integration of Open Mind, Open Heart and Open Will. It is beyond what we could have imagined as we entered the U.

I see this movement up the right-hand side of the U in this supervision group. We sit in the stillness, and then slowly a face smiles, a body twitches, a head moves, an expression changes, a forward motion appears, the energy changes and an idea emerges of something to try. *Wow, I just had a thought, I just realised I could, maybe I could try, what about if we, how about I suggest, why don't I try. . . . I have a plan!*

Each time the group members embraced their courage to go through the journey of the U, they opened the possibility of leaving the session having *crystallised* an intention and vision and developed a *prototype* to *enact* that came from beyond their thinking mind, from the integration of their Open Mind, Open Heart and Open Will.

The journey through the U is timeless. The process can occur in 15 minutes, over a whole session, over many sessions or a lifetime. We are always emerging, evolving, unfolding; we are a living system.

For the supervision group as a whole, we explored what had been emerging that led to the group member moving into spontaneous action. This inquiry led to us contracting for a further four sessions. We moved up the right hand side of the U, *crystallising* our intention and vision to work with more emergence. We *prototyped* a way of working together and began to experiment with *creating by operating as a whole*.

'And now we are into the second contract, it seems like we are operating at a different level. It feels more flowing, there is an ease as the supervision process moves around between us. There is a richness and texture to our encounters that is a combination of us all'. *(Group Participant)*

Once into the new contract, I invited everyone to contribute to this chapter. The U is not a static process, where we can confidently rejoice when we reach our journey's end. As a group we went through one journey and were beginning another.

In this new journey around the U, the Voices of Judgment, Cynicism and Fear arose. I engaged with my curiosity and wonder. I leaned into our contracting principles and welcomed all of the feelings and concerns and doubts with compassion. I recalled the Chinese Taoist parable to ultimately connect to the place beyond good and bad, right and wrong. I drew on my courage and opened to an emergent process, and began writing.

The journey around the U is a huge act of faith, as we have no idea how it will unfold (Senge et al., 2004).

Conclusion

In order to hold the complexity of issues we now face, and to support today's coaches, supervisors and their clients and client systems, we need new thinking and that cannot be born from past habitual thinking patterns. We need the journey down the U into the unknown to sit in a place of '*presencing*'; to connect to a deeper source, to find what is emerging for us in response to two fundamental questions: '*Who is my Self?*' and '*What is my Work?*'

'Presencing signifies a heightened state of attention that allows individuals and groups to shift the inner place from which they function. When that shift happens, people begin to operate from a future space of possibility that they feel wants to emerge' (Scharmer, 2007: p. 1).

This requires that we make our own inner psychological and spiritual exploration to cultivate the capacity to listen and inquire into our head, heart and belly wisdom; to sense into ourselves and the field; to hold steady in the deep discomfort of 'not knowing' and to allow for an emerging future to arise, a vision and intention to crystallise, a prototype to form from an integration of head, heart and will that embodies creating by operating from the whole.

In this way we can come together in groups and in community with listening and curiosity to Open our Mind in the face of the Voice of Judgment; with compassion to Open our Heart in the face of the Voice of Cynicism; and with courage to Open our Will in the face of the Voice of Fear. In this space the emergent future arises.

Acknowledgements

The author would like to thank and acknowledge the special contribution of the members of the supervision group, Claire FitzGerald, Amanda Horne, Sandy May and Lisa Taylor.

References

Almaas, A. H. (2008). *The Unfolding Now: Realizing Your True Nature Through the Practice of Presence*. Boston and London: Shambala.

Birch, J. (2020, October). Supervision of Supervision: Something Becoming. *Coaching Today*, (36), 27–31.

Campbell, J. (1949). *The Hero with a Thousand Faces*. New York: Pantheon Books.

Chinese Taoist Parable. https://secularbuddhism.com/who-knows-what-is-good-and-what-is-bad/.

Chodron, P. (2009). The Practice of Tonglen. www.youtube.com/watch?v=QwqlurCvXuM.

Diamond Approach. (1976). Ridhwan School. www.diamondapproach.org/ridhwan-school.

Ellis, C. (2019). In S. Holman-Jones, T. E. Adams, & C. Ellis (Eds.), *Handbook of Autoethnography*. Abingdon: Routledge.

Gendlin, E. T. (1978). *Focusing*. New York: Everest House.

Gendlin, E. T. (1990). The Small Steps of the Therapy Process: How They Come and How to Help Them Come. In G. Lietaer, J. Rombauts, & R. Van Balen (Eds.), *Client-Centered and Experiential Psychotherapy in the Nineties* (pp. 205–224). Leuven: Leuven University Press. http://previous.focusing.org/gendlin/docs/gol_2110.html.

Hawkins, P., & Shohet, R. (1989). *Supervision in the Helping Professions*. Maidenhead: Open University Press/McGraw Hill.

Hawkins, P., & Smith, N. (2006). *Coaching, Mentoring and Organizational Consultancy: Supervision and Development*. Maidenhead: Open University Press/McGraw Hill.

Huebl, T. (2020). Collective Trauma Summit. https://thomashuebl.com/.

Lyon, I. (2019). 21 Day Nervous System Tune Up. https://irenelyon.com/.

Murdoch, E., & Arnold, J. (2013). *Full Spectrum Supervision: Who You Are is How You Supervise*. St. Albans: Panoma Press.

Palmer, W. (2012). Leadership Embodiment Training with Leadership Embodiment Foundation. www.leadershipembodiment.com/.

Palmer, W., & Crawford, J. (2013). *Leadership Embodiment: How the Way We Sit and Stand Can Change the Way We Think and Speak*. Scotts Valley: CreateSpace Independent Publishing Platform.

Porges, S. (2011). Polyvagal Theory. www.stephenporges.com/.

Psychosynthesis Trust. (1989). Psychotherapy Training. https://psychosynthesistrust.org.uk/.

Rowan, J., & Jacobs, M. (2002). *The Therapist's Use of Self*, Maidenhead: Open University Press.

Scharmer, C. O. (2007). Addressing the Blind Spot of Our Time. Executive Summary of Theory U: Leading from the Future as It Emerges. www.presencing.org/assets/images/theory-u/Theory_U_Exec_Summary.pdf.

Scharmer, C. O. (2009). *Theory U: Learning from the Future as It Emerges*. Oakland: Berrett-Koehler Publishers Inc.

Scharmer, C. O. (2018). *The Essentials of Theory U, Core Principles and Applications*. Oakland: Berrett-Koehler Publishers Inc.

Schwarz, R. (2000). Internal Family Systems Training. https://ifs-institute.com/.

Senge, P., Scharmer, O., Jaworski, J., & Flowers, B. S. (2004). *Presence: Human Purpose and the Field of the Future*. New York: Random House.

Sumerel, M. (1994). Parallel Process in Supervision. www.counseling.org/resources/library/ERIC%20Digests/94-15.pdf.

Van Der Kolk, B. (2014). *The Body Keeps the Score*. New York: Penguin Books.

Yalom, I., & Leszcz, M. (2005). *The Theory and Practice of Group Psychotherapy*. New York: Basic Books.

Chapter 6

Nature as dynamic co-partner in group supervision

Catherine Gorham

A Light Exists in Spring: Emily Dickinson

A Light exists in Spring
Not present on the Year
At any other period –
When March is scarcely here

A Color stands abroad
On Solitary Fields
That Science cannot overtake
But Human Nature feels.

It waits upon the Lawn,
It shows the furthest Tree
Upon the furthest Slope you know
It almost speaks to you.

Then as Horizons step
Or Noons report away
Without the Formula of sound
It passes and we stay –

A quality of loss
Affecting our Content
As Trade had suddenly encroached
Upon a Sacrament.

(Source: 1896, Dickinson)

Introduction

Nature offers an abundance of unpredictable, unique moments that draw us in, causing us to stop and wonder – what a gift for supervision! Don't be deceived by

DOI: 10.4324/978100314345-7

the necessary practical considerations described in this chapter – the essence of this approach is poetic, and I hope that its magic shines through.

In fact, this work is all about relationship. As you read this, you and I are in relationship; nature is inviting us both to connect in this co-created space. What kind of space would you like it to be? If you could choose anywhere in nature you'd like to be reading this, where would you be? Would you be warmed by the sun or cooled by the dappled shade? High up on a mountainside with views across the peaks or nestled down in the curves of the valley? Mesmerised by the scent of lemon groves in the stillness or the smell of salty sea breeze and chatter of seagulls? What is the physical impact on your body as you allow yourself to settle in this space? Wherever you choose to sit or wander, please do stay awhile with me.

You will find your own pace as you explore this chapter and your own meaning for the words on the page; in fact, you may find your relationship with me and with nature ebbs and flows as you read – maybe even your relationship with the different parts of yourself. The immediacy of your experience here parallels the dynamic characteristic of supervising with Nature, which is one of its many gifts and a reason for its potency. From now on, I will refer to the entity of Nature as co-partner, with a capital 'N' to differentiate it from nature or the natural world as 'the phenomena of the physical world collectively, including plants, animals, the landscape, and other features and products of the earth, as opposed to humans or human creations' (Lexico, 2020).

The theoretical landscape – why this works

Several years ago, I undertook formal ecotherapy training – intrigued by the internal shifts catalysed when connecting with the outdoors, both in my personal resilience practice and in my professional coaching and supervision work with clients. At that point I didn't understand why something changed in me in the moment of connection, but I knew, at a somatic level, that it had the potential to be a valuable asset in my 'self as instrument' toolkit, and I felt compelled to explore more. It soon became evident that the principles of ecotherapy provided me with a theoretical explanation for my inner noticing whilst enabling me to explore more deeply how this might enrich my practice. Since then, I have become passionate about supporting other practitioners in understanding the technical nuances required when taking clients outdoors – it is so much more than coaching or supervision + outdoors. I, therefore, make no apology for the fact that I make many references to the modality of psychotherapy in the following pages. My view is that we as coaches and supervisors are all in the business of psychological safety and being aware of the psychological considerations when working in this way is paramount.

Wilson's biophilia hypothesis (1984, cited in Jordan, 2015: p. 9) states that we as human beings are hardwired to connect with nature, which explains the biological shift in us, with a propensity towards feeling better, when we go outdoors. Lewis (2017) identified that therapists taking clients outdoors experienced a higher degree of spaciousness in themselves as practitioners than when working indoors. That sense of expansiveness is a powerful platform from which non-conscious thoughts and feelings can be more easily accessed. In addition, Nature's presentation offers a canvas onto which the inner landscape can be projected. Buber's 'I-thou' theory 1923 (cited in The-Philosophy-com, 2012) describes our completeness or identity (I) as determined by our relationship with what surrounds us in the moment. For example, as soon as we connect to a tree nearby, we frame our unique relationship with the tree as another 'I' by projecting our internal landscape outwards onto it, thereby enabling us to understand our difficult feelings more clearly, as an infant would with its mother (Klein's 'projective identification'1997, cited in Jordan, 2015: p. 67). For these reasons, supervisees may quickly develop a sense of attachment to natural objects involved in their process, offering the opportunity for even a photo of a tree or a flower to facilitate a shortcut somatic reconnection with a shift in state long after the supervision session has finished.

The dynamic and unpredictable characteristics of working outdoors also create infinite opportunities for immediate shared experiences between practitioner and client (which Marshall, 2016 describes as 'eco-intimacy'), and I shall include several examples in the following pages.

The therapeutic frame/scaffolding

One of the key ecotherapy principles that I believe is also fundamental for outdoor supervision is the therapeutic frame (Jordan, 2015: pp. 32–33). The concept of the therapeutic frame in counselling and psychotherapy includes boundaries, the financial contract and the professional, consistent and ethical conduct of the therapist to protect the safety of the client with the private counselling room seen as synonymous with the 'frame'. Traditionally, this has automatically assigned a level of power to the therapist who, as well as hosting the space, chooses where to sit and stipulates the 'rules' in their own working area. This becomes infinitely more complex in an outdoor setting – and when supervising a group.

Hermansson, 1997 (cited in Jordan, 2015: p. 82) proposes that boundary management is a dynamic process which the therapist navigates using their professional judgement. In relation to coaching and supervision, the physical structure of an office has usually been the holding container (until recently, before the shift towards more virtual work with the advent of the COVID-19 pandemic in 2020), with either party hosting the space and with sitting positions becoming habitual or, at the very least, with limited options for how the space is co-habited, so a symbolic frame is nonetheless apparent, with only marginally more democratisation than that present in a traditional counselling relationship.

As soon as the work moves outdoors, even in a 1:1 supervision session, the dynamic shifts considerably, with so many choices in the moment as to which path to take, which bench to sit on (and how much proximity to each other), which direction to walk round a park. This invites the possibility of a much softer and less binary power dynamic between supervisee and supervisor, which can be advantageous to the relationship as well as being symbolic of the peer positioning often present within supervisory relationships. However, this can quickly feel overwhelming for the supervisee, especially if the supervision relationship is relatively new or the supervisee is new to working outdoors.

Once you consider group supervision outdoors, this then becomes one of the key challenges on a practical and dynamic level: you as the supervisor risk making every decision by committee (down to when we should plan to walk towards the toilets in a park, for example), which might simply require negotiation but may restrict the physical locality that a supervisee can choose for their inquiry. The pendulum of power inevitably shifts back to you as supervisor retaining a leadership role and being more directive at certain touchpoints. This then becomes part of the holding and containing, so it is important, but when and what those touchpoints look like are useful to contract with the group upfront.

Sometimes groups like to vary their meeting place, for example, between different parks. Giving choice to the supervisee presenting as to where they would like to be for their 'air time' isn't always straightforward if they have never been to the location before. It is not uncommon for at least one supervisee to be unfamiliar with the location if this is chosen by the group, and that can have a destabilising effect if control/uncertainty is already an issue. In such situations, I invite the supervisee to intuit where they would like to start or to connect with the essence of the container they would like for their exploration. Then, with permission, I might suggest a spot (or a walk) nearby, with the option of moving on if it doesn't feel right, which is of course then part of the data. The number of choices available can feel overwhelming and exposing – so I might choose a smaller area or limit the choices.

However, working in an unknown space can have an equally positive effect – for example, one supervisee invited playfulness into the space as we contracted together. When it came to choosing the exact spot for her inquiry in the park (which she hadn't visited before), she wanted to follow her instinct. Unbeknownst to her, she was leading the group to a children's playground, and the look of sheer delight on her face when she saw the sand pit was a sight to behold. I must admit, it is the only time I have ever led supervision from a sand pit, but I would recommend it because the fluidity of the landscape as you move is a fabulous tool!

I sometimes catch myself being triggered to feeling over-responsible, especially in a group setting. I have to be mindful of the risk of moving into Controlling Parent or Nurturing Parent (from Berne's Transactional Analysis theory (1961) and cited in Hay, 1993: p. 55) and creating a dynamic of power/powerlessness. As supervisors, we are accustomed to watching our internal process and how it shows up in our contracting; however, in an outdoor setting, this can easily become magnified as physical needs are also a consideration. Contracting for group supervision outdoors also needs to accommodate who is responsible for what, with infinitely more spot contracting than is required either in an indoor group and/or individual supervision session outdoors.

OUTDOOR SUPERVISION FRAME

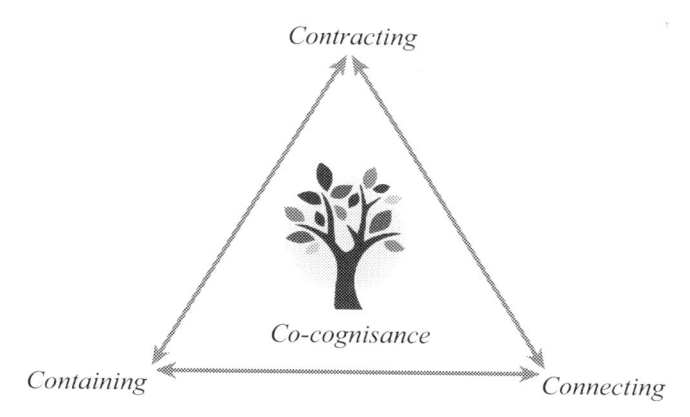

Contracting

Co-cognisance

Containing   *Connecting*

Figure 6.1 Outdoor supervision frame

Outdoor supervision frame

I trust you are already getting a sense of how complex the frame needs to be to hold these added layers of complexity in group supervision outdoors. I have, therefore, designed my own model to provide the necessary scaffolding:

Contracting

Given the particular risks of this approach relating to non-privacy, unpredictability and potential for emotions to escalate in the moment, some additional contracting upfront is critical. The tighter the contracting, the more the process can be allowed to unfurl in the moment, like a fern in the spring sunshine that feels secure in its space.

Psychological safety in this context comes from a sense of trust in the supervisor, the container (locality and holding of emotions, see Containing p. 84) and the process itself. Trust is built by being explicit about permissions at the outset: for example, permission to request a move to another spot (a quiet, secluded corner can suddenly feel violated if others arrive), to press the pause button, to name what's going on physically or emotionally if this becomes uncomfortable. Fear and a sense of personal vulnerability can escalate rapidly in an outdoor setting – whether this be externally based – for example, a fear of geese, squirrels, loose dogs or meeting someone known to one of the supervisees – or internally based, such as a fear of feeling tired, cold, thirsty, exposed or emotional or a shame associated with an external fear.

My supervisee, Ann, hadn't declared her fear of geese. This became evident when we encountered a large group of geese on a river path. Once the group moved her away (with a touching degree of care and gentleness) and her immediate physical fear began to subside, it prompted a rich conversation about her shame of the fear – and her shame generally.

Unpredictabilities are part of the magic of this approach and can become figural to the work, as in the previous example, or dealt with practically depending on what occurs.

A group of people arriving with a radio in the woodland of a quiet nature reserve prompted an immediate move by the Supervision Group to walk by the river. Interestingly, it turned out to be a very noisy day for mating male marsh frogs with their raucous chuckling croaks which were almost comical, so noise in the system still became a theme for inquiry!

The original therapeutic frame signals consistency; that is, these are the 'rules' for how it works; where you sit/I sit and how you pay me; a private confidential space without interruption and so on. In outdoor group work, there is an ongoing flavour of inconsistency in the environment where random things happen. These add to the vitality and immediacy of the experience; for instance, I went back to the nature reserve two weeks later, and all the mating had finished – the same spot offered a beautiful peacefulness. The potential inconsistencies – which can affect expectations especially if a group chooses to visit somewhere they have worked previously – have to be compensated for by consistent responses by the supervisor. These might be in the form of naming what is arriving unexpectedly in the space and inviting any internal noticing to be shared (e.g., annoyance about the radio). What does this mean for us right now? How is an interruption relevant to this inquiry? The spot contracting needs to provide the scaffolding to hold anything unexpected.

My recommendation would be to contract individually with supervisees first as part of the intake conversation (including assessing appropriateness for outdoor work – see also Risks, This section refered to is now: p. 89) ahead of the initial group contracting conversation in which supervisees' individual responsibility for their own physical needs are balanced with the collective responsibility for the group's welfare.

Connecting

As we arrive physically, we need time to transition – often from the urban to the natural – and we need space for attunement:

1 Attunement with the different parts of me I am inviting in as supervisor and the natural space itself (ideally, I will have done both prior to the session),
2 An invitation for the supervisees to attune to the different parts of themselves they want to be present as supervisees,
3 Between us as partners in the supervision process including Nature and
4 Attunement to those of whom the supervision is in service.

The Supervision Group were a group of coaches offering voluntary coaching to NHS staff during the Covid-19 pandemic. Supervision was identified as being 'in service of NHS clients and their patients'.

The process offered for attunement depends on the style of the supervisor – I tend to suggest a period of silence at the beginning of group sessions, beginning with stillness and then walking together silently, shifting awareness from inwards to outwards.

This is the point at which I position our work as being at the invitation of Nature. The modality of ecotherapy has evolved beyond a human-focused, results-oriented approach of 'using' Nature – Level 1 – to a whole-systems, reciprocal circle of healing – Level 2 – to reflect today's concerns about humans' destructive impact on the planet (Jordan & Hinds, 2016: pp. 70–71). This positioning encourages a softer tread on the earth as we enter as guests in the space.

The sense of connecting is dynamic in itself, ebbing and flowing in the moment, yet overall deepening in intimacy as the work progresses. Nature has a way of inviting others to participate as equal partners because of our implicit sense of relational knowing – beyond language – enabling us to adapt to emerging challenges. This parallels the early years development described by Stern (1985) and cited in Lyons-Ruth et al., 1998: p. 286. Wilson's biophilia hypothesis (1984), '*Biophilia is the innately emotional affiliation of human beings to other living organisms*', cited in Intercon, 2020 and the immediacy of the experience, nurtures a mutual sense of responsibility within a group (See Containing section). The degree of shared responsibility tends to extend organically far beyond that which I've observed in an indoor environment, as evidenced by explicit care and concern for each other. This could be partly because physical needs are more evident in the moment, such as a person's need to sit, move, have a break from the sun and more. What's powerful is that Nature is inviting supervisees to connect more consciously with their own and each other's vulnerability; in this way they also become more active co-facilitators rather than witnesses as in an indoor setting. The shared vulnerability invites further intimacy, and so the cycle continues.

Containing

Winnicott's concept of a 'holding environment' (1960, cited in UKEssays, 2018) in a therapeutic relationship offers a useful metaphor to represent the natural world holding outdoor psychological work and bearing witness to it. Winnicott used the term 'holding' to refer to the trusted and safe supportive environment that a therapist creates for a client, similar to nurturing and caring maternal behaviour towards an infant (Good therapy.org, 2020). However, the essence of being held by the supervisor is only part of the Outdoor Supervision Frame. Equally important is the sense of the supervisory and emotional processing being psychologically contained (Bion, 1970, cited in Jordan, 2015: p. 106) – within the supervisor (able to hold a more dynamic and fluid unfolding process outdoors), the supervisees individually and within the supervision group.

The qualities of the outdoor holding container impact significantly on the degree to which supervisees feel held in the space. Some kind of structure – natural or manmade – offers scaffolding and edges for the work. For example, I run groups in a London park, and we often start in the rose garden because the wooden structures round the edge provide a circular container within which we can arrive together and connect energetically, held in the space. After the first supervision issue has been explored, enabling the group to settle into its identity – more able to hold its own edges and with less need of the scaffolding structure – I invite the supervisee presenting for the next round to choose the spot for their inquiry. Variety of location adds interest for a group session but also serves two other benefits:

1   It encourages physical movement which, in my experience, stimulates emotional processing in itself and
2   It offers the chance to embrace the different meaning that individuals place on different natural environments.

It is worth considering how to maintain the sense of the group's entity (i.e., the edges of the container) as you walk between different settings in a park among members of the public; for example, should this be organic or a mixing of pairs, and so forth? Supervisees can appreciate direction on this, especially if the group is fairly new and the visceral entity of the group hasn't yet developed.

The energetic connection supports the containing, but it is also important to contract around the edges of the container, that is, the thresholds beyond which the holding process would no longer feel safe or appropriate to continue. These thresholds are unique to each individual and dynamic; they are often held unconsciously until violated or at risk of being violated in which case there may be an immediate somatic reaction in the form of a rawness, unease or sense of threat to physical or psychological safety appearing in the space. This links back to the permissions piece, in which supervisees are encouraged to stay attuned to and to name what's being triggered – which is of course part of the work.

Co-cognisance

According to Proctor's model of supervision 2010 (cited in Cutcliffe, J.R.; Hyrkas, K.; Fowler, J. (eds).: 25), the supervision process should address three needs in the supervisee: normative, formative and restorative. In my experience in this outdoor context, the group supervisee effect has a strong normative influence (which would most likely be true indoors or outdoors) but the potential formative and restorative effects are exponentially greater with Nature as co-partner. There is something about the immediacy, uniqueness and vitality in the moment which is refreshing in its potential reframing and therefore potency. The non-conscious is suddenly accessible in this shared experience – not only for the supervisee presenting but for the other supervisees and the supervisor. I have been emotionally moved on many occasions by the simplicity and complexity that co-exist in this space of exploration.

The Boston Change Process Study Group (cited in Jordan, 2015: p. 49) refers to 'moments of truth' arising from 'moments of intersubjective meeting' (Lyons-Ruth et al., 1998: p. 286) – when unpredictabilities occur where the implicit minds of the client and psychotherapist (and in this case, Nature) meet and share a joint experience leading to a fresh insight into the other's subjective reality – speaking personally, these can be truly remarkable and beyond rational comprehension.

> *A supervisee presented her issue in the rose garden of a London park and a fellow supervisee in the group observed that, whilst talking, she had adopted a 'Buddhist sitting position' (i.e., the Lotus position) which was surprising given she was sitting on a park bench. The supervisee presenting was curious about what that position signified, and the discussion moved on. Five minutes later I looked up to see a Buddhist monk arriving on the next bench and the poignancy of that brought a sense of shared intimacy to the group whilst giving the supervisee a sudden realisation that the moment contained a message of acceptance.*

On another occasion,

> *A supervisee brought an inquiry about her next career move, as she felt on the cusp of terminating her secure employment and setting up her private practice as a coach. She was seeking confidence to 'open the doors to her future' as she described it at the outset. We walked slowly through the park, using the bridge across the lake as metaphor for the 'before' and 'after' states of her decision. Once we were embodying the 'after' stage by moving at a faster pace to represent agency and momentum, I was suddenly drawn to an avenue of tall oak trees which seemed to be inviting us in. As we reached the last tree, I spotted a set of keys which had been accidentally dropped! Of course, we handed them in, but the supervisee was delighted with the sign she was already equipped to open the door to her future!*

The outdoor supervision process

Whether indoors or outdoors, my supervision group process invites each supervisee, with equal air time, to bring an issue they are curious about/stuck with/wanting to build on – and relating specifically to a client or a general theme or themselves as coach. The other supervisees are invited to make an offer to the presenting supervisee, coming from 'I' – that is, what they are noticing is coming up for them when they witness the person presenting, which could be an image, feeling, question, words and so on. In an outdoor environment there is of course a vast palette of colours, textures and objects in proximity to each other and dynamism playing out in the moment and I encourage all the supervisees to notice where their attention is drawn in relation to the issue.

It would take some practice for outdoor supervisees to be as present as the supervisor to Nature's gifts around them, given they are holding their own emotional processing at the same time. It might be helpful to make a distinction here between generic supervision groups outdoors (i.e., where the supervisees are attracted to the expansiveness and novelty of being supervised outdoors) and specialist supervision groups where the supervisees are already coaching with Nature as co-partner and therefore want to have Nature present in their supervision as a parallel process to their own outdoor work. I would propose that those two groups of supervisees are distinct, and their needs would best be served separately.

What do I mean by Nature as dynamic co-partner?

By being outdoors, we are already embracing the natural world as a witness, as a non-conscious holding environment. Berger and McLeod (2006: p. 81) introduced the concept of Nature as a partner. The following example of alternative approaches illustrates the difference between the two concepts:

We stand in a group, enjoying the extra sense of spaciousness that being outdoors offers and feeling held by the trees and birds around us.

Nature as witness

I notice and point out a blackbird nearby who has witnessed the issue being presented.

Nature as co-partner

I notice and point out a blackbird nearby who has witnessed the issue being presented – and offer this question to the supervisee:

> There is a blackbird close by who has chosen to stay and listen to you presenting, what might he have noticed?

This immediately prompts a sense of separation from the issue in the supervisee, allowing new perspectives and an invitation to observe their own projections onto the blackbird.

The supervisor's own process

Multi-dimensional awareness

As supervisor – and coach – I am accustomed to staying present to what's going on in my client, in myself and in the relationship space that we occupy. However, in this work I am also holding a level of awareness for Nature as co-partner. This requires frequent filtering of invitations to connect, for example, whether it's the right moment to interrupt a supervisee to question the significance in the system of a heron landing or a bee feeding on nectar as we've walked past. Of course, despite these intentions, I won't capture all the data appearing in the space at any moment, mirroring the supervision process experience for us and our supervisees.

Which parts of us relate to the natural world and how?

My supervision training with the Coaching Supervision Academy instilled in me the concept of 'Who I Am is How I Supervise' (CSA, 2020). We are made up of multiple selves (Lester, 2012: pp. 10–11) and to be at our best as supervisors, we need to be as aware of these different parts as possible – including how they interrelate, when they are triggered, when they serve us, and our supervisees, and when they don't – so that we can regulate them.

In this context, a fundamental question is which parts of us are more likely to be opened up or closed down when we relate to the natural world, and how does that ebb and flow according to the landscape we are in? This usually requires a prior inquiry into the unique relationship developed with nature in childhood and since then. For example, a supervisee with fond memories of family holidays, playing on the beach and freedom to explore may more easily access the playful and carefree part of themselves (Natural Child ego state, Hay, 1993: p. 55) when being supervised (and when coaching) outdoors. The supervisee will bring their own somatic response to Nature which may or may not match that unconsciously being offered by the supervisor – and this needs to be explored at the contracting stage. For example, if the supervisor's relationship with nature is mainly spiritual, and the supervisee is primarily interested in ecology, a sense of incongruence may be created.

Therefore, when establishing a new supervision group working in this way, whether virtually or literally outdoors, it is critical to explore individual preferences so that there can be learning from each other.

Risks

Assessing whether outdoor work is appropriate

Given the potential for non-conscious emotions to arise unexpectedly outdoors, it is important that the psychological containment (Bion, 1970, cited in Jordan, 2015: p. 106) of all supervisees is assessed ahead of the first outdoor group session. Individual conversations beforehand may suffice; personally, I have always chosen to hold the first group indoors, before meeting outdoors, and cover comprehensive contracting at this point, including individual responsibilities. For instance, if one supervisee turns up for an outdoor session without the right clothing/footwear, this can restrict the whole group's experience. If a supervisee arrives in a state of overwhelm, external sensory stimulation may be unhelpful and inappropriate; therefore, this requires individual and group contracting. The supervisee may be encouraged to choose a much more contained (i.e., visibly holding) outdoor space for their own inquiry (such as a shady corner of woodland with limited variety of colours/textures, fewer members of the public, etc.).

Nature's gifts

Nature as soother

The natural world is a paradox of predictabilities and unpredictabilities – we find comfort from the constancy of the ebb and flow of the tide, the circle of life and the seasons that give us meaning and hold us in their transience. This systemic lens (mode 7, Hawkins & Smith, 2008: p. 170) can be applied as a metaphor to any supervision issue.

Mindfulness can be a tool for de-escalating high emotions as it invites internal and physical stillness; for example, inviting a supervisee to stop and really notice the intricacies of a natural object (either staying at a literal level or inviting a metaphorical interpretation) can have a powerful soothing and stabilising effect, at the same time prompting an alternative perspective.

Memories accessed through any of the senses can take us away to a place with positive associations.

I'm often asked what I do about the weather when I explain my work is outdoors! The weather can add to the sense of holding, bringing us more into a felt sense of our own bodies and the interface between the inner and outer worlds. Of course, everyone has their own physical threshold when it comes to the weather, and this can be the subject of group negotiation.

> *When delivering a master class for coaches at a lighthouse in an exposed location, on a very windy day, the participants worked in pairs, to explore their personal relationship with the natural world. They were invited to choose two different locations to compare the somatic holding effect of each: one much more open to the sea and horizon at the water's edge (the tide was out) and one by the sea wall next to the mainland, which offered a physical protective structure behind. The coaches reported this to be an emotionally moving exercise; one said that whilst the open sea spot felt more exposed physically, she welcomed the sense of the wind taking her emotions away up the coast, which she found cathartic.*

Nature as poet

Nature isn't designed around straight lines, and neither are we! Nature offers both simplicity and intricacy and reflects the supervision process which can drill down and then zoom out to the system view.

Metaphors are absolutely everywhere. I have a daily practice of self-compassion with a tree objectifying my internal compassionate supervisor; the vibrant green of the moss on the bark represents to me softness, compassion, gentleness, protection. Meaning-making is personal, though, and every supervisee may take something different from what Nature offers, in parallel process to every coaching client having their own meaning.

Nature as a systemic lens

Working in this way is an emergent process. Nature offers opportunities for naming what's right there and making sense of that in the context of the inquiry – for example, the sting of the nettle or the toxic plant – what's toxic in the system? It's about creating separation from the issue – a fly has just landed on that leaf – flies have extremely large eyes that cover nearly the whole head – what would a fly notice afresh about this issue?

Vistas present a canvas for exploring metaphorically what's in and out of view; as in supervision we might focus in on an issue then take a step back – changing perspective can be provocative; for example, if the tiniest acorn cup is offered to the supervisee as a holding container for the issue, what would be the impact of that?

Nature as mirror

We see vulnerability all around us in the natural world which connects us with our own.

Water, whether a puddle, pond, lake or ocean, is of course an invitation to look literally at reflections and constellations; for example, suddenly different parts of the system are touching each other – what sense do you make of the water lily and trees suddenly being connected? Which relational positions in the system is the supervisee seeing and not seeing?

For those with an auditory preference, Nature's sounds offer a mirror to the inner auditory landscape, whether that be a bird singing representing a dominant inner voice or narrative or to the difficulty of isolating one sound amongst many, reflecting a state of inner noise or overwhelm.

Sunshine is a valuable gift in this work.

> *I led a supervision group one late afternoon, and the sun suddenly offered a beam of sunlight right on the path of the shaded woods we were walking through. It seemed so clearly an invitation for the supervisee to step into the light. I suggested the supervisee chose whether to have the sun on her face or on her back and to embrace the effect of the warmth on her as she held the issue. The rest of us stood back to witness Nature as supervisor. The supervisee immediately noticed her own shadow alongside which prompted in her the question of how she was getting in her own way. It was a powerful moment – and fleeting as the light moved – but long enough for her to feel the somatic change in her as she projected her own assumptions onto her shadow self.*

Group dynamics

With this modality, there is an ongoing negotiation around individuals' tolerance thresholds for mud, wet, wind, cold, sun and the like. The physical conditions connect us with the edges of our inner landscape and our tendency to move towards/away from, engage with fear, express our needs and so on. Part of the work in holding an outdoor supervision group is to facilitate those negotiations – unlike indoors, there is nowhere to hide, and the vulnerability of the supervisor can also be immediately evident; for example, when I was frightened of a stray dog suddenly joining our supervision group on the beach!

Virtual

In my experience, most supervision groups don't take place outdoors – and supervisees may not even be based in the same country! There is no reason why Nature can't be equally valuable as a co-partner within a virtual process. Many of the principles are the same, for example, around somatic connecting with the self and others in the group and attunement to Nature as a mirror to the inner landscape. Contracting is simpler, with fewer physical thresholds such as cold and sun, although privacy might still require attention, as might video and audio equipment. Frequent spot contracting would be essential, though, to retain the intimacy in the group and to compensate for less available body language data. 'Containing' within the virtual supervision frame requires particular attention in a different kind of 'open' space, with the supervisor drawing attention to the energetic holding of each other and bringing awareness to the edges of the container.

The process is different in that images/sounds/objects can be intentionally brought into the space by the supervisor and/or supervisees and visualisation is another powerful option which retains the immediacy of the experience for the supervisees. Likewise, the supervisee offering a choice of objects in the moment ensures that a degree of surprise and spontaneity is maintained. It is helpful if any images brought by the supervisee are evocative, including opportunities for exploring relationship, proximity, difference and the like – for example, a photo of a multi-headed teasel with one head in flower – the textures stimulate interest and the different heads are in relationship with each other.

Outdoor supervision vignettes

All names have been changed and details edited so that they are non-identifiable, even to the supervisees themselves.

Inquiry:
*   Corinne, the supervisee, felt that her coachee Samantha was out of reach. Corinne noticed she was working hard to engage Samantha, but the more she pushed, the farther away the coachee moved.*

Setting: London park.

Supervision process (20 minutes): Corinne was invited to select a tree in the park which represented Samantha. From a distance of maybe 100m she chose a tree that was right at the edge of the park boundary. She led the way towards it and as we all walked closer, we could see that its branches extended over the railings into the street beyond. The tree had grown towards the light, so the side exposed to us as a group was relatively bare. This felt very symbolic – the tree was physically edging away from the park. The other supervisees asked Corinne to tell them more about why she chose this tree given she had done so from a distance without seeing the nuances of its position. She said she had been drawn to it instinctively given its proximity to other trees and the park boundary and was surprised that it was actually occupying more space in the street than in the park. I invited Corinne to observe what she noticed in herself as she viewed the tree; she said she suddenly felt compassion for Samantha, connecting with a sense of fear and vulnerability she had missed during the face-to-face coaching. I questioned whether it had indeed been a "face-to-face" experience given the tree was facing away from her. I and the rest of the group stood back to observe as Corinne related directly to the tree – Nature was acting as co-partner, we were witnessing. Corinne visibly softened in front of us and reached out with gentleness to the point of intersection on the trunk where the main branch veered off towards the street. Just below that the tree was at its strongest and most stable. Suddenly Corinne recognised that she could welcome and work with that part, that was enough, she didn't need to push Samantha to bring in more of herself than she was ready for. The group held Corinne as she took her time to notice the emotional unfolding in herself which allowed her to connect with Samantha with more softness and compassion. As we were coming towards the end of Corinne's inquiry, I invited us all to walk back to our starting point 100m away and to take another look at the tree from a distance, encouraging everyone, including Corinne, to share any more thoughts or feelings. Corinne realised that she had also held back the warmer, relational parts of herself from connecting with Samantha, as her focus on achieving the right outputs for her client was triggered into overworking.

Inquiry:

Rahim, the supervisee, was concerned about a pattern he'd noticed in himself – that he was getting too emotionally involved in the content of his coaching sessions which was leaving him feeling generally depleted.

Setting: River path.

Supervision process (30 minutes): Rahim had explained his inquiry to the rest of the group and requested that we walk together along the river because he wanted to dislodge the stuckness he felt about this issue. I invited him to notice where in his body he was noticing the stuckness, and he said it was sitting buried deep in his stomach: 'It's been there for a long time'. I asked him how he felt about it and he said, 'Angry', because it was getting in the way of him doing his best work. He then chose to stop at some wooden decking which was right at the water's edge, and we sat down alongside him, giving him space as I could see that he was drawn by the river's invitation to connect. Aware of not wanting to interrupt that energetic connection, I softened my voice and quietly asked him how the river represented his own system. He recognised the movement of the water as a metaphor for him being in flow in his practice and that some of the boats moored alongside were disrupting the pattern on the water's surface as it swirled around them, noisily buffeting their sides. He described the boats as his clients, each carrying their own story, tempting him to step in and take one of the empty seats. Then two swans swam past together, elegant and at ease. In that moment we witnessed Nature offering Rahim an alternative framing of his own process: he and his clients swimming along side by side for a while, separate entities but in connection. He didn't have to get caught up in their content. The position he had chosen on the decking had enabled him to observe himself and interrupt his habitual response. He took a photo of the swans as an anchoring tool to return to the new felt sense he had experienced whenever he needed. When asked how his stuckness was feeling, Rahim replied: 'It's now much smaller and close to the surface, suddenly I feel kindness towards it'.

References

Berger, R., & McLeod, J. (2006). Incorporating Nature into Therapy: A Framework for Practice. *Journal of Systemic Therapies*, 25, June, 80–94. doi: 10.1521/jsyt.2006.25.2.80.

Berne, E. (1961). *Transactional Analysis in Psychotherapy*. New York: Grove Press.

Bion, W. R. (1970). *Attention and Interpretation: A Scientific Approach to Insight in Psycho-Analysis and Groups*. London: Tavistock Publications.

CSA. (2019). Coaching Supervision Academy. https://coachingsupervisionacademy.com/csa-diploma/ [Accessed: 20 July 2020].

Dickinson, E. (1896). A Light Exists in Spring. In M. L. Todd (Ed.), *Poems by Emily Dickinson Third Series* (p. 103). Boston: Roberts Brothers.

Good therapy.org. (2015). Donald Winnicott (1896–1971). *Good therapy*. www.goodtherapy.org/famous-psychologists/donald-winnicott.html [Accessed: 29 July 2021].

Hawkins, P., & Smith, N. (2008). *Coaching, Mentoring and Organizational Consultancy: Supervision and Development* (2nd ed.). Berkshire: Open University Press.

Hay, J. (1993). *Working It Out at Work. Understanding Attitudes and Building Relationships*. Watford: Sherwood Publishing.

Hermansson, G. (1997). Boundaries and Boundary Crossing: The Never Ending Story. *British Journal of Guidance and Counselling*, 25(2), 133–146.

Intercon. (2020). *We Are Hardwired for Loving Nature. Intercongreen*. https://intercon-green.com/2013/06/13/we-are-hardwired-for-loving-nature/ [Accessed: 20 July 2020].

Jordan, M. (2015). *Nature and Therapy*. Hove: Routledge.

Jordan, M., & Hinds, J. Eds. (2016). *Ecotherapy – Theory, Research and Practice*. London: Macmillan Education/Palgrave.

Klein, M. (1997). *Envy and Gratitude: And Other Works 1946–1963* (Intro. By H. Segal). London: Vintage.

Lester, D. (2012). A Multiple Self Theory of the Mind. *Comprehensive Psychology*, 1(5). doi: 10.2466/02.09.28.CP.1.5.

Lewis, R. (2017). *A Qualitative Study of Psychotherapists' Experience of Practising Psychotherapy Outdoors*. Dublin: Dublin Business School.

Lexico. (2020). Nature. *Lexico*. www.lexico.com/definition/nature [Accessed: 4 August 2020].

Lyons-Ruth, K., Bruschweiler-Stern, B., Harrison, A. M., Morgan, A. C., Nahum, J. P., Sander, L., Stern, D. N., & Tronick, E. Z. (1998). Implicit Relational Knowing: Its Role in Development and Psychoanalytic Treatment. *Infant Mental Health Journal*, 19(3), 282–289. Integra-cpd. www.integra-cpd.co.uk/wp-content/uploads/cpd-resources/Lyons-Ruth_1998_Implicit_Relational_Knowing.pdf [Accessed: 3 August 2020]. https://doi.org/10.1002/(SICI)1097-0355(199823)19:3<282::AID-IMHJ3>3.0.CO;2-O.

Marshall, H. (2016). Taking Therapy Outside – Reaching for a Vital Connection. Keynote Presentation at CONFER Conference: Psychotherapy and the Natural World. CONFER [Accessed: 25 May 2018].

The-Philosophy-com. (2012). Buber's I and Though (Summary). *The-Philosophy*. www.the-philosophy.com/buber-i-thou-summary [Accessed: 4 August 2020].

Proctor, B. (2010). Chapter 3 Training for the Supervision Alliance. In J. R. Cutcliffe, K. Hyrkas, & J. Fowler (Eds.), *Routledge Handbook of Clinical Supervision, Fundamental International Themes*. Routledgehandbooks.com. www.routledgehandbooks.com/doi/10.4324/9780203843437.ch3 [Accessed: 3 August 2020].

Stern, D. (1985). *The Interpersonal World of the Infant: A View from Psychoanalysis and Developmental Psychology*. New York: Basic Books.

UKEssays. (2018). Holding and Containing – Winnicott (1960). *UKEssays*. www.ukessays.com/essays/psychology/holding-and-containing-winnicott.php [Accessed 3 August 2020].

Wilson, E. O. (1984). *Biophilia*. Cambridge, MA: Harvard University Press.

Chapter 7

Moving bodies

Countering digital disembodiment

Louie J N Gardiner

> *Everywhere I am, I am.*
> *Everywhere I am, I find myself . . . moving.*[1]

Introduction

I offered to write about embodiment in coaching supervision groups. In so doing, I realise I have created a conundrum for myself. Embodiment is a uniquely personal state. This means I cannot speak of anyone else's experience; firstly, because I am not them, and secondly, because what we as human beings experience is often beyond the reach of words. I could tell you what I do in group supervision and how I establish the conditions for me and my supervisees to work together, but this would not give you any sense of the aliveness that is inherent in the actuality of embodiment, as it materialises in each of us every time we engage with others.

Through my doctoral research I have come to appreciate that there is no knowing without a knower. There is no such thing as knowledge. Words on paper or on screen are mere scribbles, dots and lines unless or until someone comprehends and does something with them. The expression of knowing is in the expression of the knower. This means, I must turn to *me* to discover what I might have to say about this topic. I am in and of the living, breathing, moving being~doing body that is me. While I am living, I am learning. While I am learning, I am moving.

Animation[2] is the fundamental indicator that I/we are alive and living and learning. But, for many, our recognition of this is so far from our awareness. We simply go about our lives; moving all the while and paying little, if any, attention to what is actually and potentially being revealed to us, if only we were to pay attention to what is in play within us. This is where this chapter invites you to go. I open my invitation to you by going there myself.

In starting to write this chapter, I did not consciously set out to do **this**. I did not consciously set out to do this, **this way**. I found myself being and doing this, this way, by following the clues and cues I noticed in myself in an initial online encounter with a group of people I had not met before – in the midst of a COVID-19-constrained 2020. Thinking about group supervision, I realised I could follow myself and explore my own interior journeying as I entered this new

DOI: 10.4324/978100314345-8

group. I surrendered to what was coming, wondering what this might reveal about embodiment in group supervision contexts. So, I started with me: attending to this being~doing body that is me, entering a group for the first time . . .

Pre-entry

I find myself here in this space; on the precipice of engaging with a group of people whom, mostly, I do not know. A collection of individuals invited together, gathering around a common intention. How did I get here? Someone opened the space and invited me in. My being~doing body brought me here. Yes – even into this digital realm. My body carried me out of my house, into my working space in the cabin in my garden, across the threshold, removing my outdoor shoes, putting on my slippers, easing myself into my chair, turning on the lights, plugging in the monitors and pressing the power button on the computer. I feel awe as I pause long enough to ponder on all that my being~doing body has already done to get me to being here, now. A multitude of micro- and macro-animated acts have been orchestrated without my even having to think about them while I consciously focused on one simple thing – to get to the Zoom call at the prescribed time. I made it, just . . . or perhaps I was a minute or two late. I cannot remember.

What I am acutely aware of is that the introverted child in me does her very best to avoid those (awkward to me) moments of arriving into a space full of people I do not know, believing I will be expected to engage in some kind of 'small talk' or, worse, that I will simply be ignored. Oh! How uncomfortable I (used to) feel in those moments. I find myself re-calling countless times as a child, when I was the newcomer arriving into an established group. I did not know 'them'; 'they' did not know me . . . and because of those early experiences, I came to believe that I would be isolated . . . ridiculed . . . marginalised . . . pushed out . . . Wow! I notice how I put 'them' into a uniform, generalised One, as if they all will be thinking and feeling exactly the same thing about the 'me' that is the Other. Those resonances from such a long time ago still linger, putting me on alert to be on alert. And in the process, **I make myself** that Other.

Entering

As I press the virtual button on my screen to enter the digital room, expecting to see unknown faces, a reverberation, imperceptible to anyone who is not me, ripples through my body. I find myself confronted, first, with my own head and shoulders, and my furrowed face looking back at me. My head is facing into a screen with other faces, apparently looking at me. But are they? Are they looking at me or at someone else? Or are they doing what I catch myself doing – see me looking at ME? What is going on in me that has me look at me?

Hmmm! I feel an uncomfortable squirm in my tummy that awakens me to something that has troubled me about this digital realm. When I see myself looking back at me, non-consciously, I have invited an extra person into this virtual space. What if everyone else is doing the same? If they are – even if for only some of the time – it is as if we have twice the number of people in the room than are actually there! When I look at me – which I find myself doing, reflexively now, in this moment – I carry myself into an observer position in relation to myself. Instead of attuning to me from the inside, I notice that I am looking at how I am showing up; what I look like; what I see myself doing and, curiously, what I hear myself saying. Now that I am awake to what is going on with me, I realise how disconnecting I find this out-of-body experience – separating not only from myself but from everyone else in the Zoom room. I feel stunned and disappointed with myself that I had not noticed what was showing up in and through me until this moment. I also feel excited and thrilled by the tumble of insights, cascading in slow motion within me as I start considering what is different when I am actually in a physical space with others. Although I may only see one or two people within my binocular gaze, I have the possibility (but no guarantee) of seeing and hearing more of their being~doing bodies in play, engaging with me. More of my faculties may come into play, but this depends largely on what else is going on in me and the degree to which I am present, attending and attuning to what is dynamically happening in me and between us. I slay one fiction[3]: being in physical proximity does not assure accessing all the cues and signals that might actually be available to the persons present.

My reflection turns to my existing supervision groups, some of which are held by the shared praxis[4] of Presence in Action.[5] This praxis opens the space for each of us to engage 'all of our being' when we come together. We reach for our Emotions Palettes[6] and use these to help us tune into, recognise and name the feelings alive in us. I feel a sudden wave of grief move through me. I miss these people coming together with me in a shared working space. I miss them talking and processing and moving spatially across the P6 Constellation floor mat[7] (see brief illumination and Figure 1 later in this chapter) that holds our interior exploration. I miss holding the space for each precious person in the circle to show up with whatever has been running them ragged until they move into revelation, resolution and release. I take a moment to pause. I notice my mind has carried me away from being here, now, with these people. I have shifted context. Ah! I have gone to somewhere more familiar, recalling people I know. Is this my self-protective pattern coming out to reassure me, by reminding me of those who value and validate what I do and how I work? The feelings in my body indicate that this is not what is going on for me. If it were, I would be feeling anxious, concerned, earnest; and instead, I am feeling sadness, wonder and gratitude – for who they are and for the fact that I get to work with and learn from them. Them showing up is giving me contrast – opening my reflective space to notice similarities and differences, in this scenario, between new and established groups. Since undertaking my PhD research, I have come to recognise that when this abductive[8] pattern comes out to play, it is time for me to get out of the way of myself and to follow the scents and trails that are unfolding before me. I feel curious and excited, wondering what small discoveries I may encounter along the way.

Engaging

I return to the group experience tipping me into writing this piece. When I am staring at this monitor, seeing people I have not met before who are sitting somewhere that is not here, I am faced with a peculiar, paradoxical mix of sensory deprivation and overload. Reliant only on the communication channels of sight and sound, I see multiple moving heads and shoulders, fuzzy faces with varying degrees of pixelation, numerous unfamiliar places and oscillating, variable sound quality. I am unable to grasp the 'all-ness' of a person, so much of which will be happening off camera – how their bodies move or remain virtually still; the small and large gestures they make; the tics and twitches that may play out in their hands, arms, feet and legs; any fiddling or doodling they might do; where their eyes and attention go; whom they look at and whom they avoid engaging with; what they wear and what smells accompany their physical presence.

None of this is accessible in a flat screen full of faces looking at flat screens full of faces. When internet bandwidth is poor, I might even lose sight and/or sound of a person altogether or they might lose me. Depending on what is at play in my encounter with that person, this severing of connection might evoke visceral relief or distress in me and/or them! Perhaps they simply hit the 'leave' button . . . to escape the discomfort of a particular enquiry or illumination? Perhaps they simply felt bored and digitally exited, having already emotionally checked out? Perhaps someone physically interrupted them, and they chose or were forced to leave without warning? Perhaps? Perhaps? Perhaps? Who knows? No one other than they can know until/unless anyone else is told. Now, that kind of abrupt departure might be much harder for a group member to follow through on if we were in the same room, a few feet apart. It is not impossible for someone to suddenly get so activated that they cannot hold themselves in the space anymore. In fact, in all my years of supervision practice, this has happened to me once, and nothing I said or did could reach that person in that moment. What about me as the supervisor? Would I ever find myself so activated by something happening in the group that I might engineer dropping off a digital call – effectively closing the room and leaving everyone 'lost in cyber space', wondering what happened? Nowadays, I cannot imagine resorting to that . . . though I do recall a time as a middle manager, 25 years ago, when I did indeed run from a team meeting I was hosting in tears! I am mindful to 'never say never' and to acknowledge that even being together in the same physical space offers no guarantee of averting abrupt departures. Nevertheless, in digital encounters, the scope for (non-)consciously noticing early-warning clues or signals of distress in another is, I believe, dramatically reduced. The opportunity to prevent people leaving or encouraging them back is virtually impossible (excuse the pun) without them bringing themselves back into relationship.

Switching off to switch on

I return to myself and the 'new' group experience I am facing. In these opening moments, I look at the others, and again catch myself watching myself. I am still.

Still? I am never still! What am I doing? Why am I here? Why now? I have no immediate answers to these questions. But I have faith they will be answered, not by trying to 'get' the answers but by turning to attend to what is presenting and becoming in this encounter with me and with these people.

My being~doing body brought me here, and I have been sitting in this seat for some time. My 'yes' to being here still expresses itself through my psychological attention, returning me to these seemingly bodyless faces. Disembodied heads float before me. Including mine. I notice my mouth is a straight-line caricature, making my lips look thinner than they usually are. I close my eyes, turning inwards to feel – to connect with what is going on within me. I **feel** the tightness in my lips. I know my body is signalling trepidation – a familiar mix of anticipation and fear. It runs from my gut and shows up in my lips, silencing me. Keeping me tight-lipped: '*Say nothing in case . . .*' I discovered this connection when someone once reflected to me that my lips had gone white and 'unusually thin'. That clean reflection helped me attune to what was going on internally. Now I know. But usually, I can only feel from within what is happening; not see from the outside-in, as I can from this online viewpoint. Another clue! I nearly missed it. I close my eyes – **not** to block them out. I close my eyes so that, by not seeing me, I **feel** me. However, in completely shutting down my visual channel, I can no longer see the others in the Zoom room. I drift back in time, momentarily disconnecting from them and our shared context. I remember doing this as a child: '*If I close my eyes, they will not be there!*' But this is not what I am doing here.

I smile. I am no longer that wee girl wishing away those in whose presence I experienced distress. In this moment, I remember I can do something about this. I want to **see these people** and **feel me**. I move my cursor to the top right of my image; right click my mouse, and then on the drop-down menu, click [Hide self-view]. Instantly I am released from my crazy self-preoccupation. My attention is freed, and I find myself changing from [Gallery view] to [Speaker view] because I now notice that I have not been able to see clearly who is speaking. Oh wow! Now I can really see each person who speaks – these are precious souls, not an amorphous, impersonal wall of digital avatars to which my mind had reduced them. Of course! I am reminded of how 'up close and personal' my in-person work sometimes is with my supervisees. I am aware that some supervisors might not actually get this close to someone's face under 'normal' circumstances. But in my supervision groups, sometimes we do. So, on the screen, although poor image quality and pixelation might mask some nuances of what passes across someone's face, I can appreciate this different way of achieving that degree of intimacy through this digital medium.

Another insight tumbles forth as I make a connection with what happens with those of my supervisees practising Presence in Action: how, when they come to my workspace or some other private location, we co-create the conditions in which they simultaneously experience and develop their capacity to be held and to hold profound personal processing using the P6 Constellation floor mat. The framework supports first-person inquiry. It comprises six outlying 'portals' (Facts, Fictions, Feelings, Purpose, Outcomes, Decisions) held at the centre by

'Presence'; the latter of which invites a person into a self-centering inquiry to 'notice what they are noticing', using the other portals to discern the nature of what is presenting within them. In short, this representation offers an external framework for a person to metaphorically 'step into themselves' to discover what is manifesting in their interior realm (see Figure 7.1).

I enter into the space with them, accompanying them as they talk and walk. We move across the space, entering each portal as they recognise the nature of what they are expressing, for example, emotions, interpretations, recalling past events, imagining future happenings and more. I follow what they are saying, noticing their movements and gestures. I reflect back to them what I notice emerging from them, with nothing added and nothing taken away. Sometimes I find myself standing incredibly close, face to face, holding them in my gaze as they meet themselves in whatever they are processing. In those moments, it is as if all others in the room dissolve into the background. Sitting in an actual circle around the mat, the group physically frames and 'holds' our processing space; with each person in the round, focussing on what is unfolding with those on the mat; while also endeavouring to attend to what is rising and falling within themselves.

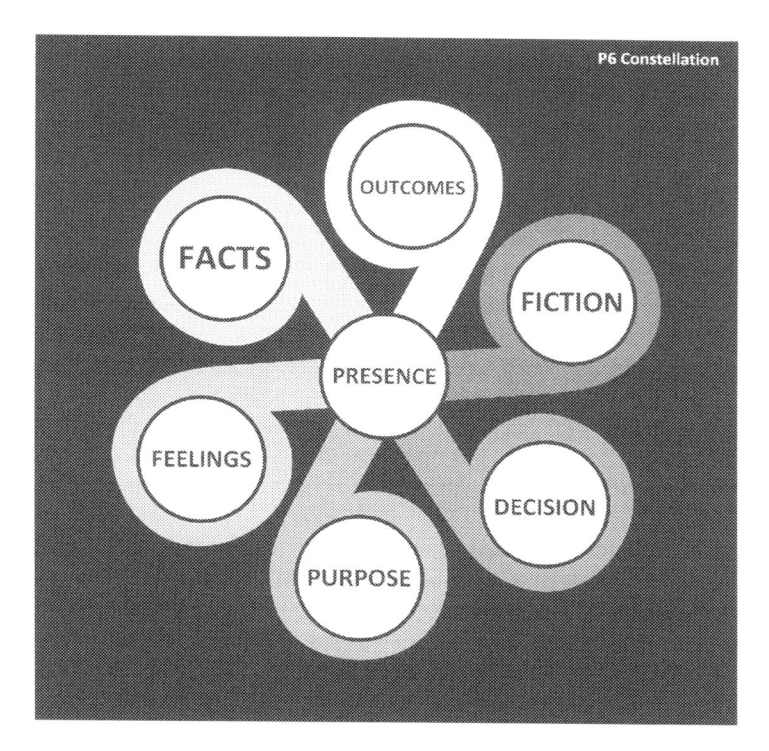

Figure 7.1 P6 Constellation™, framing self-centering inquiry (L J N Gardiner, 2018)

Another insight lands within me, catapulting me forward into future digital encounters. I know how I can bring some of this alive on the screen! In readiness for these unanticipated moments of intimate personal processing, I simply need to prepare everyone in the Zoom group to be alert to turning off their video and audio – without waiting for an explicit request – so that the person processing and the person hosting see only each other, free from any other visual or auditory stimulation.[9] The challenge for those in the digital 'circle' is recognising that their energetic presence is as vital in holding the encounter as it would be if they were physically 'holding' space. Furthermore, in readying to support and reflect back to the processing person, these witnesses need to be particularly alert to themselves. What might non-consciously unfold in their own behaviours, when they find themselves in the virtual and invisible holding circle, being neither seen nor heard? What else arises for them, as they attend to what unfolds between the two people visible on screen? While off-video, this is not the time to actually leave the room to get a cup of tea or to drop attention by answering an email! However, if anyone's attention does drift somewhere else, this will signal something on which to reflect that may be of use both to the individual drifting off as well as to the group process. I reveal this very dance throughout this chapter – in which my interior sense-making continuously moves between each present moment and my past and future imaginings. This is part of our human condition which, rather than denying, we can hone and learn to use reflexively, to reveal what is showing up in and through us.

Severing the old for new to emerge

Once again, having drifted off into my past and future musings and having come to a momentary resolution, I bring myself back into the Zoom room, to this group that has barely begun. Freed from my own processing, I notice I am listening again. Listening and noticing what is unfolding; noticing, noticing, noticing. Something is forming in the unfolding of our interactions. I am noticing who connects to whom; who mentions whom; what one says to another. He verbally affirms what she says . . . and her too. She acknowledges her . . . and him . . . subtle alliances and sub-groups forming. I wonder what is going on? Where is my place in this? Damn! I have already put myself at the margins. I have been sidling my way to the edge. My misleading mind has picked up a frayed thread from bygone times and has been attempting to spin a tiresome yarn. My being~doing body has been onto this mental racket all the while, and here, now, I recognise it is time to sever the thread before the yarn runs away with me. Momentarily, I move my digital mouse and click on [Show self-view]. I allow myself to see that I am one member of this group. I gaze across our images on the digital wall in front of me. We are the ones. We are the chapter authors of this book. I am one of them and I take my place. I inwardly nod and silently acknowledge myself. I have a place here. I have two chapter contributions to make, and this is one of them. I move my mouse and click [Hide self-view], bringing my full attention back onto these others who are gathered to give of themselves. They have something to say, and I want to hear them. I am ready, open, connected and curious.

Coming home to ourselves

Through this experience, I am reminded again that my body catches on long before my mind does. On this occasion, my mind is challenged, only as my words find their way to the surface, trickling onto this digital screen in front of me, as my fingers tap and tickle across my laptop keyboard. In these pages, you are witness to what has been flowing and unfolding, as I have been following the trail of jumbled fur balls that have been popping out of my metaphorical mouth. Without my being~doing body twitching and pulsing and frowning and fretting, none of this would have become available to me or to you. Without my mouth and its thin lips; my facial muscles and vocal chords; and my lungs to draw in and exhale air to create sound and . . . and . . . and . . ., I would be unable to speak. Without these eyes straining to focus after hours and days and years looking at my computer; and these ears ringing with tinnitus; and this dry, crinkled tongue urging me to drink; I would have no way of connecting to all that is beyond the me that is held by the thinning, aging skin that enwraps this being~doing body, who calls herself Louie. Without the mushy, squishy convoluted mass encased in my skull, connected through skeleton, muscles, nerve cells and hormones and body fluids to my sensory organs, I would have no capacity to think. I would have no access to my fast-spinning, flawed mind that is in daily need of mindful, effortful, slow-process honing. All of my being is needed to bring coherence to this extraordinary sense-making facility that arises from all that my being~doing body is and does and makes, from all that I encounter.

I **am** my being~doing body. I am not embodied **in** it, for that suggests that some part of me can be disembodied **from** it without actually dying! To say we are disembodied is a construct of our minds – meaning-making – that is not born out in reality. I come home to this; to me.

Teasing out the threads

As this reverberates and settles within me, I find my attention drifting ahead again. I want to draw together the threads and insights that have been emerging and to make explicit how they translate into group supervision.

Being a person, first and always: My first-person illumination reminds us of the reality that every individual entering a new group faces an onslaught of familiar and unfamiliar sensory stimulation. Over time, in relation to a specific group of people, this is likely to diminish. Nevertheless, on every occasion the group gathers, each person comes with their own unique experiences coursing through their bodies. Their patterns of being and doing; their meaning-making shaped by and shaping past, present and future realities and projections will all show up subliminally and explicitly. Our bodies are our primary resource for accessing and attuning to all of this within the context of our relational realms and wider world. We are the instrument giving us direct access to what is, what has been and what might be. We diminish, disregard or deny ourselves access to this at our own peril and at the risk of confusing or compromising our interactions with others.

Being in groups to know ourselves in groups: Being the recognised supervisor of a group is, in my view, a profound privilege carrying personal and professional responsibility. How we as supervisors hold or host these spaces will vary depending on those with whom, when and where we are working. Context matters. In the Presence in Action community-in-practice, we come together in varied 'containers' in which I take on different roles – as supervisor, trainer and community member. Together we rely on a foundational praxis to support us to move between hosting, processing and witnessing, and so, along with every other community member, you may see me walking across the floor mat while others host and witness me. In these community spaces, I do my interior work with them when I discern it is helpful to do so. As supervisor, you will find me drawing on my attunement to myself in service to the processing of another and the group as a whole. As trainer, additionally, I may reflect theoretical underpinnings to illuminate the distinctions and nature of the work we are undertaking. In consciously holding the space and working with the edges in all our encounters, I am seeking to serve the intention of each while attending to the individuals, relationships and situational context. Making such distinctions clear, and practising our praxis, enables us to transition between our different roles as is fit-for-purpose. Recognising I am continually in process, I am mindful of the challenges I and others face when I and we come into relationship. Irrespective of our shared containers and my role within each, I endeavour to stay alert to what goes on **for me**. In this chapter, I have been attuning to what was manifesting in me as a participant in a 'new' group, meeting online for the first time. I found my attention dancing between this present-moment experience and reflecting on my experiences as a group supervisor moving from in-person to online hosting. I delighted in experiencing surprising insights that revealed some new practical actions for handling the conundrum of creating intimate online encounters. I summarise these together with some of my current practices in the table at the end of this chapter.

Being the instrument of our praxis takes more than practice: Once I recognised that my being~doing body was my primary instrument for encountering the world, I realised two things. Firstly, I had nowhere to hide – everywhere I am, I am. Secondly, I could no longer blame another for what issued forth from my being~doing body – everywhere I am, in all that I do, I find myself being and doing. I took a while to move beyond my own resistance to what was undeniable. Finally, I said 'yes' to taking on the responsibility to hone my response-ability. Decades on, this evolved into a praxis which infuses how I show up in in my relations with others and how I coach and supervise others. Core to this is a self-centering~extending dynamic that calls on me to be receptive[10] to what is calling for my attention, readying me to responsively follow and flow to where this may lead, in relation to those I am serving. Comprehending and becoming able to articulate the **nature of my praxis, what underpins it** and **what brings coherence to it**, has made the world of difference to me and to the self-assuredness

I experience. Not knowing what is coming and becoming – while knowing the current limits of my knowing – has become a liberating experience evoking relief, joy, excitement, anticipation and humility. Attuning to not-knowing is, for me, the essence of supervision; within the context of Group Supervision, this becomes infinitely more complex with each additional person present. As supervisor, I am called to serve the intention of the group, to hold firm to the boundaries that keep the nature of our engagement clear, while simultaneously surrendering to what might unfold within and between us. Sitting with the humility of not-knowing helps me remember that my role is **not** about second-guessing **what** is going on **nor** knowing **what to do**; it is about knowing how to open up to what is presenting in each of us and to what comes alive within and between us. Group supervision reminds us that we are in relationship with others and with life; as such, it can resource us to attend to and extend ourselves differently in service to other groups in which we find ourselves.

Being in and of the world means adapting to the territory: As the world changes, we change . . . or we die. COVID-19 invoked us, simultaneously, to retreat from each other physically while geographically extending, through digital means, at pace. It catapulted millions of people into connecting online for the first time and countless others into learning to work in their own homes, isolated from colleagues, family and friends. My in-person supervision groups became flat-screen encounters overnight. Entering into, and engaging with, the group of this book's chapter authors in the way that I did brought to light what had previously been tacit[11] in me: the all-pervasiveness of the interplay of our being~doing bodies everywhere we are. One gift of being unwittingly projected into this digital medium is how it has awakened me to explicitly augment the imperative of attuning to what is calling for our attention; and inviting us to dare to talk about what is showing up in and through our being~doing bodies. This means attending to our physical/physiological sensations and emotions; as well as whatever else we may (not) be noticing, thinking, imagining and remembering. Everything that plays out in our interior realms comes together and manifests through our patterns of being and doing, whether or not we are online. If we ignore this, we end up denying and depriving ourselves and others the opportunities of benefitting, and benefitting from, all that might become.

Being~doing bodies being and doing differently: As I turn towards the closing of this chapter, I find myself reflecting how I might distil these insights, usefully, for others hosting group coaching supervision sessions in digital realms. Suddenly, it seems obvious! Let me illuminate what I have been using. In 2018, Jo Birch and I undertook a small research project in which we extrapolated Seven Simple Rules for Coaching Supervision.[12] These are embedded in my practice and reflected in the section 'Teasing out the threads'. In Table 7.1, I summarise my insights from this chapter and align them to the most applicable of each of the Seven Simple Rules.

Table 7.1 Applying the Seven Simple Rules of Coaching Supervision for transforming online encounters

Simple Rules	Amplifying practice and making digital-space adjustments
• **Attune to self**	• When in a Zoom call, select [Hide self-view]. • Be ready with practical resources that will support engagement; e.g., with Presence in Action, each practitioner has workbooks to note what they are noticing, believing, feeling, recalling and imagining; and an Emotions Palette© – a set of cards to help attune to what they are feeling. • Notice our own being~doing patterns, e.g., physical sensations, tension, movement, tics, twitches, fiddling, gazing out of window, attention wandering, feelings, thinking, doing etc.
• **Engage with love**	• Turn on [Speaker view] to draw our attention to the person speaking. • Notice: o the words people utter and what is beyond the words o facial and gestural movements.
• **Serve the intention**	• Prepare contingencies for internet dropping. • When one person is processing and being held by another, be ready to o turn off own video and audio o stay fully engaged as self-reflexive witnesses and use notebooks to note what we notice.
• **Hold the space, work with the edges**	• Create a quiet space in which to engage. • Start and end session at agreed-upon times. • When one person is processing and being held by another, be ready to: o turn off own video and audio o stay fully engaged as self-reflexive witnesses and use notebooks to note what we notice.
• **Illuminate and explore what is calling for attention**	• Notice. • Notice what we notice in/about ourselves and others. • Notice what tips us into judging self and others.
• **Dare to call it out**	• Offer factual reflections rather than interpretations of what we notice.[13] o I notice I am feeling/said/did. . . o I notice you said/did. . .
• **Attend to the individuals, relationships and situational context**	• Ideally schedule sessions when the internet is not used by others in our households. • Ideally use a laptop and close all other internet tabs. • If our workspace might be disturbed (e.g., by children, pets or partners), wear headphones to a) protect the privacy of all participants and b) support everyone's listening and participation.

Notes

1 (Gardiner, L. J. N. *Attending, Responding, Becoming ~ A Living-Learning Inquiry in a Naturally Inclusive Playspace*. PhD University of Hull, PhD pending publication).
2 (Sheets-Johnstone, 1981, 1999, 2009, 2011, 2016, 2018).
3 I take 'Fictions' to be '*what my mind does with . . .*' whatever I witness, experience and feel; that is, it is meaning-making, which includes judgements, conclusions, assumptions, myths, metaphors, stories, interpretations and the like about myself, others or 'the world'. 'Fiction' is one of six portals within the P6 Constellation framework which serves as a guide to reflective and reflexive self-inquiry (Gardiner, 2014a).
4 Praxis: the fusion between practice and theory.
5 (Gardiner, 2019, PhD pending publication). Presence in Action is a self-centering praxis underpinned by the principles of Natural Inclusion, complexity thinking and primal animation. It is supported by the representation of the P6 Constellation, a simple Acuity Practice and embodied knowing expressed through seven symmathesic agency behaviours. Please refer to earlier chapter where I say more about all this.
6 The Emotions Palette[c] is a set of cards used in conjunction with the 'Feelings' portal within the P6 Constellation. The cards support individuals to access, discern and express the range of feelings they are experiencing at any given moment.
7 A representation of the P6 Constellation on a rug or on portable floor mats (Gardiner, 1999, 2014a, 2014b, 2014c, 2017, 2018).
8 (Gardiner, PhD pending publication).
9 I note that if two people are in the centre of a physical circle of people, some would be behind, to the side and in front of each of us. Neither of us would see everyone all at once, as we might on a monitor.
10 (Gardiner, 2019; Rayner, 2003, 2004, 2010, 2013, 2018).
11 (Polanyi, 1958, 1959; Polanyi, 1966).
12 (Birch & Gardiner, 2019).
13 Reflective Contribution is used within the praxis of Presence in Action. It is a precise and particular alternative to the conventional practice of giving feedback.

References

Birch, J., & Gardiner, L. J. N. (2019). Seven Simple Rules: An Alternative Lens. In J. Birch & P. Welch (Eds.), *Coaching Supervision: Advancing Practice, Changing Landscapes* (pp. 21–34). London: Routledge.

Gardiner, L. J. N. (1999). *PAI: Point Attractor Inquiry Process*. Sheffield: Potent 6 Ltd.

Gardiner, L. J. N. (2014a). Changing the Game of Change-making. *Coaching Today*, 12, 6–11.

Gardiner, L. J. N. (2014b). The Scottish Referendum: Complexity Perspectives. *e-O&P: Journal of the Association of Management Education and Development*, 21(2), 6–17.

Gardiner, L. J. N. (2014c). The Sweet Bitter of No. *e-O&P: Journal of the Association of Management Education and Development*, 21(3), 38–42.

Gardiner, L. J. N. (2017). Portals, Patterns and Paradigm Shifts. Edinburgh: EMCC.

Gardiner, L. J. N. (2018). Portals to the Collective Mind. In *24th International Coaching, Mentoring and Supervision Conference* (pp. 11–14), April. Amsterdam: EMCC.

Gardiner, L. J. N. (2019). Attending, Daring, Becoming: Making Boundary-Play Conscious. In J. Birch & P. Welch (Eds.), *Coaching Supervision: Advancing Practice, Changing Landscapes* (1st ed., pp. 103–125). London: Routledge.

Gardiner, L. J. N. *Attending, Responding, Becoming ~ A Living-Learning Inquiry in a Naturally Inclusive Playspace*. PhD University of Hull, PhD forthcoming.

Polanyi, M. (1958). *Personal Knowledge – Towards a Post-Critical Philosophy, 1962, 1973*. London: Routledge & Kegan Paul Ltd.

Polanyi, M. (1959). *The Study of Man (Routledge Revivals): The Lindsay Memorial Lectures, 2013*. London: Routledge.

Polanyi, M. (1966). *The Tacit Dimension*. New York: Doubleday.

Rayner, A. D. M. (2003). Inclusionality – An Immersive Philosophy of Environmental Relationships. In A. Winnett & A. Warhurst (Eds.), *Towards an Environment Research Agenda: A Second Selection of Papers* (pp. 5–20). Basingstoke: Palgrave Macmillan Springer.

Rayner, A. D. M. (2004). *Inclusionality: The Science, Art and Spirituality of Place, Space and Evolution*. Llandeilo: Bridge Gallery Publishing.

Rayner, A. D. M. (2010). Inclusionality and Sustainability – Attuning with the Currency of Natural Energy Flow and How This Contrasts with Abstract Economic Rationality. *Environmental Economics*, 1, 98–108.

Rayner, A. D. M. (2013). Alan Rayner – The Essence of Natural Inclusionality, 28 August. *Youtube*. [Downloaded 28/08/2013].

Rayner, A. D. M. (2018). The Vitality of the Intangible: Crossing the Threshold from Abstract Materialism to Natural Reality. *Human Arenas*, 1, 9–20.

Sheets-Johnstone, M. (1981). Thinking in Movement. *The Journal of Aesthetics and Art Criticism*, 39(4), 399–407.

Sheets-Johnstone, M. (1999). *The Primacy of Movement*. Amsterdam and Philadelphia: John Benjamins Pub.

Sheets-Johnstone, M. (2009). Animation: The Fundamental, Essential, and Properly Descriptive Concept. *Continental Philosophy Review*, 42(3), 375–400.

Sheets-Johnstone, M. (2011). Embodied Minds or Mindful Bodies? A Question of Fundamental, Inherently Inter-Related Aspects of Animation. *Subjectivity*, 4(4), 451–466.

Sheets-Johnstone, M. (2016). Foundational Dynamics of Animate Nature. *Zwischenleiblichkeit und bewegtes Verstehen [Intercorporeity, movement and tacit knowledge]*, 51–67.

Sheets-Johnstone, M. (2018). If the Body Is Part of Our Discourse, Why Not Let It Speak? Five Critical Perspectives. In N. Depraz & A. Steinbock (Eds.), *Surprise: An Emotion? Contributions to Phenomenology* (pp. 83–95). Cham, Switzerland: Switzerland Springer Nature.

Chapter 8

Virtual small group supervision – research *informing* practice and practice *being* the research

Kathryn M Downing

It has been an almost five-year journey for me, from beginning as a supervisor to becoming an inquiring practitioner–researcher, during which I conducted an intentional inquiry into my practice as a supervisor with two of my groups. I did this in the context of researching, observing, comparing and contrasting with three other groups supervised by colleagues, while holding all of those experiences up to the existing academic and practice literature. As Bateson (1994) writes: "*Insight, I believe, refers to that depth of understanding that comes by setting experiences, yours and mine, familiar and exotic, new and old, side by side, learning by letting them speak to one another*" (p. 14). This has been a magical journey.

I completed a Diploma in Coaching Supervision in the U.K. in 2015 and shortly thereafter enrolled in the Doctor of Professional Studies at Middlesex University, London. I wanted to study and research how the practice of coaching supervision contributes to our profession, and to develop personally and professionally as a supervisor.

My research led me to consider, experiment, notice, learn and integrate. I hope that as you read this, comparing and contrasting with your own experiences, that you will feel some of that magic: openings of possibilities, insights or reflections in your own practice. Perhaps you will recognise aspects of yourself and discover something new or provocative.

The ultimate conclusion of my research was that supervision in virtual small groups is effective; the supervisors and coaches "learned and developed, in their own unique ways, personally and professionally through integration of inquiry, reflection, experimentation, and action" (Downing, 2021: p. 15). In this chapter, I will focus on three primary functions of the supervisor – the first is creating and nurturing the bonds between group members, taking into account the multiple relationships within the group; the second is co-creating with the group members structures and processes that are uniquely designed to meet their learning needs; and third is being a guardian of reflective practice by managing the actions and interactions that contribute to a safe and trusted space. Supervision is a co-created learning environment. I therefore also discuss the group members' roles and responsibilities.

DOI: 10.4324/978100314345-9

The beginning

In the design of my research and recruitment of coaches and supervisors, my aim was to include previously established supervision groups. In my conversations and discussions with potential participants, it was immediately clear that the relationship they had with their supervisors was foremost in their minds and their wish to ensure that nothing would negatively impact these. One of the groups I was supervising declined to participate in the research because they were concerned that my role as researcher alongside my supervisor role would impact how we would be together; one group member expressed that they wanted me to be their supervisor rather than observe them as a researcher.

Coincidentally, at about this time I attended a research conference at Oxford-Brookes on coaching and supervision at which Beinart and Clohessy (2017), authors of a recently published collection of research on supervisory relationships in the clinical supervision setting, presented. Here was a collection of rich data that I dove into in order to deepen my understanding about what I was hearing from the coaches and supervisors. Their research, primarily in the clinical dyadic supervision setting, found that the relationship between supervisor and supervisees is "the most significant aspect of supervision" (ibid., p. 7).

Supervisory relationships

Throughout my 18-month research with the five groups, the primacy of the supervisory relationships remained as the most important ingredient of a meaningful small group supervision experience (Downing, 2021). Hawkins (2011) writes that, "It isn't what the supervisor does, but the attitude and perspective they bring and hold in the supervisory relationship" (p. 173). In the widely used Seven-Eyed Model for supervision, Eye 5 is the relationship between the coach and the supervisor, utilised for identifying parallel process as well as exploring the relationship itself (Hawkins & Smith, 2013: pp. 196–197).

Basing his research in psychological tradition, De Haan (2012) states that the relationship between the supervisor and supervisee is "the most important active ingredient" (p. 141) and defines relational supervision as having four qualities – focus on the relationships through the material brought by the supervisee; a solid productive relationship between the supervisor and supervisee; use of the supervisor–supervisee relationship as a model for the development of the relationship between the coach and their client and the supervisors' ability to trust themselves to use appropriate interventions, rather than being bound by a particular model (ibid.).

The group supervisory relationships are composed of a multiplicity of relationships, each of which needs tending. These include the individual relationships between the supervisor and each coach; between the coaches with each other and between the supervisor with the group as an entity.

Cultivation of the relationships

I have found that relationships are cultivated and attended to through small actions and gestures by each coach and myself, beginning in the recruitment and selection process and continuing throughout the engagement. My openhearted presence, with intentional attention to the group, is essential: it is an invitation for the coaches to engage. This means honouring adult learning principles (Knowles et al., 2015) to embrace what arrives and to explore, consider, and inquire without moving to solution or persuasion. Presence creates the connective tissue and empathic resonance chambers for the groups (Whitehead, 2015).

In my supervision groups, I have noticed my way of being contributes to the flourishing of the relationships. Embodying qualities of warmth, care, grace and positive energy have been identified by various supervisees as important to their relationships and their sense of a safe and trusted space. These qualities were noticed in my facial expressions, like smiles and the warmth that imbued the energy of the room; a lightness in tone and tenor when challenging; regularly asking permission of group members to pause, to inquire, to notice or to shift and

Figure 8.1 Virtual small groups (Illustration by Kelly Hudson)

relatively consistent calm; perhaps the fresh flowers that were in the frame of the Zoom window had welcoming connotations.

There are implications for the supervisory relationships of conducting virtual supervision. In our groups, we used Zoom as the video meeting technology. How does hosting and facilitating a gathering on Zoom compare to an in-person meeting?

In face-to-face groups, three qualities are significant: being in person, physical touch and hospitality. Coyle (2018) points out the importance of the physical setting in creating close proximity, and the role of touch (e.g., a hand on the arm). Block (2009) devotes attention to the physical set-up, including room design, light, amenities and the seating arrangement. Both authors include "hospitality" in their discussions, the importance of welcoming attendees and providing food and beverages. These are in service to the bonding of the team or group, and to the creation of the necessary conditions for dialogue.

How does one attend to these elements in the virtual setting? I explored ways in the virtual realm to convey hospitality and found that the welcoming and hosting of the group becomes more collaborative. How each person arranged their personal space, and the lighting for their face had an impact on how we saw them and how we experienced our collective environment.

Additionally, the virtual supervisory relationships were impacted by the supervisor's ease with the technology – when the supervisor was at ease and accepted the accompanying "messiness" of the technology, the coaches experienced the environment as safer. Many supervisees embraced this acceptance and transferred it, by implication, to acceptance for what they brought to the session – the "messiness" of their coaching.

The ability to see all of the group, using Zoom's "gallery mode" gave a visual representation of a circle, which gave members a sense of being in a physical group. The intensity of the small window in which to focus on facial and a few small body expressions enhanced listening and understanding of verbal contributions. The invitation into a small part of each participant's personal space conveyed contextual information and enhanced the sense of intimacy.

Contracting

In supervision, as in coaching, contracting – the articulation of logistics, structures, processes and agendas – is a requisite part of the co-creation of the "container" which is used to describe the energetic field within which the group convenes and operates. This is the place for dialogue (Isaacs, 1999; Bohm, 2004). Isaacs (1999) describes a "container" for the dialogue as "a setting" in which we collectively hold "the intensities of [our] lives" (p. 243), going on to articulate the four essential practices that create this as "the active experience of people listening, respecting one another, suspending their judgments, and speaking their own voice" (ibid., p. 242). He identifies the potential shift from conversation to reflective dialogue through the welcoming of curiosity, a willingness to explore what is going on for each of us and noticing more possibility to share our own stories and perspectives (ibid., pp. 272–273).

At different levels, there are varying amounts of negotiation; any deviations in implementation are permission-based. There are three levels of contracting: the initial level of logistics and supervisor choices; the second level of the overall process, structure and operating principles for the group and the third level of the flow, rituals and processes within each session. There are choice points for each supervisor and for the group, for the elements within each level of contracting. While I address perspectives from the supervisor's vantage point, coaches considering supervision have corresponding choice points.

Contracting level #1

There are many decisions to make in the initial design of a virtual supervision group. The supervisor will determine the parameters of the group and provide information to supervisees who are considering joining; there is less co-creation in this level of contracting. In the setting of my research supervision groups, the parameters were established externally by an organisational Supervision Center, which had several operating principles and had been established to provide ongoing professional and personal development for coaches certified by the organisation. The coaches paid for the supervision, and the certified supervisors were paid as subcontractors by the sponsor. The supervision engagements were 10 sessions over about one year, and all sessions were 90 minutes duration, conducted virtually using Zoom as the videoconferencing technology. Small groups provided a cost-effective approach; groups of six were preferred.

The supervisors did not take a proactive role in the selection of group members. Rather, coaches would sign up for a group with a particular supervisor and join whomever else had also enrolled, or a group would self-form and request to work with a supervisor. There were no requirements for the coaches to be actively coaching or to have a certain number of clients. In my research, I came to learn that the coaches' professional experience and the extent of their engagement in actively coaching impacted the learning outcomes for the group. My preference is to work with similarly situated coaches, for example, a group of actively coaching coaches or a group of emerging coaches. I do not tend to take into account their prior supervision experience.

As points of contrast, the supervisor might also consider the composition of the group and whether they want to attract newly certified coaches, actively coaching coaches or seasoned and experienced coaches; whether they expect group members to have similar levels of experience and training, shared methodological approaches to coaching, supervision experience or other variables. Sheppard (2018: p. 30) describes three different levels of coach development within the supervision context – new to supervision, experienced and very experienced – and suggests the focus for each may be different. For example, a new supervisee may be looking for reassurance and a focus on tools and competencies; an experienced supervisee may be looking for "an elder sibling"; and the very experienced supervisee may be looking for essentially a "peer" (ibid.).

The next task of the supervisor is to set out the initial parameters through an interplay of preferences and practicalities. The elements that need defining are supervisory approaches (discussed in the next section), group composition (profile of coaches, size, composition and selection of the group) and logistical decisions (frequency of meetings; length of sessions; choice of technology; costs, invoicing and refund policy; rescheduling and cancellation provisions and pre-work, if any).

Supervisory approaches

There are numerous models for coaching supervision (Bachkirova et al., 2011), including the Seven-Eyed Model (Hawkins & Smith, 2006), the Full Spectrum Model (Murdoch & Arnold, 2013), the three worlds and four territories (Munro Turner, 2011) and the Three Pillars Model (Hodge, 2014). Having selected a model or a more emergent or eclectic approach, the supervisor might reflect on how much they want to control and the degree to which they are open to co-creating with the group. This is the consideration of how to facilitate.

In considering the style of facilitation, Proctor (2008) defines four types of groups:

1   Authoritative group, in which the supervisor has control of the group process – essentially, individual supervision observed in a group setting.
2   Participative group, where the supervisor is primarily the supervisor but invites the other group members to co-supervise to some extent – the supervisor "actively teaches and directs group members in co-supervising each other" (ibid., pp. 32–33).
3   Co-operative group, where the group members are active co-supervisors, and the supervisor has "overall responsibility for the supervision work and for the well-being of the group and has to be vigilant in monitoring and facilitating the work of the group" (ibid.).
4   Peer group, further discussed in Chapters 11 and 13.

My preferred style is co-operative with occasional utilisation of the participative style. However, my own group supervisor uses the authoritative style. Supervisors might reflect on their preferred style and open a conversation with the group, leading to a group agreement. Once you have recruited, selected and formed the group, the next step is contracting at the next level.

Contracting level #2: overall structure, process and operating principles

The agreements for process and structure include rules of engagement, expectations around working, playing and learning together and the respective roles and responsibilities of the supervisor and the coaches. There needs to be enough discussion of the process and structure to establish the expectations of the supervisees, and to convey to them the security of knowing the basic group operating principles.

The key elements of the process and structure are co-created. In the research groups, and now in my current groups, I engage the group in this discussion, and as a group we consider and decide on each aspect. If the coaches are relatively new to supervision, they are likely to arrive with less clear expectations than those with more experience of supervision. My role in the contracting process changes accordingly, as does the sense of collaboration and co-creation. Re-contracting throughout the year becomes increasingly collaborative as the coaches gain experience in the group. Past experience and knowing what worked "then" does not necessarily always translate to what will work "now" in a new group.

What work do the coaches want to bring to the sessions?

It is most often agreed that the coaches can bring a wide variety of subjects, including a particular client case, a recurring issue or theme, the development of self as coach, topics related to their coaching practice or whatever is on their mind or in their heart related to their lives. The inclusion of self-exploration provides space for supervisees to bring issues of stress, depletion, burn-out and other concerns.

In the discussions of what to bring, I raise the option of coaches bringing cases, issues or themes that are going particularly well, not just those with which they struggle. When we are working at our best we can recognise, articulate and explore our current capabilities. It gives us opportunities to catch up with our development and often provides us as rich a learning opportunity as discussing where we are stuck or unsure. Some coaches embrace this, while others find it more challenging to talk about their successful interventions than their difficult ones.

The second level of contracting is how we organise the content within the session. Some coaches prefer to arrive and see what is uppermost, either in their mind or in the group as a whole, in the moment, and divide the time in response to need. Some prefer to assign a lead presenting coach for each session, with a bit of space held toward the end for any "hot" issue in the group. Some groups require written case studies or descriptions in advance, and those submitting these determine the cases considered. Some groups choose to meet two weeks in advance of the session and decide who will bring which items.

I have discussed two key elements previously that I feel deserve more elaboration. There are 10 additional matters that we address in contracting:

1 **Perspectives on supervision and our purposes for coming to this group** – this is to develop our shared purposes.
2 **Confidentialities** – our agreements to ensure what happens in the sessions, the clients and their organisations are held with confidentiality.
3 **Recording of the supervision sessions** – whether or not to record sessions, under what circumstances, and what happens to the recording. Recordings may be requested by coaches, like when a session is missed; for reviewing a

session; for taking a segment to my supervisor for exploration in supervision of my supervision.

4 **Reflection question** – I may provide a reflection question a few days in advance of the session if the group requests.

5 **Rituals** – I may discuss ways of beginning the session with a brief "how are you arriving?" to invite contribution from every voice in the room and in closing with "what are you taking or sitting with as a coach, or a person as you leave this session?"

6 **Ethics** – what codes of ethics the individual coaches use and how we will find a collective way forward with ethical dilemmas.

7 **External communication** – establishing the principles for appropriate one-to-one communications outside the group between the supervisor and a group member.

8 **Resources** – when relevant, I may send articles, book titles, podcasts or videos following a session. There is no requirement they are viewed or utilised.

9 **Rescheduling** – this is negotiated with each group. In a group of two, if one cannot make it, I typically offer to reschedule. In a group of six, I only reschedule if three or more cannot make the agreed-upon date.

10 **Supervisor's supervision** – I request agreement to discuss what happens in the group, while ensuring protection of confidentialities, with my supervision supervisors. If any member of the group feels uncomfortable with my request, I do not take the issue to supervision.

Periodically, groups will revisit many of these agreements and amend or revise them as we learn about how we interact as a group. Each group designs the container uniquely to meet their individual and collective needs.

Contracting level #3: ongoing flow, rituals and processes

Contracting around the flow, rituals and processes within each session is necessary and ongoing. Interventions are permission-based and the agenda and how items will be organised is dynamic; the inquiries the presenting coach wants to explore, and how the inquiries will be conducted, may change from coach to coach. This type of adaptive contracting happens throughout the session. Our process, at each step, is mutually agreed upon.

Stewardship

I use the word "stewardship" to signify the actions and interactions that reinforce and expand the safe and trusted space. So far, I have focused on the co-creation of the container through the cultivation of supervisory relationships and contracting around structure and process. Here, I explore and describe circumstances, actions and interactions that can diminish or tear the fabric of the safe space, decreasing the capacity of a coach, a supervisor or the group as a whole to self-disclose, reflect and learn together.

Managing group dynamics

The supervisory relationships in a group setting are complex and dependent on the supervisor's skill and capacity in facilitating within those dynamics. The supervisor's management of the group processes is as important as their supervision and necessitates the establishment and management of the relationships within the group to create a safe space.

The supervisor has numerous responsibilities – to notice the abundance of nuance, complexity, multi-dimensionality and emergence within the field and tend to them in the service of the personal and professional development of the coaches (Downing, 2021; Bernard & Goodyear, 2019: p. 193). Consistent with this, Ögren et al. (2014), found that, in the clinical supervision setting, the supervisor's ability to work with the group dynamics is essential in creating a safe container for the learning: "To favour constructive and prevent destructive group processes, the supervisors must be well acquainted with the dynamics that characterize small work group, and at the same time, be able to handle his or her role as supervisor and leader" (ibid., p. 650).

The supervisor sets the overall tone and, by her or his presence in moment-to-moment actions, invites the group to forge relationships within it.

The qualities for stewardship of the container include keeping the session within the defined purpose, facilitating so that every voice is included and honouring the contract with the presenting coach. Ensuring the voice of each coach is heard in the space through facilitation conveys equal opportunity for each coach's experience and views. In the research study, I found that coaches' shared vulnerability, preparation and levels of participation also impacted the container.

Expansive acceptance (Downing, 2021), empathy, and appreciation and gratitude are integral to the relationships and contribute to overall trust. My summarising of key aspects of the dialogue, identifying the relationships between the various comments and synthesising their reflections and inquiries was appreciated by group members. My groups also mentioned appreciation for a pause, after the presenting coach concluded their inquiry, for each of them to reflect on what they were taking away or sitting with from the discussion.

There are seven primary types of actions and interventions that strengthen and expand trust and safety – expansive acceptance; shared vulnerability; self-disclosure by the supervisor; challenge and possibilities; empathy, appreciation and gratitude and experimentation. I discuss each of these briefly.

Expansive acceptance

Expansive acceptance invites and encourages coaches to cross a threshold into a place of showing up just as they are.

> "*We know the truth, not only by reason, but also by the heart*"
> *(Pascal, 2016: p. 118)*

My acceptance of what the coaches bring is expansive; I move into reactive negative judgment rarely and affirm their observations and increased awareness.

In one case during my research, a coach shared that she was very judgmental of everyone. I responded that it was good that she recognised that, and I invited her to use our time together to play with noticing when she moved into judging. Another coach shared a deep fear that she was out of her depth with the client. I responded: "I really marvel at you saying you're feeling out of your depth, because I think that's such an important thing for us to feel and own, that we are skilled in a certain frame and not in others. . . . I think it takes great wisdom to say I'm out of my depth. I think it's a very strong statement of recognition of what's going on [with the client]".

A colleague supervisor and her group shared reflections that included a quote from Ram Dass (Dass & Das, 2013) of his teacher asking, "Don't you see it's all perfect?" (p. 104). I was intrigued in those few moments about how it would be to live into that phrase. I decided to experiment with its application in two ways: with myself, in the continuing practice of self-compassion, self-kindness, and acceptance of my foibles and idiosyncrasies, and with one of the research groups, as collectively we had continued to notice our own stories.

When I introduced this notion one coach said, "I just have such a hard time with that. My whole identity is about 'it's not perfect'. It's not all perfect and seeking more perfect . . . it's identity-shaking to hear that quote, or to be in that question". I continued to reference the quote in our sessions and that proved transformative for three of us. One necessary ingredient was the repetition of this response before it could be felt fully. As one coach shared, as we were concluding the year, the "honoring our wholeness of however we show up. . . . I feel seen, I feel heard, I feel taken care of and I feel in relationship with each of you individually and collectively". I feel humbled by the mysteries of how we interacted, created the container, used the idea of "it's all perfect" in service of not being perfect, in service of looking at our failings, our mistakes, our foibles together. This is an illustration of what I mean when I use the phrase "expansive acceptance" (Downing, 2021).

Shared vulnerability and empathy

Shared vulnerability strengthens the dimensions, flexibility and vitality of the container. Vulnerability was demonstrated through the courage and willingness of the coaches to share their stuckness, their struggles, and their fears. Vulnerability invites vulnerability. Coyle (2018) found that the quality of shared vulnerability – the mutual sharing of challenges, difficulties, and failings – was critical in effective small teams. This is descriptive of the small group setting where the coaches are asked to bring the messiness of their practices to the group. Brené Brown defines ordinary courage, distinct from heroic courage, as "the inner strength and level of commitment required for us to actually speak honestly and openly about who we are and about our experiences – good and bad" (Brown, B., 2007: p. xxiv). This is about our ability to be vulnerable in a small group and a reminder that vulnerability is a key element in creating the safe container (Brown, B.C., 2012; Isaacs, 1999).j

When coaches share their concerns and self-judgment and the members of the group respond with empathy, the space for vulnerability within the container increases very likely from a recognition that a similar struggle is common to many people. The coaches often notice how reassuring it is to recognise they are not alone with particular client dilemmas or self-doubt; it lessens the sense of isolation that comes with having a solo practice.

Vulnerability requires a vigilant inquiry into one's practice, which is challenging. It requires a balance of curiosity and the courage to explore, opening one's self to feedback; to puzzle about; to notice; to challenge one's beliefs and ways of being; to steadily excavate one's stories and to cultivate self-compassion, self-kindness and perspective. The opportunity for growth arises from the commitment to shape and re-shape one's self and one's practice in moving toward mastery (Dweck, 2016; Kegan & Laskow Lahey, 2009; Mezirow, 1991). It requires bringing the self as instrument to the foreground; self-awareness is a frequent focus of inquiry and challenges us to this work: "[T]o know one's self requires a fierce and courageous willingness to explore the many layers of one's inner landscape, a territory that can be elusive and enigmatic, confusing and paradoxical" (McLean, 2019: p. 3).

An empathic response to vulnerability creates resonance in that moment. These are the experiences Ferrucci (1990) describes as the power of empathic connection: "In addition to being a vehicle for awareness, empathy is also an instrument for transformation. It temporarily changes the structure of our being by taking us to an entirely different wavelength . . . empathy frees us from our private maze and show us new and unenvisaged modes of being, greatly enhancing our imaginative and creative abilities" (p. 30).

Parallel process describes a dynamic arising in one place that mirrors a similar dynamic arising elsewhere. In the case of coaching supervision, we see this in the coach–client relationship where feelings that arise may mirror those of the client in their work system; or between the supervisor and coach mirroring the coach–client relationship (Tracey et al., 2012). Tracey and her co-authors note there is little consensus of the definition of parallel process in the psychoanalytic realm, except the recognition that parallels in the client–therapist relationship sometimes show up in the therapist–supervisor relationship and that this can be bi-directional (ibid.).

Often, when I named something that appeared to be a parallel process, this was met with a collective group sigh. I interpreted this sigh to be one of relief that what was going on for them was also going on for the client or in the client's system, or for me and our system. It offered another possibility to the fear that feelings had arisen through some 'wrongness' on the part of the coach. Each new possibility, and more curious attention to their behaviour and feelings, brought new potential to inform their work with the client.

Vulnerability is essential. Inviting and role modelling vulnerability within the group is a key responsibility of the coaches and the supervisor. The supervisor may model vulnerability through self-disclosure of his or her own coaching dilemmas, which is discussed next.

Self-disclosure by supervisor

Self-disclosure by the supervisor of challenges within their own work as a coach has been found to be a significant catalyst in strengthening the dimensions, flexibility and vitality of the container. In the clinical supervision setting: "Supervisor self-disclosure predicts the strength of the supervisory working alliance. That is, the more frequently a supervisor self-disclosed, the greater was the agreement between the supervisor and the trainee on the goals and tasks of supervision and the stronger was the emotional bond between the two" (Ladany & Lehrman-Waterman, 1999: pp. 156–157). Supervisor self-disclosure of this nature goes some way towards addressing the problem of supervisees placing the supervisor on a pedestal, which Sheppard (2017) found as one of the ways coaching supervisees hinder their supervision experiences.

In one of the supervision sessions in the research study, I shared a case and asked the group to supervise me. This surprised the group, and one coach expressed that he saw me as "a masterful coach who shouldn't get stuck with a client". My willingness to be vulnerable, to self-disclose, had a profound and lasting impact on their experience of the container. Throughout the remainder of our time together this episode was often referred to as "pivotal" in creating safety and trust, enabling group members to bring more of themselves to the group.

Challenge and possibilities

The shared purpose of individual and collective learning necessitates challenge: offering differing perspectives and opening up alternative possibilities. The

"I'm just laughing because it's a little ironic. You want us to hear a case that you're doing...You're the master coach. It is ironic."

Figure 8.2 Supervisor self-disclosure (Illustration by Kelly Hudson)

number and nature of the challenges are dependent on many factors, including the group members' relationships with each other and with the supervisor. When a group member is committed to the growth of the others, there are often more challenges in service of the exploration of deeper self-reflection. To the extent that relationships are distant or weak, there are fewer corresponding instances of challenge. It takes a good working alliance for challenge, just as in coaching.

I hold the question about when and how often to challenge in every session, and across the arc of the year with each group. The elements that I balance are my in-the-moment intuition, the strength of the working alliance of the presenting coach with me and with others in the group, whether there are potential ethical issues and the potential for shame to arise. On reflection I often consider the degree of challenge that seems appropriate; on occasion, I consider my challenges were too much or too little and this provides material for exploration in my own supervision.

Appreciation and gratitude

When the interactions among the group members are abundant with appreciation, gratitude and empathic resonance, the group can nurture vulnerability, self-disclosure, experimentation and reflection.

"Belonging feels like it happens from the inside out, but in fact it happens from the outside in. Our social brains light up when they receive a steady accumulation of almost invisible cues: We are close, we are safe, we share a future" (Coyle, 2018: pp. 25–26).

I first noticed in the research groups that there were cultural and social assumptions within the groups around consistent gratitude for and acknowledgment of the collaboration, sharing and inquiry in service of the group's learning. These elements were not explicitly contracted; they were, or became, unspoken norms. For example, a presenting coach thanked the group members, often by name, for what they had offered during the inquiry. Group members offered appreciation to the presenting coach for particular elements of the case that resonated with them. In concluding the session, the ending reflections were frequently of appreciation for the relationships and the learning, especially so if a challenge had created a new insight. I continue to experience this in newly formed groups. It may be a cultural norm within my communities or more broadly within the coaching profession.

Experimentation

Experimenting with processes in the moment in a session, with the permission of the group, may bring fresh energy and often fun, which strengthens the container. I invite experimentation in the supervision process. One coach commented: "There's value in disrupting and disorganising, just changing it up . . . it was fun".

Example: Candice was the presenting coach and I asked what she wanted from the group at the end of her presentation. She wanted others to share what they had done in similar client situations. I asked if the group would try something new, briefly, before we responded directly to Candice. They agreed. I invited the group to share: "What came up for you? Visuals or feelings or stirrings – just what did you notice in yourself as Candice described the case?" We took turns responding. Felicia and Andy moved straight to offering a solution; they did not name anything that had come up for themselves. Debra shared she had felt tenderness and care; Ellen found herself in many different places as she tried to notice what she was observing and stay present to Candice's descriptions. I shared an image that Candice was an adult figure, and her client was a younger person, and that they were not standing together as equals.

I then asked the group to share what they noticed about themselves as coach in the responses to what was stirred in them. Andy and Felicia, who had jumped to solutions, both noticed and reflected on the challenge of letting go of their solution-orientation and moving into coach mode. Debra discovered by not taking notes, she had found herself more able to be fully present: "My ideas or thoughts just floated away. . . . I've never noticed that before". Ellen shared she was unable to stay present. Candice discovered a theme as she listened to the others – over the past 90 days, she had noticed her move away from "positive regard" with some of the clients, in this case after some additional information had been given to her about their lack of resourcefulness. She was able to see herself in the responses from the group.

The experiment stayed with us – this idea of learning how to simultaneously observe inner processing while staying present to others. Ellen shared: "There was an ask to pay attention to what we're noticing in ourselves . . . staying present for myself . . . and [the presenting coach] . . . and of course thinking about the story and how would I coach, and oh yes, I had a similar client. I found myself being in many different places". It was difficult for her. Some of the coaches noticed the links between what they were experiencing in the session and other experiences in their personal and professional lives.

I opened the conversation with the group on future experimentations. One response was: "I thought this was an extremely powerful call . . . you're holding a really special container for us to allow us to bring ourselves in a different and special way". This was a wonderful learning experience for me as supervisor and for the group. We continued to experiment, and I have since incorporated experimentation with my other groups.

Time together as a group

Supervision groups develop capacity for stewardship of the container over the course of the year. As they get to know each other better; there is often more vulnerability, more sharing, and more challenge. The groups learn and develop through the year together; with laughter, learning, exposure and creativity come stronger relationships. They also come to know me better as a supervisor, which can lead to a stronger relationship with me and within the group.

Looking back on the year of sessions in the research study, one coach commented: "Honouring our wholeness of however we show up. . . . I feel seen, I feel heard, I feel taken care of, and I feel in relationship with each of you individually and collectively". Another coach shared: "It's special, it's safe and it's intimate. I feel this worry inside me that brings me to tears, which is, is it fragile". Our relationships, and the space within which we worked, required continuous intentional attention. We showed up just as we were and that was good enough. The container was healthy enough. I take that learning forward to my current groups.

Contributions to decreasing safety

There were five kinds of occurrences that negatively impacted the safe and trusted space. As Coyle (2018) observed: *"This idea – that belonging needs to be continually refreshed and reinforced – is worth dwelling on" (p. 24)*. The first were societal and cultural norms that inhibited some coaches from bringing certain parts of themselves or their experiences into the group. Second, a coach's life narrative impacted and sometimes kept them from bringing something into the space. Third, the coach had an experience proximate to the session that negatively impacted his or her sense of safety in the session. Fourth, the coach was triggered by content, an intervention or the process within the session and was unable to regain a centered stance and be present within the session. Fifth, the supervisor or one of the group members said something that triggered the whole group, which decreased the sense of safety within.

What we keep hidden

I am imagining that the container was, as yet, insufficient to hold situations that were considered culturally or socially inappropriate or uncomfortable to discuss. What kinds of issues were not coming into the group? This is an area that is ripe for my own reflection and exploration in supervision.

Today, in the midst of the pandemic and the global Black Lives Matter movement, issues of systemic racism, diversity and inclusion are coming into my supervision groups. Previously, these had rarely been areas of exploration. Coaches are now proactively bringing these very important issues into the supervision space. I wonder what I could have done, or what we as a group could have done differently, to have invited the tougher-to-talk about issues into our work? I wonder, more generally, how other supervisors invite in or address difficult issues, whether cultural or societal, such as about death and dying, loss and grief or the host of other topics we don't routinely discuss.

Our personal narratives

Each of us brings our individual life narratives into supervision and these influence the sense of trust and safety experienced within the group. When I was researching with my groups, I asked them to bring recordings of coaching sessions and this request brought life narratives into the bright light of day. There were coaches for whom it was an impossible request, afraid of learning they were not masterful coaches, and there were coaches who readily brought recordings. Another coach discovered it was safer to reflect on recordings with the group than on her own, because on her own her inner critic was too fierce. The contrasts in these reactions highlight the distinctively individual nature of who and how we are and the influence of our own stories on our perceptions of safety within the container.

One of the coaches framed her inquiries in the sessions with her inner critic's voice. She inquired about what she was missing, what she had not done or had done wrong, what she should be doing. She was focused on improving, becoming a better coach. She resisted receiving positive feedback or considering her strengths – the inner critic would not allow her to accept she was good enough.

This coach was not unique; I have a similarly loud inner critic, as do other coaches. Our inner critics push us to identify areas to develop, to shift and to pay attention to. They do not assist in our ability to notice, articulate or deepen what we do well. I wondered why the groups focused more frequently on what was not going well. How could I provide a space in which to nurture coach development – and encourage moments where the coaches could explore what it was that they were doing well and celebrate those instances that made visible their learning and development?

This inquiry has led me to more explicitly invite coaches to bring moments when they were feeling truly present or when there was a meaningful interaction with the client. We reflect on those times with the purpose of identifying their strengths, to assist the coach in pausing to notice and acknowledge their development. This is, at times, a more vulnerable disclosure in a group setting.

Events proximate to the session

In the research study, incidences around the time of the session were shown to influence how coaches arrived in the session. Sometimes these also impacted the coach's ability to recover and be present, participate and reflect. Many kinds of events had this impact, for example, awaiting medical results, arriving late, not feeling prepared, being forced into retirement, feeling overwhelmed. The outcome was that the coach or supervisor was not fully participatory within the group and described feeling increased anxiety, fear or shame.

Example: a coach arrived late for a session. We welcomed her, acknowledged that things happen sometimes and that it was good to have her. Her journal entries following the session were filled with shame. She had felt disruptive arriving late and was doubting her value in heartfelt terms; she also wrote from her head that she knew this wasn't true. "At this point a week later, I'm finding myself wondering if I was more disruptive in this session than value add. I'm questioning what value I bring to the group and if I'm leveraging the opportunity. . . . I'm finding myself feeling small and insignificant in this moment".

A week following the session, she was not feeling safe. Over time, she regained her sense of safety.

Individuals impacted within the session

Individuals, on occasion, react negatively to the process, interventions or the content of a session, which lessens their sense of safety or trust within the container.

I have witnessed a handful of micro-moments, when an individual in a session reacted, sensing a loss of acceptance or worthiness. Here are a few examples: a coach felt I was inquiring from a place of negative judgment. A coach had responded in a different manner to others and wondered if they "were not getting it?" A coach was presenting their case and a colleague moved from inquiry to judgment, essentially telling them what they "should have done".

In each case the impact remained for different lengths of time; some were significant enough to need repair, some dissipated on their own.

Actions of supervisor or coach

The sense of safety, trust or courage within the container could be lost for a moment, a session or longer, by an action of the supervisor or a coach. These are the moments in which the supervisor's attention to what is happening is useful and may also be challenging. "However, rooted and grounded in respect, empathy and authenticity a group facilitator may be, there will be times when one, or more, do not seem accessible" (Proctor, 2000: p. 117).

Continuous partial attention (Stone, 2009) is the concept that in our technology-laden lives, we are seldom fully paying attention. In one of the sessions, in mid-inquiry, another coach in the group "knew just the model that needed to be used with the client" and sent it to us in an email. My internal response was to move to judgment – I experienced her reactivity and move to action to be disruptive of the flow. I reacted with a facial expression – a grimace conveying my judgment into the collective field.

> Who noticed? Who felt similar feelings? Did my reactivity to her reactivity impact any one's sense of safety except my own?

My internal dialogue was that I had crossed a boundary, unintentionally and in-the-moment. I believe it was felt by the group and it made the container feel momentarily less safe for all. If I had noticed through Eye 6 of the Seven-Eyed Model (Hawkins & Smith, 2013: pp. 196–197) this unwelcome reaction, perhaps I could have regained my centered presence and worked with what had just happened. In this instance, I did not. In my experience, working with Eye 6 deepens over time.

Guardian of reflective practice

The supervisory relationships are the most important elements impacting the supervision space. I opened this chapter by stating that supervisors are the

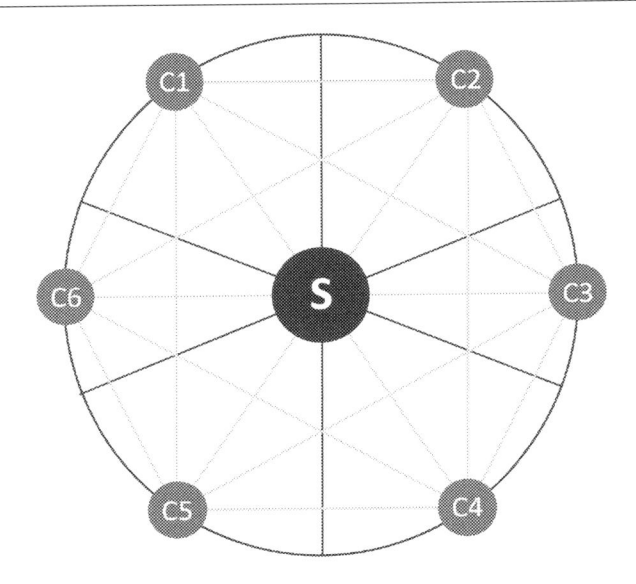

Figure 8.3 Multiplicity of relationships (Illustration by Kelly Hudson)

guardians of reflective practice through managing the actions and interactions that contribute to the safe and trusted space. As I share my learning and reflections, the multiplicity of the relationships within the small group setting are in the foreground. These include individual relationships between the supervisor and each coach; among the coaches with each other and between the supervisor and the group as an entity. The calculation of dyadic relationships is 22 relationships[1] in a group of six coaches, as illustrated in Figure 8.3. (There are many more relationships possible beyond dyadic, as relationships between more than two individuals often exist.)

One of the primary responsibilities of the supervisor is to manage the group dynamics, which requires facilitation that is informed by awareness, sensitivity, monitoring and intervention. This will create the possibilities for the four essential practices that are necessary for reflective dialogue: "The active experience of people listening, respecting one another, suspending their judgments, and speaking their own voice" (Isaacs, 1999: p. 242). That is our guardianship role.

In conclusion

The stay-at-home orders and school closures resulting from COVID-19 changed many aspects of working virtually. It became, for many, the preferred and only option for coaching and for engaging in supervision. There was broader acceptance of the physical settings of group members. The supervisor's acceptance of the fullness of the coaches' lives within the context of the pandemic communicated the hospitality described by Coyle (2018) and Block (2009). Inviting and welcoming meeting family members, including children and pets, impacted groups and individuals. For some, it demonstrated acceptance of the struggles in the situation and for some, it was a distraction and annoyance.

All of the responses created material for supervision when we explored the coaches' relationships with their clients in these unprecedented times.

Supervision is an organic and emergent process of being in relationship with self, supervisor and group members. Relationships with clients, client systems and life in the wider world are also present. The choice of engaging in small group supervision can provide a richness of experience and learning not possible in the one-to-one supervision experience. I have found group supervision sessions to be richly and deeply rewarding, valuing the relationships and bonds within the group, the increasing sense of not being alone in the challenges, and the witnessing of shared humanity in our foibles, idiosyncrasies, challenges and successes. Many of the coaches I have worked with have also found these kinds of experiences. Together we have found moments to celebrate seeing ourselves, and being seen and held, in the conundrum of "wherever you go, there you are" (Kabat-Zinn, 1994).

Note

1   Dyadic relationships equation: $((S*C1) + (S*C2) + (S*C3) + (S*C4) + (S*C5) + (S*C6)) + (group*S) + ((C1*C2) + (C1*C3) + (C1*C4) + (C1*C5) + (C1*C6) + (C2*C3) + (C2*C4) + (C2*C5) + (C2*C6) + (C3*C4) + (C3*C5) + (C3*C6) + (C4*C5) + (C4*C6) + (C5*C6)) = 22$ supervisory relationships.

References

Bachkirova, T., Jackson, P., & Clutterbuck, D. (2011). *Coaching and Mentoring Supervision.* Open University Press.

Bateson, M. C. C. (1994). *Peripheral Visions: Learning Along the Way.* New York: HarperCollins Publishers.

Beinart, H., & Clohessy, S. (2017). *The Effective Supervisory Relationship: Best Evidence and Practice.* Hoboken: Wiley-Blackwell.

Bernard, J. M., & Goodyear, R. K. (2019). *Fundamentals of Clinical Supervision* (6th ed.). Pearson Education.

Block, P. (2009). *Community the Structure of Belonging.* San Francisco, CA: Berrett-Koehler Publishers, Inc.

Bohm, D. (2004). *On Dialogue* (2nd ed.). Abingdon: Routledge.

Brown, B. (2007). *I Thought It Was Just Me (but It Isn't).* New York: Gotham Books.

Brown, B. (2012). *Daring Greatly.* New York: Gotham Books.

Coyle, D. (2018). *The Culture Code.* New York: Bantam Books.

Dass, R., & Das, R. (2013). *The Polishing the Mirror: How to Live from Your Spiritual Heart.* Boulder, CO: Sounds True.

Downing, K. M. (2021). Creating the Container for Reflective Practice in Virtual Small Group Supervision (unpublished). Middlesex University.

Dweck, C. S. (2016). *Mindset: The New Psychology of Success* (Updated ed.). New York: Random House.

Ferrucci, P. (1990). *Inevitable Grace Breakthroughs in the Lives of Great Men and Women: Guides to Your Self-Realization*. New York: Jeremy P. Tarcher/Putnam.

Haan, E. D. (2012). *Supervision in Action: A Relational Approach to Coaching and Consulting Supervision*. Maidenhead, UK: Open University Press.

Hawkins, P. (2011). Systemic Approaches to Supervision. In T. Bachkirova, P. Jackson, & D. Clutterbuck (Eds.), *Coaching and Mentoring Supervision* (pp. 167–182). Maidenhead, UK: Open University Press.

Hawkins, P., & Smith, N. (2006). *Coaching, Mentoring and Organizational Consultancy: Supervision and Development*. Maidenhead: Open University Press.

Hawkins, P., & Smith, N. (2013). *Coaching, Mentoring and Organizational Consultancy: Supervision, Skills and Development* (2nd ed.). Maidenhead, UK: Open University Press.

Hodge, A. (2014). An Action Research Inquiry into What Goes on in Coaching Supervision to the End of Enhancing the Coaching Profession. http://eprints.mdx.ac.uk/13707/1/AHodge_thesis.pdf [Accessed: 16 February 2016].

Isaacs, W. (1999). *Dialogue and the Art of Thinking Together: A Pioneering Approach to Communicating in Business and in Life* (1st ed.). New York: Currency.

Kabat-Zinn, J. (1994). *Wherever You Go, There You Are*. Boston: Hachette Books.

Kegan, R., & Laskow Lahey, L. (2009). *Immunity to Change How to Overcome It and Unlock the Potential in Yourself and Your Organization*. Boston, MA: Harvard Business Review Press.

Knowles, M. S., Holton, E. F., & Swanson, R. A. (2015). *The Adult Learner: The Definitive Classic in Adult Education and Human Resource Development* (8th ed.). London and New York: Routledge. doi: 10.4324/9781315816951.

Ladany, N., & Lehrman-Waterman, D. E. (1999). The Content and Frequency of Supervisor Self-Disclosures and Their Relationships to Supervisor Style and the Supervisory Working Alliance. *Counselor Education and Supervision*, 38(3), 143–160. doi: 10.1002/j.1556-6978.1999.tb00567.x.

McLean, P. (2019). *Self as Coach, Self as Leader*. Hoboken, NJ: John Wiley & Sons Ltd.

Mezirow, J. (1991). *Transformative Dimensions of Adult Learning*. San Francisco, CA: Jossey-Bass.

Munro Turner, M. (2011). The Three Worlds Four Territories Model of Supervision. In T. Bachkirova, P. Jackson, & D. Clutterbuck (Eds.), *Coaching and Mentoring Supervision* (pp. 41–54). Open University Press.

Murdoch, E., & Arnold, J. (2013). *Full Spectrum Supervision: "Who You Are, Is How You Supervise"*. St Albans: Panoma Press.

Ögren, M., Boëthius, S. B., & Sundin, E. (2014). Challenges and Possibilities in Group Supervision. In D. L. Milne & C. E. Watkins (Eds.), *The Wiley International Handbook of Clinical Supervision* (pp. 648–669). Wiley Blackwell. doi: 10.1002/9781118846360.ch31.

Pascal, B. (2016). *Pensees*. Originally Published 1669. New York: Open Road Media.

Proctor, B. (2000). *Group Supervision: A Guide to Creative Practice*. London: Sage. doi: 10.4135/9781446221259.

Proctor, B. (2008). *Group Supervision a Guide to Creative Practice* (2nd ed.). London: Sage Publications Ltd. doi: 10.4135/9781446221259.

Sheppard, L. (2017). How Coaching Supervisees Help and Hinder Their Supervision. *International Journal of Evidence Based Coaching and Mentoring* (11), 111–122.

Sheppard, L. (2018). Part 3 How to Work with New Stages of Supervisee Maturity. |*Coaching at Work*, 3(13), 28–32.

Stone, L. (2009). Beyond Simple Multi-Tasking: Continuous Partial Attention (Blog). www. lindastone.net. https://lindastone.net/2009/11/30/beyond-simple-multi-tasking-continuous-partial-attention/ [Accessed: 19 April 2020].

Tracey, T. J. G., Bludworth, J., & Glidden-Tracey, C. (2012). Are There Parallel Processes in Psychotherapy Supervision? An Empirical Examination. *Psychotherapy*, 49(3), 330–343. doi: 10.1037/a0026246.

Whitehead, J. (2015). The Practice of Helping Students to Find Their First Person Voice in Creating Living-Theories for Education. In H. Bradbury (Ed.), *The SAGE Handbook of Action Research* (3rd ed., pp. 247–255). Sage. doi: 10.4135/9781473921290.n24.

Chapter 9

Using creative approaches in group supervision

Jo Birch

Introduction

> *I tuned into myself as I opened a large online workshop. I invited an image to appear. To my dismay, my previously available image, an intriguing copper armillary sphere, the ancient navigational tool of mariners, was nowhere to be seen. In its place, there it was . . . a raspberry jelly! Turned out from a copper mould and yet not quite flawlessly formed. Some of the smooth, rounded shape was jagged and distorted. My heart felt heavy as I saw myself reflected in the imperfect, shimmering party-piece before me.*

Engaging with imagery in supervision can be playful and light-hearted *and* is deeply personal. It requires sensitivity and daring from all involved.

Verbal language cannot always reach what is beyond our cognitive awareness.[1] The arts, image making and creative processes can bring forth messages from the unconscious, and we may subsequently come to a meaningful understanding.

Creativity is a broad term encapsulating numerous forms of expression (Gash, 2017: pp. 4–8). In this chapter, I focus on easily accessible ways to use creative approaches in coaching supervision groups through imagery and drawing, writing, objects and plasticine. This is just the beginning – there are so many more ways we can extend the creative repertoire using paints, movement, sound, storytelling, writing, play, sand trays, drama and much more. The principles of the work described here could apply to any of these forms of expression.

Practitioners using creative approaches gain much wisdom by starting with their own personal immersion in creative work – exploring and processing their own material, getting a deeper sense of the experience of spontaneous expression, creating and being facilitated through an inquiry. This provides opportunities for the practitioner to notice the impact of the invitation, the clarity of purpose and contract, the format, facilitator interventions, time, space and more ahead of using the approaches themselves in their work with others.

Following an experiential principle in which we 'do', then seek to understand, I invite you to join me in three short creative exercises. I share my images and processing, along with background information and simple rules to guide your

DOI: 10.4324/9781003143450-10

exploration and future practice. Each exercise will begin with a short centering practice, a process to bring your awareness into you as a living, breathing human being, helping you to lay gently to one side your cognitive connection with the demands of the day. Trust whatever needs to appear will do so through the image making. All the exercises here are applicable in coaching supervision groups – and the possibilities are as infinite as your own imagination!

As you and I move through the chapter, we will make the most of ourselves as an asynchronous 'group'. As such our processing is, of course, separate. However, in a regular coaching supervision group we would be attending in the moment to the 'issue bringer', other group members and the dynamics arising within each of us and among us.

Many of the questions I will pose for you are those you may explore as a supervision group – especially the initial inquiries around creating space, your relationship with creative approaches and connection to this point in time. Each of these, and other avenues, offer potential insights witnessed by peers within the group environment, opening the possibility for greater understanding of your individual and collective similarities and differences. This acknowledgement of multiple experiences and personal perspective is critical in engaging with creativity.

Creative Kit

You will need some resources for the chapter – your Creative Kit. As with preparation for any supervision session, after your internal preparation through centering and other pre-session practices, the essential requirements continue with the space:

- Quiet, private space
- Your imagination
- Selection of paper or card in different colours, sizes and maybe even textures
- Selection of crayons, pencils and pens
- Plasticine (or clay, playdoh etc.)
- Pen/pencil and writing paper or journal

Contracting

I would love for you to participate, bringing the concepts and opportunities alive in you as you read through this chapter. If you are willing to have a go, let us look at the contract between us – and, as we do so, I will mention some considerations for coaching supervision group contracting.

Firstly, allow yourself to be curious about your own journey. We will all have had messages ('feedback') on our creative ability at some point in the past.

What are you believing about yourself and your creative talents? Your ability to draw, or even to imagine?[2]

It may serve you to get your immediate thoughts out onto paper. Look at them. Take a moment to consider your statements, perhaps immediately connecting with their origins.

What is drawing you towards creative approaches at this time?

This exploration may surface some of your expectations of yourself, me and this chapter.

In the supervision group, it may be important to spend some time uncovering thoughts and feelings regarding this work before embarking on creative approaches.

Now, please collect your Creative Kit. In the in-person setting, the resources often are brought by the supervisor; however, as you read the chapter, as in working in the online setting, we will each attend to the materials that we wish to bring. Collecting resources is an important part of the preparation for coaching supervision groups using creative methodology online. It is entirely possible to spontaneously use readily available materials around the home, office or outdoors; however, if you have agreed to work with creative approaches in a group, preparing your own Creative Kit beforehand signals your readiness and represents part of your commitment to the group contract.

Next, we will attend to the space. In the physical space, much of the setting of the room will be managed by the supervisor – bringing resources and ensuring there is adequate light, air, appropriate seating and privacy for everyone. In the virtual environment, each participant will be responsible for creating their own dedicated space for the work. Think about your own space.

What, if anything, needs to be put in place, or changed, for it to best serve you in carrying out this personal inquiry?

In setting up a coaching supervision group, you might consider how you and group members attend to the environment in which you will work. The physical space affords group members a container for the work – a door to enter and a process of leaving the room at the end of the session. Creating this distinction in the online environment is just as important. The supervision group experience is a clearly contracted activity. Group participants may consider whether the desk at which their day-to-day work is conducted best serves reflective practice or what adjustments need to be made and how to manage the transition from the encounter into something else.

Managing the space for the work is particularly important when working with creative approaches, as this work can stir up thoughts and feelings that have not been consciously present for us, and there are some '*emotional risks connected to the process of stimulating and working with images*' (Moon & Nolan, 2020: p. 28). It is clear in the invitation – we use creative approaches to gain new insights and connections and yet some take us by surprise. Many people experience vivid dreams which may raise unexpected feelings.

In introducing creative techniques into the supervision group environment, we can generate laughter and frivolity *and* deep personal work. It is therefore imperative that supervisors attend to the creative process, the group process *and* hold the contract for the work. Chesner and Zografou (2014) talk about 'structural hygiene', meaning 'respect for form and boundaries' and suggest that without a strong container creative expression may be reduced.

> *Having explored the space for our work, how else might you give yourself 'form'?*

You may wish to create a time-bounded space for yourself and review the extent to which this has served you after the exercise. As we move through the exercises, I invite you to self-facilitate your images through reflective writing and I suggest you begin with three-minute writing sessions and trust you will adjust as necessary.

To further resource yourself, consider your self-care: drink plenty of water; take breaks and rest; make a dedicated space and time for your creative and reflective work (here and elsewhere) and, of course, use your own supervision for additional support.

> *How are you attending to your self-care?*

In setting out this contract with you I invite you to immerse yourself in the exercise and notice if, and when, you stray into interpreting, analysing and judging your work, or connections that appear for you. In self-facilitating, allow your insights to arrive, notice when you begin to 'try' or 'think' them into being. This helps you to see what moves you to this space and therefore might may move others when you are facilitating them.

> *Pause. Notice what is arising in you right now.*

Following the initial centering practice, there will be a *focus* for each invitation into creative expression. The focus provides the anchor to which we can return later in our sense-making.

In a group situation we would explore how we might work together – how we as supervisor and group members contribute. Throughout this chapter we will use as our guide four simple rules for engaging with creative approaches. You will see them pop up as we go through the first exercise, and there will be more detail later in the chapter.

In accompanying you, I will use myself and my own creative inquiry as we travel together through the pages.

Exploring you as a practitioner – exercise 1

Exercise 1: Conveying the image to paper

Pause. Take a moment to 'arrive' into this journey with me. Notice your chair, or the floor, supporting you and move or stand if you wish. Bring your breathing into your awareness and take three conscious breaths, giving attention to the air coming into your body and allowing a longer exhale as the air moves out.

Tune into yourself as a practitioner – as supervisor, coach, organisational leader.

Who are you? Allow an image to appear. Notice yourself as the image arrives. Notice any judgements or censoring. Give attention to whatever is present.

Take a moment.

When you are ready, convey something of that image to paper, without words, using any of your available drawing and colouring resources. Accepting whatever arrives . . . and noticing.

Take about two minutes to make your marks on the paper. Then return to this chapter.

As with any of these exercises, any form of representation is perfect – whether it is a detailed sketch or some colours on the paper. As we are working in different time zones and spaces, I now invite you into a reflective writing process – following a similar process that we would use if we were in the same room together.

Glance at these prompts; begin where you begin; write without thinking too much.[3] Incorrect spelling and punctuation are fine, and there is no need for your writing to make sense.

Write for three minutes. Glance again as necessary.

- *As you look at your image, what do you notice? (Keep describing what you notice just as it is.)*
- *What part of the image in your mind is here on the paper?*
- *What's happening here?*
- *What's this? (Turn to what intrigues you.)*

Invite the image to express itself.

The story of your image might be unfolding – read the words you have written to this point. Trust your intuition to lead you to the next useful prompt and write for a further three minutes:

- *Where did you begin the image?*
- *Where have you placed it on the paper?*

- *What kind, or colour, of paper have you used? What else can you say about that?*
- *What kind of crayons and colours have you used?*

Notice with childlike curiosity.

Stay with your image for as long as you can. The image has the message, not your logical, cognitive thinking!

After three minutes, or when your writing begins to slow or you sense enough has been written for now, and without disrupting your engagement with the process, take a moment to read over your words.

Notice specific terms, for example, as in my own writing with which I opened the chapter:

- *I wanted an **armillary sphere***
- *There it was . . . a **raspberry jelly***

Reflect what is.

Through reflecting on what has shown up, we notice unique terms that may be key to a connection perhaps between the present and the past, or another place and time . . . or open a new avenue of exploration.

- *An armillary sphere? Where have I heard that before, or what does this object mean to me?*
- *A raspberry jelly? Where do I know raspberry jellies from?*

We are still very much in the image, beginning to connect with our own experiences that have brought this image into being, here today. Only *you* can have these connections. My association with the *raspberry jelly* is mine. Your images and associations with the jelly will arise in you and be uniquely yours.

Keep yourself to yourself.

The final stage of the inquiry is linking with the focus, the purpose of the inquiry, back at the beginning. This holds us in the contract for the work: even if links are not yet visible, and no insights have arrived, the contract for the work remains essential.

In this case, the focus of this exercise was to invite you to connect with yourself as a practitioner.

What are you noticing about the connection between your image, your writing and who you are as a practitioner?

In facilitating others, it might be tempting to bring this question much earlier in the inquiry and accept the initial information present. However, by staying longer in the inquiry and in the image, you may allow something unexpected and new to arise from the creative process. Your 'thinking' might be encouraging you to stick with what is immediately present!

Some background

Tuning into creative approaches, through imagery, drawing, music, movement and other forms of expression, evokes a range of feelings and thoughts. Not everyone is willing to take this step; therefore, contracting and agreement are essential. This approach has the capacity to enable us to work differently with the data available to us, helping us access new perspectives and break free from internalised circular thinking that can so easily perpetuate as we attempt to 'think' our way through complex issues.

When we work on the telephone or 'audio only' with clients, we amplify and enhance the capacity of our hearing – we notice tiny changes in breath, pace, tone and timbre that might go un-noticed when we have a plethora of visual clues in the in-person environment.

Such is the gift in creative work. By focussing in on creative expression, we open our senses to new possibilities beyond rational thinking. Seeley (2011) encourages practitioners to bring creativity into their work within corporate settings, moving away from reliance on cognitive thinking:

> *Our living bodies, senses, emotional responses, imaginations and intuitions are routinely dismissed as reliable sources of information and the practices which could cultivate these ways of knowing with rigour are largely neglected and underdeveloped.*
>
> (Seeley, 2011: p. 3)

She uses illustrations of organisations using dance, singing and drama techniques to access strategic thinking and enhanced productivity.

We, as human beings, have been using art and creative processes throughout time to express and convey our inner world without words (Gash, pp. 12–17; Sheather, pp. 8–11). As western sciences of the human mind took shape, Freud developed his theories of the unconscious and began to notice the limitations of verbal expression.

> *He noted that his patients frequently said that they could draw their dreams but were unable to describe them in words. This observation inspired and eventually confirmed the belief that art expression could be a route to understanding the inner world of the human psyche.*
>
> (Malchiodi, 1999: p. 29)

Subsequently, Jung discerned that, in addition to rational 'thinking', there existed within us a kind of knowing characterised by images, myths and symbols. This knowing, residing largely out of our awareness, was directing choices and decisions. It was here, within our unconscious, that healing and development occurred (Stagg, 2020). Jung was committed to a regular practice of image making, and experienced the profound nature of this work:

> *The creative process so far as we are able to follow it at all consists in the unconscious activation of an archetypal image and in elaborating and shaping this image into the finished work. By giving it shape, the artist translates it into the language of the present and so makes it possible for us to find our way back to the deepest springs of life.*
>
> (Jung, C., 1922: p. 130)

In our image making, we may find archetypal conflict[4] between dark and light, good and evil, our dreams and our fears portrayed in a seemingly innocent pattern or marks on the paper.

I return to my opening image and speak from the image:

In the image:

> *I'm a raspberry jelly – a party piece connected to Jo's childhood. Not that she had a jelly mould at home. They were for 'other people' – in the Boarding Schools of girl's novels or in the pranks of Saturday morning comic characters.*

Reflecting, resonating and noticing associations:

> *A party piece? Oh . . . I am immediately taken back to those days of playing the piano in the Music Festival – an enduring trauma. Feeling like a party piece, up there on this enormous stage rattling the keyboards in time with my knocking knees.*

The person-centred approach of Liesl Silverstone is a key influence in my work:

> *Allowing the **client** to know what the picture meant. No interpretations. No guess work. No me knowing best.*
>
> (Silverstone, 1993: p. 2)

In facilitating images, supervisors support supervisees to create the bridge between the expressed image and themselves (Silverstone, 1993: p. 7).

The image creator might not immediately know what message is being conveyed (Sheather, p. 16) and the act of creating may be the 'work' itself (Silverstone, p. 5). Sometime later the insight may appear. This is perfectly illustrated by the quote attributed to Isadora Duncan, the free-spirited American dancer at the turn of the 20th century:

> *If I could tell you what it meant, there would be no point in dancing it.*
>
> (in Seeley, 2011: p. 6)

Imagery is often portable allowing us to sit with it, take it with us as a camera image and return to it as necessary, allowing meanings to emerge when they are ready.

Your relationship with this chapter – exercise 2

As we move into the next exercise, we use ourselves in relationship. You, me and the chapter. This approach is suitable for any relationship – whether parts of ourselves or a relationship with another person or inanimate object (as here with this chapter) or a complex system of inter-related players in an organisational contract.

You may use objects from your Creative Kit and you may be drawn to something else around you.

Exercise 2: Using objects

Pause. Take a moment to 'arrive' into this journey with me. Notice your chair, or the floor, supporting you and move or stand if you wish. Bring your breathing into your awareness and take three conscious breaths, giving attention to the air coming into your body and allowing a longer exhale as the air moves out.

As you breathe, allowing the air to flow freely in and out, please tune into the relationship between you and this chapter. Noticing. Allowing. Resonating.

*Tuning into **you** first, look around with a soft gaze and choose an object to represent you. Trust whatever arrives.*

Take a moment to breathe before tuning into the chapter.

Find another object to represent this chapter (or part of the chapter).

Bring your two objects together, if possible – on the table, tray or floor.

Attend to the object representing you first. Take your pen or pencil and write freely for a few minutes[5] on these questions:

* *What have you chosen?*
* *What are you noticing about your object?*
* *What are you believing, thinking and/or feeling about your object?*
* *What more can you say?*
* *What are you noticing now?*

In attending to the second object, return to these questions once more and again write freely.

After a few minutes, pause.

* *What do you notice about how you have placed them?*
* *Look again, what else do you notice?*

You may wish to spend some time with your objects before moving into the next section, where I will convey something of my experiencing.

Returning to my own inquiry

When I tuned in to my relationship with this chapter through this exercise, I found myself instinctively moving towards two objects without thinking at all: Dora (representing me) and a pair of my walking boots (representing the chapter)!

Figure 9.1   Dora and the boots

*Dora is small toy; she looks like a dalmatian dog. She **is** a dalmatian to me! She has been my totem for a few years – representing my relationship with spontaneity and expression, a symbol to encourage me to be free flowing, taking inspiration from the spirit of Isadora Duncan,[6] the American dancer. I look closer at Dora today. I smile. No two dalmatian dogs are alike. Dora is perfect, she fits in my hand and sits on my desk.*

I'm more curious. There is a connection between Dora and an old TV character from a series set in the North of England – my adult home, the birthplace of my daughter, the grey sea crashing on the sea wall, my favourite place to be. A strong sensation runs through my body, and I feel my lungs expanding as if I am standing on the wall drinking in the spray of the water. Joy floods through me in the moment. The sea is grey, deep and unpredictable. Yet as predictable as the moon – moving in rhythm with natural forces.

Turning to my old walking boots . . . another smile! Walking is slow – often I choose to cycle. I breath out a big sigh. The beginning of the walk. Always takes me a while to settle in. I find myself stopping to adjust my laces, take off a fleece, put on a fleece, grapple with the backpack . . . creating various distractions for myself until I find my stride. And then, at some point, I might look up to find an enormous sky or stunning landscape scene, or look down into a fresh, bubbling brook or close my eyes to hear the sound of an unknown bird. Joy!

I notice I positioned Dora in front of the boots. She seems to be going a different way – or at least facing another direction. Yes, facing a different direction. I'd say she was striding out. She looks clear and calm (to me!)

I again stay 'in the image', encouraging the words to flow and only later allowing connections to emerge – recognising that there are many layers to this. I might uncover more insights as time passes, enabling Dora and the boots to reveal more.

I will return to Dora and the walking boots in the next section.

Guiding our work

I wanted a way to more clearly describe my way of engaging with creative approaches and invited my colleague Louie Gardiner to build on our earlier work together. In 2019 we discerned a set of Seven Simple Rules alive in *coaching supervision* practice (Birch & Gardiner, 2019) which is now the basis of our supervision training programmes.

Drawing on the same bodies of theoretical knowing, we engaged in a similar process of inquiry for working with creative approaches. We became aware of three core assumptions:

- The image speaks for itself
- Everything is something
- What's personal is personal

We turned to ourselves to find out how these assumptions shaped our practice and were able to distil four repeating behaviours. These are expressed as simple active 'doing' statements – four simple rules for engaging with creative approaches:

- Invite the image to express itself
- Reflect what is
- Notice with childlike curiosity
- Keep yourself to yourself

Noticing, naming and consciously adopting these generative behaviours helps practitioners bring consistency to their practice.[7]

Conveying these simple rules through an image held by a heart was an intuitive next step for me and can be visualised in Figure 9.2 (Birch & Gardiner, 2020).

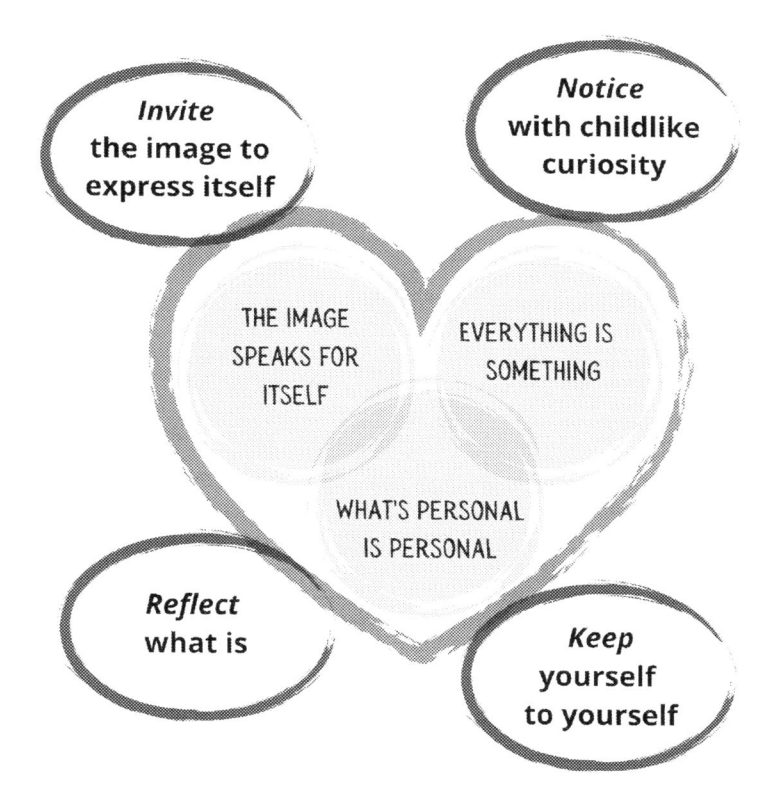

©2020 Birch J. Gardiner LJN

Figure 9.2 Creative approaches: Four simple rules and three assumptions [© Birch and Gardiner (2020)]

I instantly recognised the heart as the symbol Silverstone used in every mandala produced at the end of each certificate course[8] and at other times in group images.

Twenty years ago, I trained with Liesl Silverstone, a pioneer in the person-centred field, and subsequently joined her small team of trainers. For the next five years in resourcing ourselves to deliver the Certificate in Person-Centred Art Therapy course (described in Silverstone, 1993), the trainers worked together, with Liesl, to deepen our own practice. This was a profound learning experience. My work with her anchors the theoretical basis for this chapter.

Over time I have come to realise the heart also symbolises the essence that holds this work – the sensitivity and love we extend to each other as we embrace creative approaches.

In our earlier study with coaching supervisors (Birch & Gardiner, 2019), 'engage with love' emerged as one of the essential behaviours in the practice. Love is a complex phenomenon – hard to define, yet inextricably linked to our development as humans, our ability to form healthy attachments and to feeling joy in spontaneous play and exploration (Schore & Marks-Tarlow, 2018). Love is vital in developing robust coaching and supervision relationships and in engaging with creative approaches.

No simple rule stands alone; all are interdependent and inter-related. The invitation, for all of us, is to embrace the set of four rules and observe how they show up and enrich our practice – helping us to notice ourselves, enhance our engagement and therefore the quality of our work.

1 Invite the image to express itself

Bringing the image into view *is* the task – in whatever way this arrives, whether visually, through art and mark-making; kinaesthetically, through handling objects and clay or through the body in movement and dance or aurally, through music and sound. We invite expression and only later find words. This cannot be hurried. We are bringing forward something that is not yet able to verbalise its purpose, meaning or message. We stay with the image as long as is possible, noticing and setting aside any pull towards analysis or interpretation.

In any coaching supervision session, we might end with more questions than we had at the start, and that may also be true when using creative approaches.

2 Reflect what is

I encourage you to use simple reflections as your primary mode of inquiry. A key skill of this work is in offering observations, not interpretations – and becoming adept at noticing the difference. This is especially complex in coaching supervision groups in which the supervisor is attending to their own practice, as well as to group members as they engage with each other.

The supervisor is often 'modelling' a 'way to be' which is absorbed by group members. As with any learning, we can read the words and hear the instruction, but 'knowing' arises in the body – the moment we suddenly 'get' the practice.

Table 9.1 Reflecting what is

Reflect what is	Interpretation
What can you say about this object?	What can you say about your spotty dog?
Your face is changing.	You look angry.
You altered your position as you spoke.	You have become uncomfortable.
You picked up that object.	You were quick moving that object.
I'm really curious about this piece.	This piece is really interesting.

In holding the simple rules of engaging with creative approaches we endeavour to amplify repeating patterns of generative behaviour – those actions and ways of being that enhance our encounter. Supervisors can share these with group members, and the 'being' of the supervisor and participants will shape what happens in the process of the group.

Offering an interpretation can lead the supervisee off track. In my own exploration the dog (to me) is a **dalmatian**. A **spotty dog** would also be true of 'the object' and, indeed, has connections for me from my childhood. In some scenarios, I might need the connection with spotty dog, but today, *in relating to the purpose of the exercise*, I need the pathway to, and from, the dalmatian – that's the link that leads me to the sea wall, not the spotty dog.

Facilitating me:

You mentioned the sea as predictable as the moon – moving in rhythm with natural forces.

Yes! That's it. I need to move in a natural rhythm – my natural rhythm. I need to write this chapter from inside and it will find its way.

The use of wider *process reflections* can hold the moment in time, the context for the image, the contract for the work and more. Moving away from the direct image or object, we can hold out the symbolic meaning of the piece and through these we link the exploration, for example:

Facilitating me:

You have brought your natural rhythm, in front of the stop-start process at the beginning of a walk. What are you noticing about these and your relationship with this chapter?

Ah yes! As I turn to the purpose of this exercise, drawing out the connection, I notice today I have found a new rhythm with the chapter. After lots of stops and starts, distracting myself with worries about theory, or referencing, or my inner voice issuing various unhelpful warnings, this image brings me a feeling of freshness, excitement and a bubbling idea about using myself more fully in the text and I find myself eager to tap on the keys. I am being called to trust my inner rhythm and work from there, whatever the challenges. Yes, that's it.

In this example, the knowing is *arising* in me – that is the gift in this work. I am not *thinking* it into being – drawing from past knowing. Creative approaches enable new knowing and insights to come into awareness.

Every reflection focusses on 'what is' and is offered from childlike curiosity, not a place of judgement.

3 *Notice with childlike curiosity*[9]

Moving into a place of innocence: seeing as if for the first time; making the joy of discovery more significant than the question itself; asking simply because something draws your attention.

- *What's this?*
- *What's happening there?*
- *What more do you know about that dalmatian?*

Some methods of working with art advocate moving the exploration along, inviting 'what if' kinds of questions; however, my lived experience suggests these are often less helpful than simply staying present to the in-the-moment process. Given the potential for unexpected connections to appear, developing the skill of walking alongside the 'image bringer' enables the client/supervisee to go where they go and to explore at their own pace.

- *What have you used to create your image?*
- *What can you tell me about the colours?*
- *What did you do with the paper?*
- *Are you in this image?*

4 *Keep yourself to yourself*

I have noticed that as humans we quickly discern patterns and interpret data based on past experiences to process the vast quantity of information we encounter. When engaging with creative approaches, we want to notice and hold back any urge to comment from our need to know or to create order.

In coach training, participants are encouraged to notice interpreting and leading questions, however, I believe this work presents the opportunity to take these skills to a new level. I had been a person-centred psychotherapist for many years before training with Silverstone. I was amazed by how many subtle interpretations and judgements came into my work. Remember, judgements come in the 'positive' form too!

- *That's a beautiful image*
- *That little dog is alongside those boots*
- *I love that contribution you made just then*

Also, notice questions that serve *your* understanding rather than the expansion of the supervisee's understanding.

What is the connection between the dalmatian and the northern TV programme?

As supervisors, we do not need to know the answers or piece everything together – the supervisee will be making their own sense during and after the session.

In exploring Dora and the walking boots, as I moved around the imagery hearing myself and the unfolding exploration I may have stayed fully in the metaphor and brought the piece to an end something like this:

Yes, I'm noticing that I need to get those boots on and simply enjoy the walk, trusting that along the way I'll find my pace and discover something joyful. I'll take the dog!

Imagery gives us a language of its own without the need to make the meaning explicit.

There is one other aspect here relating to the in-person supervision group. Here we hold the physical space, appreciating that art or the placing of objects are external representations of an individual's inner process. As such, the piece is deeply personal, and any art or objects would only be touched by the image creator (the supervisee).

Exploring your practice – exercise 3

In previous exercises, we have used our current situation – me writing the chapter and you reading and participating. In this exercise, we move into exploring our practice – yours and mine. We will use plasticine, clay or Play-Doh.

Please set a five-minute timer to begin after the centering exercise.

Exercise 3: Using plasticine, clay or Play-Doh

Pause. Take a moment to 'arrive' into this journey with me. Notice your chair, or the floor, supporting you and move or stand if you wish. Bring your breathing into your awareness and take three conscious breaths, giving attention to the air coming into your body and allowing a longer exhale as the air moves out.

As you breathe, allowing the air to flow freely in and out, please tune into an issue arising from your work – a supervision or coaching relationship, or something else to which you would like to give attention.

Now, take your eyes away from this chapter, closing them if you wish. You may speak your thoughts out loud if you wish.

> *Allow your hands to work with the material as you consider your issue. There is no need to pay any attention to the movement of your hands and the material. Allow them the freedom to work the material and simply see what evolves.*
> *Begin your five-minute timer.*

When the five minutes is up, take a look at your creation. You may, as I have done, photograph your work (see Figure 9.3).

How are you feeling?

As before, let's enter a writing process, asking open curious questions, letting the words flow freely, noticing any need to change or correct, accepting whatever arrives.

- *What do you notice?*
- *How do you describe your creation?*
- *And what else do you notice?*

Trust what avenue of inquiry seems most relevant.

- *What medium did you choose?*
- *What more can you say about this specific medium?*
- *What do you notice about the colour you chose?*
- *What did you notice in your hands?*
- *Where have you placed the piece(s) now? On the tray, table or floor?*
- *Re-read your words – what do you notice?*
- *What else do you notice?*

Take some time to be curious with your own creation. When you are ready, after a word about coaching supervision groups, please join me in exploring my creation.

In using this exercise in a coaching supervision group, one person would bring their issue, engaging with their own clay, plasticine or Play-Doh whilst the others also let their hands work as they listen. The issue bringer would explore their creation as previously described, and group members would offer what has been created by their hands whilst listening – recognising that their creations may or may not have relevance to the 'issue bringer'.

Let's see what I make of my creation. I chose to explore a supervision relationship with a coach in which his schedule has changed and the only time we would now be able to meet coincides with an existing personal commitment of mine. Do I let go of my commitment or say 'no' to the coach?

Figure 9.3   Plasticine

> *I notice I have two pieces. My hands worked with the plasticine for a while and then I broke it into two. The first piece came from what had been created to that point. It is green and has ten or eleven indentations. It has a smooth arc and a rough edge where the piece was torn. It is a nice shape. . . . I smile when I look at it. I like it – I am pleased at how it has turned out although I have no idea what I mean!*
>
> *The second piece is a curved bowl. It is open . . . an open receptacle. There is one indentation on the inner surface, but the rest is pretty smooth. It's not a perfect shape of anything. And yet I like it and how it sits with the other piece. Separate and obviously from a similar piece of plasticine.*
>
> *I have used a particular shade of dark green – the only thing in that colour that comes to mind is a symbol of a tree from my primary school. I liked that school. I chose plasticine because I like that it takes work. It isn't the nicest material to work with, but warm hands soon make it pliable and interesting.*

In reflecting, I noticed that my mind focussed initially on the coach and how he might be feeling. I am fond of the coach, and we have worked together for some years since the very beginning of his coaching journey. I feel happy about our work together, remembering the changes he had made over the years. I felt worried about ending our work – in that moment, catching a thought that I was indispensable! However, when I shifted my attention and brought myself into 'me' and my own needs in the relationship, my hands tore the plasticine into two parts, and the bowl-shape arrived.

As I reflect on the bowl, it seems to be the space I created for my own activity. I paused, simply observing the two pieces, linked and yet separate. My insight arrives – our work is over, and I feel sad. I pause in this space a while and allow this to settle in me.

Closing our contract

Thank you for accompanying me through this chapter. We are now drawing our work to a close.

In closing group supervision sessions, I will not invite any further creative work – acknowledging the propensity of creative approaches to open unexpected pathways to previously inaccessible material. Holding the container for this deep work well inside the boundary of the supervision session itself ensures those who engage in creative expression have time and space to attend to what emerges.

You may, however, wish to reflect on your journey using the reflective writing process we have utilised throughout the chapter, noticing any key insights that have emerged.

Taking the work forward

There are infinite ways to bring creative approaches into your work with coaching supervisees in a group setting. However, these three exercises, together with the four simple rules, will provide a theoretical basis and a platform on which you can further develop your skills.

These simple exercises can be used in attending, supporting or responding to

- The structure of the group – check ins, check outs;
- The group members – introductions, describing cultural background, identifying similarities and differences;
- Group dynamics – the relationships between group members/supervisor
- Issues brought to supervision – cases, themes and other issues.

Many other techniques are available through which to extend your repertoire, including those that enable you to attend to the group experience as a whole or offer new avenues into case work and individual explorations.

Continuing your development

My own skills were greatly enhanced through personal experience – my immersion in expressive opportunities and through experiential person-centred art therapy skills training – subsequently leading those courses and others. Each experience has brought new opportunities for self-awareness. If you consider that Dora has been my totem for many years, and that the purpose she serves is to help me to be freer and more spontaneous, you might begin to understand that creative expression does not come easily to me! I can be stiff, constrained and, at worst, frozen to the spot with fear! However, I believe we are always working on our own 'stuff', and I trust that my 'psyche' knows what it needs to do to heal – to move forward, develop and grow. That trusting leads me into various areas, seeking out art, dance, movement, drama and improvisation and clowning,[10] which, through the ever-present discomfort and personal challenge, extend my understanding of communication. Each of these areas frees up my physical and emotional ability to convey my inner world to myself and others – and, in turn, enables me to explore and deepen my work.

As a supervisor, you may have had years of training and experience in coaching and supervision. Moving into the world of creativity requires that you attend to yourself first – offering yourself a range of opportunities to engage with creative expression. Each can bring insights from the experience: observing your own process and being facilitated by yourself and by others – bringing you a sense of what works and what gets in the way of your own processing and perhaps that of others.

In one of my early attempts using art and creativity, I was surprised to find I was indeed holding expectations about what would be produced:

> *I invited the coach to draw the image in her mind. She drew two tiny stick people at the edge of the page. Not more than four or five skinny little lines of black pen. What on earth would I do with that!*

I later saw how many different avenues of exploration I could have taken – her choice of pen, colour, size, position on the page and even the paper she used (a scrappy torn piece). I could have been curious as to how the focus of our work today, exploring a key work relationship, was expressed in the image. If I had been able to acknowledge and accept the feelings arising in me, I would have known what to do!

What happened instead was an inadequate mumble from me, pushing down my judgements and attempting to escape the feelings of embarrassment, fear and confusion bubbling up in me like a swirling fog, swiftly turning to something else – very possibly conveying to the coach (the truth) that this was not what I expected, denying us both access to the profound nature of the process developing between us and the emotion associated with those skinny little lines.

Gaining personal experience is the basis for ethical practice – always working within our competence. Training is useful in establishing the theoretical basis for your work, learning specific techniques and enjoying a learning community. Supervision is essential and, when working with groups, it is always advisable to source your own supervision group arrangement in addition to one-to-one sessions. Understanding yourself in groups is critical to any group work. As with supervisees, supervisors engaging with creative techniques are prone to vivid dreams and the surfacing of old material. Don't forget – supervisors are just people too! Attending to your own self-care is therefore essential.

I return my thoughts to the beginning of this chapter – this work takes sensitivity and daring, for ourselves and others as we attempt to communicate through creative expression and to hold this in the contract of our work together. Our willingness as practitioners to keep engaging for ourselves, bringing ourselves to the edge of our comfort, experiencing the unexpected and acknowledging what arises is key to developing a solid, safe practice.

Acknowledgements

The author would like to acknowledge Shirley Smith for her enthusiasm in bringing this work to a wider audience through our Crucial Difference Creative Approaches series; and for Louie J N Gardiner for her creative input and editorial support.

Notes

1 For more information on creativity and neuroscience, see Gash (2017: pp. 37–47) and Sheather (2019: pp. 18–41)
2 Around 3% of the population have aphantasia – meaning they may not be able to voluntarily access visual imagery. (Zeman, 2020) This sometimes extends to sound, smells and/or sensations of touch.
3 A range of reflective writing techniques in Holder, J. (2013). *49 Way to Write Yourself Well*. Brighton: Step Beach.
4 Primitive themes and patterns that seem common since the beginning of humanity. For more reading, see Kalsched, D., & Sieff, D. (2006). Unlocking the Secrets of the Wounded Psyche: The Miraculous Survival System That Is also a Prison. *Caduceus*, 69, 1–13.
5 You may wish to use a three-minute timer.
6 https://isadoraduncan.org/foundation/isadora-duncan/.
7 For coaching supervisors, these simple rules would be additional to those evident in the practice of coaching supervision; however, we recognise that not all creative practitioners are coaching supervisors.
8 Certificate in Person-Centred Art Therapy Skills.
9 A case study demonstrating the practice of childlike curiosity can be found, along with other useful resources, in Gash, J. (2017). *Coaching Creativity* (pp. 157–159). Abingdon: Routledge.
10 Useful links include www.interplay.org/; www.5rhythms.com/; www.personcentered-expressivearts.com/.

References

Birch, J., & Gardiner, L. J. N. (2019). Seven Simple Rules: An Alternative Lens. In J. Birch & P. Welch (Eds.), *Coaching Supervision: Advancing Practice, Changing Landscapes*. Abingdon: Routledge.
Birch, J., & Gardiner, L. J. N. (2020). Creative Approaches: Four Simple Rules and Three Assumptions Crucial Difference Course Material. Creative Approaches Series, May.
Chesner, A., & Zografou, L. (2014). *Creative Supervision Across Modalities: Theory and Applications for Therapists, Counsellors and Other Helping Professionals*. London: Jessica Kingsley Publishers.
Gash, J. (2017). *Coaching Creativity: Transforming Your Practice*. Abingdon: Routledge.
Holder, J. (2013). *49 Way to Write Yourself Well*. Brighton: Step Beach.
Jung, C. (1922). Collected Works, Vol. 15, p. 130.
Malchiodi, C. (1999). *Art Therapy Source Book*. New York: McGraw-Hill Education.
Moon, B. L., & Nolan, E. G. (2020). *Ethical Issues in Art Therapy* (4th ed.). Springfield, US: Charles C Thomas Publisher Ltd.

Schore, A., & Marks-Tarlow, T. (2018). *How Love Opens Creativity, Play and the Arts Through Early Right-Brain Development*. In T. Marks-Tarlow, M. Solomon, D. J. Siegel (Eds.), *Play and Creativity in Psychotherapy* (pp. 64–91). New York: Norton & Company.

Seeley, C. (2011). *A Thought Piece on Artful Knowing for a Sustainable Future*. Ashridge: Ashridge International Research Conference, June.

Sheather, A. (2019). *Coaching Beyond Words: Using Art to Deepen and Enrich Our Conversations* (p. 27). Abingdon: Routledge.

Silverstone, L. (1993). *2nd Ed Art Therapy: The Person-Centred Way*. London: Jessica Kingsley Publisher.

Stagg, E. (2020). Jungian Sandplay for Adults. *Therapy Today*, November.

Zeman, A. (2020). An Update on 'Extreme Imagination' – Aphantasia/Hyperphantasia. www.sites.exeter.ac.uk/eyesmind/ [Accessed: 29 December 2020].

Chapter 10

Group supervision using the Mirror model

Olga Rybina

Introduction

I begin by expressing my deep gratitude to the participants of the first pilot groups, thanks to whose feedback the Mirror model (Rybina, 2016) emerged.

In 2016, supervision in Russia was a developing practice, well known among those in the helping professions, such as psychologists, teachers and doctors. However, there were few supervision groups for coaches as practitioners within the helping professions. At that time, the ICF had no regulatory guidance for coaches requiring supervision as a mandatory practice as it did with, for example, psychologists and psychotherapists. Perhaps this became a limiting factor in the development of supervision within the coaching profession.

In 2016, my own positive experience of participation within Balint groups (Balint, 1955; Balint & Balint, 1955), together with a burning desire to support practitioners working according to ICF standards, became the driving force behind the creation of the Mirror model of group supervision for coaches. It is gratifying to note that today, the ICF promotes a detailed description of the value of reflective practice and supervision for coaches. This undoubtedly increases the interest of coaching practitioners towards the opportunities for training and growth available through this format.

My own experience of participation in Balint groups, as a clinical psychologist, has highlighted several important points:

1   We need rules of interaction within the group that apply to all participants.
2   It is necessary to use the resources of the group itself as much as possible.
3   We need to create an intimate trusting space for individual reflection.
4   We need a process where everyone – both individual supervisees and the group itself – gets maximum benefit.
5   We take into account the specific skills of the professionals we supervise.

As a supervision group, we originally planned to organise ourselves as a classical Balint group for coaches but adapted it for several reasons.

The Balint group has its origins in the field of practical medicine and is designed to attend to the specifics of doctors' work. Principles underpinning communication between doctor and patient differ from those within coach–client

DOI: 10.4324/978100314345-11

relationships, and it is important to take this into account when shaping the work of a supervisory group for coaches. For example, the experience of the Balint group has been applied to training psychotherapists (Barash, 1992) and training group psychotherapists (Alexandrov et al., 1990). In these studies, the authors identify specific changes to the focus and structure of the process according to the individual features of these professions.

These experiences inspired us to find solutions that take into account the specifics of a coach's work. The main task of the coach is to manage the client's reflective process through the client–coach relationship. In the coaching supervision process, it is important to use these existing skills, of both reflection and partnership, to create an environment for their further development. In the Mirror model, we do this through mini-sessions with supervisees.

The classical version of a Balint group is related to psychoanalysis, and the leader of the group is a psychoanalyst. However, there are variants of the Balint group. For example, the Belgian author Moreau (Karvasarsky, 2000) rejected the psychoanalytical method of interpretation and, as a leader, took an active position in discussing the case "as an equal" with other participants.

We believe that this approach is the most applicable when working with coaches, because it includes the principle of partnership, which is familiar and essential in coaching. The group leader in this adaptation becomes a facilitator of the group process *and* a partner in the discussion of the case. Moreover, in the Mirror model, a coach with supervisory skills, not a psychoanalyst, would be the leader.

In the classical version of the Balint group, the moment-to-moment reactions of the participants are welcomed and are not regulated in any way. The leader of the group records and analyses these spontaneous emotional and behavioural reactions. Therefore, in this original model, the efficacy of the work depends on the skill of the leader in interpreting and making sense of the unfolding process in the group.

We were challenged to create a model in which

- The specific role and skills of the coach are central to the process,
- The supervisor acts as facilitator and partner,
- There is a clear structure to the process,
- Supervisees have the opportunity to observe participants' reactions and use the data to expand their own awareness and decision-making and
- There is a safe-enough space for the supervisee's reflection.

All of these are incorporated in the creation of the Mirror model.

Components of the mirror model

In the Mirror model, the process of group supervision consists of four stages: organisational, contracting, reflective and final. Each stage has its own goals; the role of the leader and the tasks she sets for the participants are specific to each stage. One thing remains constant: the leader is the guardian of the process for each participant.

In developing the Mirror model, it was therefore essential to begin by defining the rules within which the group would operate. The main initial objective was the psychological safety of the participants.

Organisational stage

Purpose of the stage:

1   To acquaint the participants with the rules of this model of group work.
2   To ensure the participants understand and accept the responsibility for their choice to participate in the group.

Since the purpose of this chapter is to introduce you to the Mirror model, I will bypass the process of recruiting group members and focus on the basic rules that are consistent for all members.

1   Number of participants: 10 people max.
    Ideally, a group of six to eight people offers potential for a rich reflective process through multiple perspectives. In practice, there were occasions when the group consisted of only three or four people, and this proved to be just as effective as the larger group.

2   Those who arrive to the session more than three minutes late are denied entry. Starting a group interaction is important from the perspective of building trust and security. In one-off and short-term meetings, the willingness of some participants to discuss their case may depend on the composition of the participants. In addition, if the group is working in a long-term format, a case may already be presented in the first three minutes. Therefore, we adhere strictly to the three-minute rule, as it supports all participants in the process.

3   Complete absence of criticism.
    The supervisor has the right to stop the discussion or exclude from it any participant who cannot uphold this rule. This rule subsequently had a significant impact on the evolution of the Mirror supervision model, which will be discussed later in the section "Reflection Stage". The safety of the group, and of the supervisee, is the foundation of any supervision process.

4   Obligatory participation in the discussion. The answer "I don't know" is not acceptable!
    The rules state that all participants must contribute to the discussion. It is particularly important for participants to contribute through descriptions of their own feelings, analogies, metaphors, rational reflections, and so on,

without being afraid, or saying "I don't know" to themselves. The response "I don't know" often hides an inner belief that somewhere there is a correct, ideal option – and this clearly contradicts the principle of the supervision process as a partnership exploring multiple perspectives.

5   Confidentiality.
This is a mandatory requirement of the supervision process.

Introducing the rules is an important part of the process. At this point, everyone makes the decision to be a member of the group or not. Each group member takes personal responsibility for being an active participant in the process. This gives freedom of choice, increases involvement and transparency and is significant in creating trusting relationships.

In my initial stages of creating the Mirror Model, I introduced the rules at the beginning of the meeting and gave potential participants the opportunity to make a decision about their participation in the group. We subsequently took this initial discussion outside of the structured group process itself, and it evolved into a pre-group preparatory stage for participants. Now, before the first meeting, we send all participants a detailed description of the supervision procedure, the sequence of named stages and the goals for each stage, as well as the rules by which the group will operate.

Therefore, as the supervisor, at the beginning of the first group meeting, I am ready to answer questions and ask participants if they are ready to join the group. Before the first case is presented, each participant pro-actively agrees to participate or has the option of leaving the group.

This approach gives participants time to absorb the information about the group before arriving. This saves time in the first meeting and is more effective in addressing accountability of the participants, especially if the group meets only once, for example, as part of a training programme.

Anyone who has made the decision to participate may act as a supervisee and bring a case. In our practice, there have been times where no-one has been willing to bring a case. In these instances, the group has gathered and is ready to work, but there is no focus for discussion. Such situations become a challenge for the supervisor and for the group itself. One of the most interesting solutions of such situations is to work with the group itself as a client, using the here-and-now group process.

In my experience, a closed group works much more effectively. This means after the first meeting, no new members join the group for the agreed duration of our work together. The degree of safety and trust in such a group becomes very high. To organise the work of closed groups, together with the description of rules and procedures, we send participants a small questionnaire, which allows them to determine the presence of a supervising case. We ask two questions:

1   When are you ready to act as a supervisee?
2   What case are you ready to bring to the group?

Sometimes, the group works on a case which has previously been agreed at an earlier meeting. It is likely to be a case with a theme that is common in coaching. This format is especially useful for open groups because we then presume that only those participants interested in this specific case would attend the group.

Contracting stage

A supervision contract differs significantly from a coaching contract: it is more flexible and embraces multiple perspectives and responses – including rational and psychological. In addition, the supervision contract can relate both to the present-day situation and to past, systemic instances that repeat multiple times in the supervisee's life.

In the Mirror supervision group, all those present participate in the final agreement of the contract. The supervisor at this stage plays the role of process facilitator, arranging the order of speakers, and helps participants to formulate their questions about the case in the most useful way if necessary.

The sequence of actions at this stage:

1 Case presentation – supervisee tells the group about the particular coaching scenario that they wish to explore.
2 The group asks clarifying questions to understand the case in more detail.
3 The presenter concludes a contract with the supervisee.
4 The presenter concludes a contract with the group.

The case presentation by the supervisee can be done in free form focussing on the communication between the supervisee and his client, for example, a story about what happened during the coaching session and what worries the supervisee now. The main requirement during the story is to keep the focus on what happened in the communication between the coach and the client.

The participants may then ask clarifying questions, for example, "have you ever had similar situations with your other clients?"

As a rule, coaches bring cases for supervision, which, although they occurred in the past, they "have not let go" of emotionally. According to Simonov's Need-Informational Theory of Emotions (1997), the presence, sign and intensity of an emotion depends on several aspects: first, on the current need of a person and second, on the presence or absence of a difference between what, according to the person himself, he needs to meet this need and what he actually has.

In supervision, we deal with two sets of the supervisee's emotions at the same time. First, the emotions associated with the case itself, which is the focus of supervision, that is, with the past. And secondly, with the present – with the reasons why this case "does not let go" and remains emotionally charged and causes stress – significantly limiting the natural process of the coach in learning from the experience and incorporating the new knowledge as part of their professional development.

This fact is important to consider when determining the contract regarding the work. In the Mirror model, the contract is the agreement between the supervisor and the supervisee about the result of the supervision work with his or her case. It is important to consider the group itself as a participant in the process. Therefore, the psychological contract will be made with both the supervisor and the group.

The supervisor will usually ask the supervisee questions: "What do you expect from the group? What is important for the group to consider?"

The supervisor concludes the contract with the group with questions for each participant: "What do you want for yourself as a result of this piece of supervision work?"

As a rule, for supervisees, a good result is to answer questions about the case itself (often "what went wrong") and to answer questions about themselves and their experiences both in the past and in the present.

For the members of the group, the most valuable result of supervision is the answer to the question: "How can I use this case in my coaching practice for the benefit of myself and my clients?". Therefore, the purpose of being an active participant in the group is both to support the presenting coach and also to apply the learning to their own practice.

Example of a case:

"When my client answers the question 'I don't know', something happens to me and I switch to consulting mode. I am happy with myself in the session – the task is solved, but afterward, I think about this situation all the time. It doesn't let me go and I feel bad".

The desired outcome for the supervisee is the answer to these questions:

1   Why am I switching to consulting mode?
2   Why do I worry after a session when everything seems to have gone well?

Identified results for the group members:

- How do I stop *myself* switching to consulting mode?
- How do I become a friend to myself after a session?
- What do I do when the client "does not know"?

Reflective stage

The reflective stage consists of three consecutive rounds, which we define as thoughts, feelings and behaviour (Lazarus, 1963).

The rounds "Feelings" and "Thoughts" have the same structure: a group reflection followed by a mini-session of individual supervision with the supervisee.

During the group reflection, the supervisee is behind a symbolic "curtain" and does not take part in the discussion. In a face-to-face format, we ask the supervisor to move the chair outside of the group circle. The task of the group is to contribute and listen and, from the multitude of options discussed, discern which response best aligns with their internal response. At the stage of the mini-session of individual supervision, the group goes beyond the circle and holds the space, listening attentively, tuning into their individual experience. The supervisor and the supervisee move into the center of the circle.

The whole process looks like this:

Round 1, "Feelings":

- The group reflects on the case brought; the supervisee is "outside the circle".
- Individual supervision with supervisee; the group is "outside the circle".

Round 2, "Thoughts":

- Group reflection; the supervisee is "outside the circle".
- Individual supervision; the group is "outside the circle".

Round 3, "Behaviour":

- Conclusions of the supervisee.
- Conclusions of the group.

In adapting the process to an online environment, we can use the options of turning the video and audio functions on and off. Entering and exiting the circle means participants who are in the circle turn on their microphone and camera, while those who are outside the circle turn them off and yet stay within the overall process.

I will describe each round in more detail.

Round 1, "Feelings"

Group work at this stage begins with a question asked by the supervisor: "What feelings have you had about the story today?"

Participants can share feelings, metaphors and associations that have emerged in response to the case being shared. Everyone can talk, identifying with the coach as well as with the client.

After everybody has spoken, the presenter invites the supervisee into the circle and the group members leave the discussion.

A question for the supervisee:

- "What, of everything you have heard from the group, has resonance for you?"

This evolves into an individual mini-session of supervision. The first circle, "Feelings", helps the supervisee to understand, with the help of the group participants, which feelings and emotions this case stirred in him/her then, in the past, and which are present now, in the present. The first mini-session, as a rule, is devoted to the analysis of emotional experiences in the past, during the session and now.

The length of individual work with the supervisee varies from five to 15 minutes. It is the longest mini-session.

After the initial round, the supervisee has gained understanding about the emotions that he/she felt in the session and considered what the client could feel at that moment. Such experience increases the coach's sensitivity to his/her own emotional experience and that of his/her clients', now and potentially in the future.

In the early development of the model, after the group work, we limited ourselves to one question to the supervisee:

- What, of everything you have heard from the group, has resonance for you?

In the case just presented (when the client says "I don't know"), it seemed a huge layer of information remained unexplored. I began to see the importance of deep reflection in the moment on the received information from the group. Therefore, I adapted the original Balint process to include the individual mini-session at this point. The group reflection presented opportunities for the coach to look at the situation from different angles and to see what had previously been out of awareness. A mini-session enables a supervisee to reflect on his/her situation with the new data gained from the group. At the mini-session, the supervisor helps the supervisee to see any connection between his/her experiences and the emotions of the client. The coach also has the opportunity to consider the recurrence of these emotional reactions in other situations and life in general.

Exploring emotions in the safe environment of group supervision enables coaches to express a full range of feelings, even those perceived in cultural contexts as unacceptable, for example, anger, fear, confusion and more. As the coach becomes connected to their emotions, this creates optimum conditions for further reflections, which may develop into more concrete cognitive awareness. Very often after the first mini-session, the request describing the desired outcomes for supervision may change, with the coach realising they now hope for something quite different than what they initially thought.

At the first mini-session, the supervisor should also be prepared for the supervisee to realise they come to a conclusion in answer to their question. The supervisee may offer to complete the supervision process at this point. In such instances, the group decides together either to continue the work by selecting another case or to finish early.

To return to the example case, let's see what happens when we examine the mini-session following the group discussion.

Supervisee: "When my client answers the question 'I don't know', something happens to me, and I switch to consulting mode. I am happy with myself in the session – the task is solved, but afterwards I think about this situation all the time. It doesn't let go and I feel bad".

Supervisor: "What of everything you have heard from the group has resonance for you?"

Supervisee: "One participant's metaphor about a hunter stalking game really resonated for me. I'm the one who becomes the hunter, and the moment the client says 'I don't know' I get excited. My adrenaline level rises sharply, and I act. In that moment, the most important thing for me is to give back what I have – my knowledge."

Supervisor: "What do you think about yourself at this moment?"

Supervisee: "That I am a genius! [Pause.] I understand why I'm switching to consulting mode. . . . This story is not just about coaching. I want to be recognised at any cost and in the moment, I can get that recognition, I will stop at nothing".

Supervisor: "It looks like you have found the answer to your question. What would you like now?"

Supervisee: "I want to understand why I need other people's approval".

In the mini-session, the presenter has already started to ask questions from the "Thoughts" circle: "What do you think about yourself at this moment?"

Sometimes, the supervisee themselves goes to the analysis of an actual need, which he had not previously realised. It is important for the supervisor to remain sensitive to the context in order to manage the group process and offer options for continuing work. In our case, after the first mini-session, the contract issue, the focus for the supervisee has been changed by the process.

Round 2, "Thoughts"

At first, the supervisee is again outside the circle. This second circle helps the supervisee through the cognitive responses of other group members in addressing three key points, in terms of Simonov's theory:

1   Determine what exact personal need was "woken up" in supervisee in the process of working with the client and what need remains active now – not allowing the case to close and move to the "archive of professional cases";
2   Identify what "theoretical ideas" the supervisee had, and still has, on how to work with these needs in general and
3   Determine the difference between how the coach would theoretically expect to act in this situation and what resources he really has.

Sometimes this difference arises precisely because of the difference between "theory" and "practice", but it also happens when the coach is not ready for the actualization of these needs and has never considered such a development, even theoretically.

The whole group's work on this circle is built around the main questions: "What did the coach want? What need was driving him?"

The second mini-session with the supervisee also starts with a question:

• What, of everything you have heard from the group, has resonance for you?

In fact, this mini-session with the supervisee is a bridge between the circles of "Thoughts" in which the contributions of group members are offered and "Behaviour". After answering the question about the actual need, the logical continuation is to plan actions – how can you do it differently?

Pitfalls of Round 2

Participants in the circle may be too emphatic in offering their hypotheses. It is important for everyone to share their thoughts but not to be attached to them, or to defend or prove their point. The supervisor should also interrupt any hidden criticism of the supervisee's actions. The supervisor draws the participant back to discussing their thoughts on the situation itself.

Round 3, "Behaviour"

The last circle concluding the reflective stage is "Behaviour". Initially, this circle was conducted according to a similar process as previously: a group reflection with the answer to one question "What could have been done differently?" The supervisor would then move into a mini-session with the supervisee.

However, in the initial development of the Mirror model, when the process moved directly to the participants, their discussion of this question often sounded like criticism of the coach's actions, which threatened the psychological safety of the supervisee. In our updated version of the model (Rybina O., 2016), unlike previous rounds the supervisee is therefore the first to answer this question.

• What do you want and what can you do differently?

Only after his/her own answer does the supervisor turn to each member of the group: "What conclusions do you make for yourself? What have you learned? How do you implement these conclusions in your coaching practice?"

The clearer picture the supervisee can formulate for him- or herself in the process of supervision and collective brainstorming, the less emotional heat will remain in the memories of the case itself and the anxiety, worry or fear when thinking about its possible repetition. Negative emotions may even be replaced by pleasant anticipation of a similar experience for which the supervisee is now ready. Simonov calls this "the expectation of pleasure".

Final stage

In this case study, the supervisee concludes by noticing: "When my client answers 'I don't know', something happens to me, and I go into consulting mode. I am happy with myself in the session – the task is solved, but afterwards it I think about it all the time. It has a hold on me and doesn't let me go and I feel bad".

Results and conclusions shared by the group included:

- It is important to be aware of the need behind your actions.
- A need can influence my behaviour without my conscious knowledge. The better I understand myself, the easier I will be able to understand my clients.
- What I am like in a session does not depend only on my professional skills.
- I have had an experience of what can happen to a client when they are less important than the coach's own wishes. This is an important experience.
- My feelings during the session can help me to realise in time whose side I am on.

Partnership

It should be noted that in the original version, we strictly followed the given algorithm: three circles, in which group reflection alternates with mini-sessions for the supervisee. As experience has shown, after each mini-session, it is important to clarify the readiness and necessity to move to the next round with the supervisee. As in the previous example, after the first round and the first mini-session the supervisee may offer to complete the process. Such a decision can be influenced by the desire for deeper exploration in an individual setting or by the feeling of completeness of the process and having found an answer to the previously pressing question(s).

Beginner supervisors may make several mistakes when using the Mirror model (Rybina O., 2016). For example, they may be embarrassed to interrupt a speaker who is obviously masking criticism or advice as feelings or thoughts. It is important to keep in mind that bringing each participant back to the concept of supervision and its non-judgmental approach always has a positive impact on the whole group. In addition to a sense of safety and security, supervision participants learn how to bring their clients back into the coaching session and not replace the coaching session with counselling.

The supervisor, holding the values of the group, the structure and the process, also becomes a "mirror" for the participants, as they do for each other (both group and supervisees).

Occasionally supervision work involves feelings that provoke participants to negative manifestations, which may not only be perceived as a security breach, but also generally affect the mood in the group and the supervisor's sense of self. In relation to such situations, the supervisor can honestly and boldly share his/her feelings about what happened, demonstrating that any thoughts and feelings in the moment are important and will be accepted.

The future

Another way of working with the group using the Mirror model invites the use of drawings. At the same time, the structure of the model remains the same. We have conducted the first pilot groups to test this variation to the model and to the work.

Now we are at the stage of generalising the experience gained and commenting on its implementation in practice.

Conclusions

Practice shows that the use of the Mirror model in group and individual formats allows participants to be more attentive to the processes taking place within their coaching practice, in time identifying situations where the coach "gets stuck" in their thoughts and feelings. The suggested format of interaction helps each participant to achieve their desired outcomes and at the same time to contribute to the process of learning within the group.

Acknowledgements

The Editor and Author wish to thank Irina Judge for the introduction.

References

Alexandrov, A. A., Isurina, G. L., Karvasarsky, B. D., et al. (1990). *Modern Forms of Training and Improvement of Doctors in the Field of Psychotherapy.* Leningrad: Leningrad Publishing House.

Balint, M. (1955). The Doctor, His Patient, and the Illness. *The Lancet,* 265(6866). https://doi.org/10.1016/S0140-6736(55)91061-8.

Balint, E., & Balint, M., (1955). Dynamics of Training in Groups for Psychotherapy. *British Journal of Medical Psychology,* 28(2–3), 135–143.

Barash, B. (1992). *Methodological Methods of Improvement in the Field of Psychotherapy.* St. Petersburg: PNI V. M. Bekhterev.

Karvasarsky, B. D. (2000). *Encyclopedia of Psychotherapy* (pp. 51–53). St. Petersburg: Ed. Piter.

Lazarus, R. S., Speisman, J. C., & Mordkoff, A. M. (1963). The Relationship Between Autonomic Indicators of Psychological Stress: Heart Rate and Skin Conductance. *Psychosomatic Medicine,* 25, 19–30. https://doi.org/10.1097/00006842-196301000-00004.

Rybina, O. (2016). Professional Supervisor Course. https://5prism.ru/supervisor/.

Simonov, P. V. (1997). Brain Mechanisms of Emotions. *Neuroscience Behavioral Physiology,* 27, 405–413. https://doi.org/10.1007/BF02462942.

Chapter 11

Linking learning

A peer supervision chain

Barb Udale and Brenda Routt

Introduction

In this chapter we share with you our learnings and insights from setting up and running a Peer Supervision Chain. At the time of writing, this has been an 18-month journey that has changed and morphed as we have progressed. We hope that by sharing our experiences we may help other peer groups establish their own chains, continuing the development of coach supervision skills within our professional community.

We are two experienced coaches who met during our coach supervision training. We come from different parts of the world – Barb from Australia via New Zealand and Brenda from Texas in the US. This instantly brought diversity in backgrounds, coach training methodologies and life perspectives to our collaboration. These differences have ensured that our work together has always been stimulating, revealing and fun.

Launching and supporting a Peer Supervision Chain, like any initiative involving humans, has been a process of continued learning, frustration and joy. There have been many benefits for the individual, the dyads who work together, the group as a whole and the community of coach supervisors that we have created.

So, what is a peer supervision chain?

A Peer Supervision Chain is a group of (in this case) coach supervisors, who enter into an agreement to supervise, and be supervised by each other, on a rotational basis. During rotations, individuals provide supervision to a colleague and receive supervision from another colleague. After a specified number of sessions, the members rotate into new pairings.

One of the main benefits of working as a chain is that each Chain member is both Supervisee and Supervisor. Supervisees experience a variety of different supervisors and, therefore, different supervision styles. Supervisors are presented with a variety of cases and learning edges with which to practise.

DOI: 10.4324/9781003143451-12

The benefits of a peer supervision chain

We believe that, as coach supervisors, we need to be both well-resourced and well-practised. The Peer Supervision Chain has provided our group with invaluable opportunities to develop our supervision skills and to practise on an ongoing basis.

During our research for this chapter, we found that most of the literature available was about Peer Supervision and Group Supervision but little focused on Peer Chains. Our experience, and the experience of our group, demonstrates that this form of Peer Supervision is invaluable in building supervision confidence and has many benefits not necessarily available in other forms of supervision. For example:

- The rich experience of working with a variety of supervisors, each bringing their individual personalities and techniques, gave members the opportunity to develop their own Supervision "style" by exploring different ways of working.
- Chain members had the opportunity to practise and explore different supervision techniques in a "safe" environment. Members felt that the support that they gained from each other gave them the freedom to experiment with different techniques before using them with clients.
- The group process allows for continued learning through discussion, sharing and experimenting.

How our peer supervision chain started

Our Peer Supervision Chain began during the final in-person Coach Supervisor Certification module.[1] The idea of forming a Peer Supervision Chain was introduced by one of the cohort members who had read about the concept in Turner and Palmer's *The Heart of Coaching Supervision* (2019). Most of our class of 13 had no idea what that meant yet; all but one eagerly said, "I want in!" Those who signed up reside in a variety of locations in four different countries.

Using the suggestions in *The Heart of Coaching Supervision* as a guide, and the earlier work (Gilbert et al., 2015) as a resource, our Chain was formed with the desire to practise and hone our new-found Supervision skills and to ensure that our "community" remained in contact.

Our organising call, held about a month after graduation, focussed on the mechanics of setting up the Chain – structure, length of rotation, contracting and scheduling. The group decided to opt for a three-month initial rotation, as we believed this would allow the group to settle in, and then to revisit the effectiveness at the next chain learning call.

It was decided that the role of facilitator and administrator would rotate throughout the group, starting with the member (Barb) who proposed the Chain. This role included allocation of the dyads and the co-ordination and facilitation of the "end of rotation" chain learning call. Scheduling of the supervision sessions was left with each of the dyads.

Author Reflection
I was keen to get the Chain up and running as I saw it as a great way to ensure that my learning continued. I believed that having a network of supervisors would be vital to ensuring that I did not feel isolated as I developed my supervision practice. – Barb

At the end of the first three-month rotation, the group would complete a survey. This would assist us in making adjustments and changes to the process, as well as gathering feedback and ideas on how to improve the process and the overall experience.

Our pilot contract

The group discussed what needed to be in the contract to ensure clarity around the purpose of the Peer Supervision Chain and the roles of both the supervisor and the supervisee.

The pilot contract addressed how we would operate as a group and covered:

- Duration of rotation
- Length of calls
- Commitment to honouring the time requirements over the three-month period, barring untoward circumstances
- Participation in a designated evaluation chain learning call to:
  o Discuss lessons learned
  o Share experiences and techniques
  o Determine adjustments needed to the operations of the group

Evaluation of pilot

On completion of the first three-month rotation a survey obtained feedback from group members on the mechanics of the Chain. The aim was to use the responses as discussion topics at our next group check-in call and then adjust processes as needed.

The first seven questions required both a ranking (Strongly Agree, Agree, Somewhat Agree, Disagree, Strongly Disagree) along with a comment section. The last three questions were posed as open-ended.

Learnings from the feedback

The feedback gathered from the Chain members highlighted a number of areas where adjustments were needed and enabled a more robust discussion during the group check-in call.

Pilot Peer Supervision Chain Evaluation

1   The three-month cycle provided enough opportunity to meet my super-vision needs.
2   I found it acceptable to manage six sessions in the three-month timeframe.
3   Three sessions provided enough opportunity to support my growth as a coach.
4   Three sessions provided enough opportunity to support my growth as a supervisor.
5   Having a de-brief check-in meeting for the whole group at the end of each cycle is important/useful.
6   I want to continue to participate in the next cycle.
7   I am willing to take an admin/coordinator role for the next cycle.
8   What did you value most about this experience?
9   What, if anything, didn't work?
10 What is your suggestion to make it an even richer experience?

- Members strongly agreed that the Chain was a valuable way of continuing their learning and development. Comments included:
  "The Chain was a great opportunity to take my newly certified supervision diploma for a test drive."
  "Regardless of the role, I learn and grow."
  "Opportunity to keep the momentum and practices. It drives me to keep learning."
  "The opportunity to keep skills up, practice and stay connected to my colleagues."

- A majority of members stated that the connection and flow might be better achieved through a four-month rotation.
- On the question of the importance of the group check-in call, all of the respondents said that they either "Strongly Agreed" or "Agreed" to scheduling an end-of-rotation call. As one person said:
  "It is good to reflect on the experience as a group."
- All individuals described gaining value from the process, even though only two participants said that they would be willing to pick up the role of administrator at a later time. Most cited business obligations as the reason for not volunteering.

Changes after the first rotation

Following the survey results and the group discussion, several changes were implemented. These included:

Authors' Reflections
We focussed too strongly in the beginning on the mechanics of the Chain and missed a valuable opportunity to really capture our individual and group learnings. – Barb

Members did not have a shared understanding of the administrative function. We did not build space for the social aspect of re-connecting after completing rigorous certification requirements. – Brenda

- Moving to a four-month rotation
- Allowing members to rotate out of the Chain at the beginning of a cycle, and then rejoin for a later cycle
- Administrative responsibility staying with the member, Barb, who had managed the process for the first round
- Instituting monthly calls for those interested in sharing articles, books, conferences, association activities and techniques

Second, third and fourth cycles

As the Chain progressed through the subsequent cycles, various challenges and issues arose. Members of the Chain were still gaining value from the process and wanted the Chain to continue. However, from an administrative perspective, challenges started to bubble to the surface. The Chain had decided that individuals could opt in and out at the beginning of each cycle to allow for work and external pressures. This meant that allocating the dyads became a complicated and laborious process, as members expected to work with others that they had not worked with previously. Ideally, a new rotation would be created by each person moving one place in the Chain, therefore supervising, and being supervised by, someone new. By allowing people to opt out of a rotation the chain was "broken," and the process became a nightmare!

The other main frustration was that no-one stepped up to take the administration role, as agreed at the start of the Chain. Many said that they highly valued the experience that the Chain offered them; however at "this time" they did not have the capacity to assist. This meant that the role continued with the original administrator.

Author Reflection
At this point I was feeling a range of emotions about the Chain. I truly valued the experience of being a member of the Chain; however, I was struggling to manage the process on my own. Allocating the dyads was becoming a nightmare, as people wanted to work with those they hadn't worked with before. This, of course, was understandable but totally impractical. I have to admit

> *that I wasn't very forthcoming in sharing my frustration as I was keen for the Chain to continue, and I felt that if I made the whole thing sound hard nobody would pick up the administration role. Barb*

It wasn't until the end of the third cycle that a second member picked up the role of allocating dyads – enter Brenda. All of a sudden, the frustration of managing the Chain was a shared responsibility. This led to robust conversations between the two of us about how to improve the current process and create a Chain that better served all of its members.

Then the opportunity of writing this chapter and sharing our experiences catapulted us into serious reflection, research and conversation. We decided that we needed to increase our understanding and knowledge about how to ensure that our Peer Supervision Chain was delivering a true value exchange and was rigorous in its process.

To accomplish this, we decided to:

- Research all we could on the topic of Peer Groups and Chains,
- Consult with more experienced practitioners and
- Consult with our Chain members to gain a fuller understanding of what was working and what was not.

The second group survey

As a way of gathering information for this chapter, we decided to conduct another survey with our members in order to gain further feedback, understand the current state of the Chain and identify what changes might be needed.

Second Group Survey

- What learnings and insights have you gained from being a member of this chain as a supervisor?
- What learnings and insights have you gained from being a member of this chain as a supervisee?
- What were the contributing factors when the supervision session went well?
- When the supervision session was not as valuable, what was present? Or not present?
- What has peer supervision allowed you to do that was possibly not present in other forms of supervision?
- What needs to happen in the future for the chain to continue to provide benefits for you?

In relation to our Group Check-in Call

- What benefits did you get from the conversations?
- How could we as a group capitalise on our individual learnings?

Highlights from the survey

From the results of the survey, we were able to gain a better understanding of what was happening within the dyads. A summary of our learnings in relation to our group follows, along with the possible impact and our thoughts on how we might manage them in the future.

Contracting

Contracting surfaced regularly as an indicator of either supervision going well or as a reason why the supervision sessions may have fallen short of expectations. Poor or inadequate contracting led to several issues relating to unclear expectations. This resulted in some supervisees not feeling they gained value from the session. We believe that our group can take a variety of actions to strengthen our contracting. They include:

- Regularly discussing as a group, the contents of the Chain contract to promote clarity, increase commitment and identify issues and necessary revisions;
- Clarifying that dyad assignments with a 'new' supervisor cannot always be guaranteed. Pairs may be repeated;
- Ensuring that our Chain contract is a "living" contract and reflects the Chain's needs and expectations and
- Producing a dyad contract checklist to remind members of the importance of an agreement between partners. This will include such elements as the objectives and aspirations of our supervision together, how we will work together, how we will structure our time together and how we will manage feedback.

Collusion

Because of the many strong relationships that were formed as a result of the intensity of completing the diploma course together, some members found it hard to hold themselves and/or their partner accountable. This showed up in myriad ways, such as spending the time "catching up" or in general conversation. As one member noted:

> We did not respect the purpose of our time together, and instead had a "friendly conversation" that was NOT supervision, and we did not acknowledge that and/or make time for a separate supervision chain conversation.

We believe possible collusion can be minimised by:

- Ensuring clarity around both the Chain and dyad contracts
- Declaring a shared and communicated commitment to valuing the time together
- Agreeing on a feedback process where members are entitled to call each other out on behaviours which are not serving them

Lack of a feedback process

It became obvious that the group needed to have an agreed-upon feedback process. In several instances, issues between dyads impacted the supervision both given and received. These included people not being "present" or being distracted, supervisors coaching rather than supervising and, in some instances, individuals not communicating with their dyad partner.

We assumed that people would manage these situations in the same way they would manage paying clients; however, because of the existing relationships, this did not always happen.

One way to manage this is to develop some clarity around how we give feedback, and we have decided that we will:

- Include it as a discussion topic in our next Group Check-in Call
- Develop a group expectation on how feedback is to be handled
- Encourage dyads to include a feedback segment in their time together

Size of the Chain

It was suggested that the Chain would benefit from increasing its size, thereby allowing for more diversity of experience and thinking. This topic emerged during the Group Check-in Call and different scenarios were discussed. Questions arose for us to consider as a group. How large should the Chain be? Is there a perfect balance between current and new members? What are the criteria for introducing new members? How do we select new members?

There was some concern that by adding new members we may lose some of our strong sense of community; however, we considered that introducing new members might expand our learning through working with different people as well as ensuring that we do not become too insular.

The group decided that we would look to expand the number of members in the Chain. As part of that process one member volunteered to prepare a document outlining the process of selecting and on-boarding new members.

As we move into our fifth cycle incorporating the feedback from our Chain, our research and information gleaned from the many conversations that we have had in preparation for writing this chapter, we offer these observations and insights in the form of Key Learnings.

Key learnings we are taking forward

There was much that we learned over the 18-month life of our Peer Supervision Chain. Our experience through trial and error and finding our own Chain's path was supplemented by many individual and group discussions, as well as rich conversations with others outside of our Chain.

About dyad success

Each dyad was responsible for scheduling their sessions, and typically the supervisor initiated the booking and invitation. Chain members generally found that booking all sessions at the commencement of each cycle worked best, rather than session by session.

Comments from our second survey highlighted a variety of areas impacting the success of individual dyads, including:

- Clear contracting within the dyad

  "Clear contracting makes a substantial difference. In a supervision chain with an existing relationship, it's important not to skip the initial conversation about the 'engagement.'"

  "A clear agreement of the contract between us. One of my pairings was with a supervisor who was expert at providing clarity around the contract for each session."

  "My supervisor treated our sessions as I expect she treats her paying clients – totally professional."

- Having a feedback mechanism within the dyad

  "Honesty about what's working and what isn't – a safe space to express it."

  "Importance of asking for and receiving feedback, in both roles as supervisor and supervisee."

- A willingness to experiment

  "Be willing/open to experiment with different approaches."

  "This has been a place for me to experiment and hone my own voice as a supervisor."

- Presence and commitment

  "The need for both to be fully present or unguarded."

  "I think we were both grounded and intentional about being present. It truly felt like a walk in the garden".

  "To respect the purpose of our time together" and if it was just a "friendly conversation" that was NOT supervision, acknowledge that and/or make time for a supervision session.

About contracting

Over the 18-month life of our Chain, we have continued to understand the importance of a co-created, rigorous, clear and concise Chain contract signed and archived by all group members. This contract needs to be kept alive and flexible, with the ability to adapt and change to meet the needs of the Chain.

After the first year, the Chain members decided that the Chain contract needed to be revised. Members had noticed that we needed to be clearer about the "Why" of the Chain. The updated Chain contract was revised accordingly:

> *The intent of this Coaching Supervision Chain is to provide a mechanism to stay connected, practice supervision skills, grow professional competence, avail ourselves of supervision, and to share our learnings and growth with the group.*

It had also been decided by the group that attendance at the quarterly Group Check-in Call was an integral part of the learning process; therefore the Chain contract needed to reflect this important point:

> *A chain learning call is scheduled to share learnings, to gather feedback, learn best practices from the members, determine any revisions to the process that may be needed and to recontract for the next round. It is the expectation of the chain that this call is attended by all Chain members. If a member cannot attend the above call then it is a requirement that they complete a short reflection of their learnings and this is forwarded to the Meeting convener.*

About group learning and reflection

The Group Check-in Call is an opportunity for members to learn, share reflections and learning edges and explore techniques and topics which may be of use in our continued development. It allows us to access the wide range of expertise, knowledge and experience that exists within the Chain.

We soon realised that it was these calls that defined us a group, and that the opportunity to share and grow together as a learning community was vital to our sense of "gaining value" from the group experience.

About leadership

Authors' Reflections

Even though I took on the unofficial leadership role from the beginning, I was convinced that the group should share the leadership. When no-one stepped up to take the baton, I continued out of fear that the Chain would collapse. – Barb

> *Evolving into a leadership role occurred due to a strong need for structure and support to keep the group going. That drive, coupled with the desire to help Barb, compelled me to volunteer more time. – Brenda*

The learnings about leadership fell into two distinct areas: the relationship between leadership and the ultimate success of the Peer Supervision Chain and the significant learnings that we as the "unofficial leaders" experienced.

At the commencement of the Chain, we decided that the leadership would be shared and rotated through the group. However, we learned through our experience that someone needed to proactively step into the leadership role. In the attempt to make the group a democracy and work with consensus, we lost momentum, frustration levels of those informally leading increased, and this put the group at risk of imploding and therefore ceasing to exist.

We quickly learned that groups need leadership to thrive and grow, much like any professional group. In our attempt to be democratic, we downplayed this need. "Leaderless groups do not work" was a comment by a colleague who was a member of leaderless peer supervision group which struggled to provide ongoing value to their members, the impact being described as feeling a "bit like a rudderless boat."

Both authors are very aware that strong leadership is needed for groups to be successful; however, both of us are also aware of our tendency to jump in and take control. We learned that accepting leadership in the beginning was an important factor in the stability of the Chain. We now feel that once the systems and processes are better established it will be easier to rotate the leadership around the group.

> *Author Reflection*
> *I notice a pattern in myself that might be described as an equilateral triangle. One corner is the headiness of helping (stemming from a background in nursing). The second is thinking I have a great idea for organising and surely others want it. And finally, Ego whispers, "No one else is doing it so I guess I will." I suspect that the latter comes from experience gained in other leadership roles, but is challenging because the chain is a group of equals. – Brenda*

About administration

We soon learned that allowing members to opt in and out of rotations created a substantial amount of work. Rotating the pairs became a complex task and group members believed they would always be paired with someone "new" on each rotation. Looking back, this was an unnecessary complication and could have been mitigated had we anticipated the amount of time it required to manage.

Allowing participants to opt in and out of the Chain also meant that there was a lack of consistency in attendance at the group check-in calls. This impacted the whole group's learning by reducing the shared insights and disrupting the sense of community.

Our planned rotation of the administrative role was unlikely to happen, at least initially, as members generally declined stepping up, although some indicated that they would be happy to help later.

> *Author Reflection*
>
> *Oh, how easy is it to be caught out by the assumptions that we make. I thought that people would know and understand the challenges in creating the pairings at the start of each rotation.*
>
> *There was also the assumption that members would view their commitment to the Chain in the same way as they do with their clients and that they would be responsive to emails, complete tasks and attend meetings. Looking back, we could have been clearer about these expectations as well as maintaining the boundaries around them. – Barb*

Where we are now

Our Chain is now into its second year of operation, and we are still adapting and changing the way we work together as a group. As current leaders of the group, we decided to explore in more depth what our group members gained from the experience and what they would like to see change. We also looked at how other groups operated and participated in many conversations around the broader topic of peer, group and coach supervision development.

In discussing the value of continuing the group, it was decided that we needed to be clear about what it meant to us all to be part of this Peer Supervision Chain and what our expectations were of each other. This clarity would also assist us when considering new members for the group. It was agreed that the Chain is open to certified coach supervisors who accept and honour the value exchange of peer supervision and commit to providing the same level of professionalism and service to each other as they provide to individual and corporate clients.

As we moved forward with more experience and knowledge a series of changes were presented to the group for discussion and agreement. These included adaptions to the following:

Size and composition of the group

- Expand membership to a maximum of 20
- Develop a selection and on-boarding process for new members
- Ensure all Supervisors are certified

Membership

Chain members need to:

- Commit to the one-year cycle
- Provide feedback to Supervisors to enhance their learning and practice
- Attend the chain learning calls, to be held on completion of each rotation
- Treat the Chain as they would any other professional relationship

Author Reflection
Decisions around greater structure has a cost in that not all Chain members could commit to one year. Therefore, a couple of participants have chosen not to participate in the next round. At the same time, more than 12 other supervisors outside of our cohort have expressed interest in joining our Chain. It is exciting to help others see the value of our group and to expand our community. – Brenda

Contracting

The Chain Contract is a living document that keeps abreast of needs and issues arising in the emergent field of the group. It is signed by all members of the group and includes expectations of supervisors and supervisees, commitment to quality, attending group sessions, and protocol around cancelling/rescheduling sessions.

Individual dyad contracts are the second types of contracts required. The responsibility for the quality of the relationship belongs with each dyad. Each pair discusses and agrees on a contract for their work together at the beginning of each new cycle and at the beginning of each session.

Leadership

To formalise the leadership role for the group, we determined that this role would best be served by two people sharing the role for the coming year. The roles would ensure that:

- The Chain contract is updated and signed by all group members.
- Any issues are firstly addressed within the dyad; if unresolved, they are to be escalated to one of the leaders in confidence, where a strategy will be devised in consultation to resolve them.
- Dyad rotations are made and documented.
- Quarterly group check-in calls are scheduled, the agenda is compiled and meetings are facilitated.

Authors' Reflections

Although we had no initial plan to become leaders, the need for leadership emerged gradually. Barb and I could see administrative organisation was lacking. For me, I wondered if we were the only ones noticing. Yet, the more we evolved into formalised leadership roles, the easier it became to pose questions, make suggestions and influence change. We experienced a shift when our roles were sanctioned. As a co-leader, it often feels like a polarity between being definitive on what the contract requires in terms of behaviours and participation versus conveying to a peer that compliance with the contract is an issue. Formalization of the leadership roles makes it palatable. Having co-leaders provides shared responsibility. – Brenda

One thing that stood out for me at this point was that Brenda and I needed to continue as co-leaders of the Chain for the coming year. I think that at this point many Chain members saw, for the first time, how much effort was being put into keeping the Chain viable. Members expressed their appreciation, and I noticed a definite "leaning in" by a number of members with offers of assistance. – Barb

Group reflection and learning

Our group check-in calls aim to:

- Continue to build the community that has been created
- Provide a space for continued reflection and learning
- Use the individual skills and knowledge of members to provide professional development for all
- Provide a practice space for experimentation with new techniques
- Share updates on projects
- Support group members in using their learning and exploring ways of sharing
- Address any concerns
- Improve the processes related to the Chain

To summarise our experience, and to assist others in setting up a Peer Supervision Chain, here are some considerations that we think might be useful.

Useful Considerations in Setting Up a Peer Supervision Chain

- Research and explore what other groups have done (see reference list).
- Spend time having group conversations about all aspects of the group. The who, the why and the how!! Do not rush this period., It is essential

and keeps the channels open for learning in the moment. Some discussion points include:

o   What is the purpose of the Chain?
o   Who can be a member – what credentials are required?
o   What are the expectations of both supervisors and supervisees? Be clear on how group members show up to supervision.
o   How is the chain to run – length of rotations, leadership?
o   What structures need to be established to ensure the smooth running of the chain?
o   What needs to be in the contract?
o   How to best capture group learnings and how to add value to these learnings?
o   What might get in the way of the group being an ongoing success and one that continues to add real value to its members?
o   How will any issues be managed – for example, non-attendance at group meetings, problems within a dyad?

• Consider sharing the leadership by having co-leaders.
• Create a reflection space for the co-leaders.
• Schedule regular reviews by surveying the Chain and adapting processes to meet the needs of the members.

What's happening as we write

Writing this chapter over the past six months has been much like sailing. Tacking, letting out sails to catch the wind, at times sitting in the doldrums, only to get a gust that propels us forward. It seems the longer we write, the more emerges in the field. We formalised a short presentation to share with supervisors-in-training to stimulate interest. That solidified into 11 newly minted supervisors committing to join our Peer Supervision Chain, doubling the size of the group.

Questions we are asking ourselves

• Are we adding to our existing group, or is this a new group?
• How do we honour the original group members as we move into a new group?
• How do we "on-board" our new members?
• How do we continue to build a strong learning community?
• How do we manage our Group Calls as we expand across more time zones?
• What additional structures do we need to put in place to keep abreast of the increased numbers?

- How do we hold members accountable to the agreed contract, meeting attendance?
- How do we prepare to hand over the leadership role?

Final reflections from the authors

Ultimately, we support and promote the concept of Peer Supervision Chains. We, and our group, have found it a valuable experience that has enabled us all to practise our supervision skills and gain feedback that has generated deeper learning and reflection.

For me, the writing of this chapter has not only contributed to developing our Peer Supervision Chain into a more robust and rigorous group, but it has also provided me with the opportunity yet again to learn something about myself and the extraordinary field in which we all work. We have had some marvellous conversations between ourselves as we have grappled with what we wanted to share. Our conversations with colleagues, group members and those wise sages within our professional community have deepened my understanding as well as left me with many questions about things that I still don't know. So the reflection continues. – Barb Udale

It is one thing to spend years honing coaching skills through practise and higher and further education. Supervision takes all that work and skill development and adds another layer of support for growth. Having joined a supervision group the minute I received my coaching credentials, and continued to this day, the value to my growth, even as an experienced coach, is immeasurable. My decision to become a certified supervisor was stimulated by my desire to continue to develop my skills and to do my part in raising the bar for our profession. Supervision offers incredible support and safety to coaches for exploration and growth. Supervisors need the same haven. What better place to practise and learn than with a group of peers? Describing the mechanics and pitfalls for this chapter required much introspection and discussion. More importantly, was selecting the words to convey the importance of finding a group of peers to join for the joy of learning, the messiness of practice and the heart of collegiality. Supervision is a must to keep the bar high in our profession, regardless of the mode chosen. – Brenda Routt

Acknowledgements

The authors would like to thank all the members of the Peer Supervision Chain.

The authors would also like to acknowledge the guidance and support of Miriam Orriss and Jo Birch.

Note

1 Coaching Supervision Academy, North America, 2019.

References

Gilbert, S., Lucas, M., & Turner, E. (2015, January–February). Chain Reaction. *Coaching at Work*, 10, 44–49.

Matile, L., Gilbert, S., & Turner, E. (2019). Chapter 9 Resourcing Through a Peer Supervision Chain. In E. Turner & S. Palmer (Eds.), *The Heart of Coaching Supervision* (pp. 169–190). Oxon: Routledge.

Chapter 12

Tastes of supervision

Jeannette Marshall

Introduction

This chapter focuses on group supervision taster sessions and gives detailed information about how these may be set up, administered and delivered in a way that promotes best practice and engenders a desire to continue to engage in regular and ongoing coaching supervision.

Taster sessions provide a useful vehicle for professional bodies encouraging members to establish a reflective practice, for coach training schools wishing to introduce an established model into their programmes and for individual supervisors wanting to promote their services to a wider audience.

Group supervision experiences have been offered as a member benefit of the Association for Coaching for more than 10 years with the intention of promoting exemplary practice in coaching. My experience of delivering these supervision sessions has informed this chapter.

This chapter also explores the nature of coaching supervision and the benefits it brings. I explain how to introduce coaches to supervision and give guidance on how to structure a group supervision taster session.

Taster sessions enable coaches who have not yet experienced supervision to do so in a safe and structured group environment, mixing with peers from differing contexts and work settings, training, levels of experience and capability – bringing a richness to the overall discussions.

For the organiser, focusing specifically on what needs to be done, using a tried-and-tested approach means they can proceed with confidence, knowing that the resulting experience is likely to bring great benefit to the participants.

Group supervision, in this context, needs to be delivered by a trained, experienced coaching supervisor. They need to be capable of building rapport quickly, providing a robust group contract and managing the process for a group of individuals whose developmental needs and level of coaching experience are unknown – to both the supervisor and the other participants. The ability to think on their feet, manage the complexities of the diverse individuals and keep the whole process moving towards a productive outcome is key. Knowing how and when to intervene in the discussions to maximise the learning opportunities without preventing ongoing dialogue is a skill that cannot be underestimated in this context!

DOI: 10.4324/978100314345-13

Managing a multitude of emergent topics, being able to put participants at ease, explaining the process, keeping to time and ensuring that the group remain engaged is the foundation of a successful group supervision taster intervention. Doing all of this while creating a safe environment where transparency and openness can emerge is essential and is not for the faint-hearted.

Above all, the supervisors must be able to manage themselves, the group dynamics and be able to keep calm under pressure!

Creating a structure, giving details of what will happen and clearly describing how the process will work will do much to alleviate any anxiety that participants may be experiencing as they venture into the unknown. Ensuring that the role of a coaching supervisor is explained and understood increases the likelihood of a successful outcome and manages participants' expectations of the intervention.

The nature of coaching supervision

It can be helpful for participants to understand the nature of coaching supervision ahead of the session. Professional coaching membership bodies offer the following definitions:

The AC (2020) defines coaching supervision as *"a formal and protected time for facilitating a Coach's in-depth reflection on their practice with an experienced Coaching Supervisor. Supervision offers a confidential framework within a collaborative working relationship in which the practice, tasks, process and challenges of the coaching work can be explored. The primary aim of supervision is to enable the coach to gain in ethical competency, confidence, and creativity so as to ensure best possible service to the coaching client, both coachees and coaching sponsors. Supervision is not a 'policing' role, but rather a trusting and collegial professional relationship"*.[1]

The EMCC (2020) defines supervision as *"the interaction that occurs when a mentor or coach brings their coaching or mentoring work experiences to a Supervisor in order to be supported and to engage in reflective dialogue and collaborative learning for the development and benefit of the Mentor or Coach, their clients and their organisations"*.[2]

The ICF states that *"Coaching supervision offers coaches an opportunity to access continuous professional development through reflection and dialogue in a safe, supportive and confidential space. If we look closer at the word itself:* super-vision *meaning* over-sight, *the practice of supervision is for the Coach and their Supervisor to reflect together and have over-sight of the Coach's practice in service of them being the very best Coach they can be"*.[3]

The AOCS (2020) describes supervision *"on a 121 or group basis is the formal opportunity for coaches working with clients to share, in confidence, their case load activity to gain insight, support and direction for themselves and thereby enabling them to better work in the service of their clients"*.[4]

Although we see some difference in these definitions and statements, it can be concluded that Professional bodies acknowledge and appreciate that supervision is an activity which is "in service of" the client, and other stakeholders invested in the coaching intervention. In addition, there is a need for supervisors to engage in regular supervision and to undertake relevant Continuous Professional Development (CPD) activities.

By understanding the nature of coaching supervision, participants begin to understand the nature of the supervision contract, appreciate the need for confidentiality and participate more fully in the experience.

Why engage in supervision?

Many coach training schools do not yet include supervision as part of the curriculum; therefore, many newly qualified coaches are not well informed about coaching supervision and are unaware of the benefits it can bring to themselves and to their coaching practice. The accreditation and credentialing processes of professional coaching membership bodies seek to influence a change in coaching practice, believing that reflective practice significantly enhances a coach's work, but it is likely to take time as the coaching field changes. CPD is a commitment in most ethical codes adopted by coaches and being in ongoing and consistent supervision can play a huge part in the coach's learning and development.

As those attending the group supervision taster sessions may be coaches in training or coaches new to supervision, it could be helpful to introduce the session, with some information about the benefits of supervision, or include this in the written group contract.

The professional coaching bodies continue to embrace supervision as part of the ongoing and continuous professional development of coaches, no matter what their level of experience. Developing an ongoing reflective practice, of which regular and consistent supervision is a part, gives the coach the opportunity to implement best practice and serve as a role model when working with clients. In this way, coaches can lead by example.

Supervision provides a safe and protected environment for coaches to spend time reflecting on their practice. This enables them to reflect in an honest and open way that not only supports their learning but informs their understanding of how to maintain and enhance their own well-being.

The purpose of supervision is not only to shine a light onto blind spots and areas for development, it is also a forum for identifying strengths and celebrating successes. Taking time to appreciate where a coach currently is on their professional journey can itself be an insightful experience. As with many other industries, coaches can be so busy working "in" their businesses that they neglect giving themselves time and space to work "on" their business. Engaging in supervision allows a coach to keep up-to-date with professional developments in coaching. It also provides a space in which to share issues that affect their coaching work. Time spent reflecting on what is happening for both the coach and their client before, during and after the coaching session, with an independent observer, can give invaluable insights into what is working well (and what isn't) and how the coach can incorporate these insights into their practice.

Identifying ethical issues that emerge when working with clients is often the focus of supervision. This is an area that can be revisited as the coach gains further experience of working with clients. It is sometimes only when discussing elements of the coaching intervention that ethical dilemmas manifest themselves and are brought to the fore.

Supervision offers a "third-person" perspective of feedback for learning. If the coachee is the first person, the coach is the second person, then supervisors offer a perspective from outside the coach/coachee relationship. This enables the coach to take time to explore their process and operating methodology more effectively. Exploring different interventions and models supports the coach to critically evaluate their own performance.

Introducing supervision to coaches

When coaching first emerged as a profession, it was often the case that this "new" intervention needed to be experienced to understand what it was and how it could benefit the clients. In much the same way, coaching supervision needs to be experienced first-hand so that coaches gain a deeper appreciation and understanding of the activity. Participating in a session, sharing experiences, and potentially gaining insights, demonstrates in a practical way the benefits that supervision can bring and is an excellent way to understand coaching supervision.

Being able to attend a group supervision taster session with other peers who have also yet to experience supervision means that each person starts from a place of "not knowing". In the hands of a skilled coaching supervisor, participants come to appreciate the breadth and depth that supervision encompasses and begin to understand its value.

Much can be done to demystify the process by explaining beforehand what will be expected of participants, the role of the supervisor in this context, the parameters of the session and what is in, and out, of scope.

The contracting process is an opportunity to describe what group supervision taster sessions will offer participants:

- Facilitation by an experienced coaching supervisor
- The opportunity to reflect on the work they are undertaking
- The benefit of learning from others' ideas, experiences, and perspectives
- An opportunity to re-examine their practice, to continue to develop their skills and self-awareness and to avoid being drawn into their clients' systems
- A way of exploring boundaries and ethical standards

The effect of client systems within supervision has been highlighted in a white paper by the Centre for Coaching in Organizations (2019):[5] "*The environments in which we work these days are complex, with many factors playing in a part in the emergence of change. We can think of an organisation as a complex system, with lots of moving parts, a network of multiple relationships, all shifting and evolving over time. Within the big organisational system exist sub-systems – teams and groups for example. Supervision helps coaches to look at the world through a systemic lens, starting with the dynamics existing within the group itself, and provides a 'safe' space for participants to start experimenting with interventions to shift the patterns of those group dynamics".*

It can be powerful for a coach (whether newly trained or experienced) to normalise their experiences of working with clients, and to understand that they are not alone in encountering the challenges and other features of their work. Coach confidence can be increased by the realisation that examples of client resistance, such as cancelling, not showing up to sessions or following through on actions, are also experienced by other coaches.

Taster sessions are often one hour in duration, with the time shared between participants. There may be a tendency to imagine this time is "short", yet the learning and insights gained can be profound. Something almost magical happens when the supervisor holds a safe space in a shared learning experience where confidentiality is assured. This relational intervention can be instrumental in building coach confidence around their approach when working with clients, enabling explorations of different ideas about how they will solve problems, and gaining a range of feedback from others about issues or concerns.

Essential "set up" process

Experience shows that group supervision taster sessions work best if they are delivered within a short time frame with a limited number of participants. For a one-hour session, four participants are the optimum number, which enables the supervisor to give time to each individual and the opportunity for everyone to speak. It is helpful for participants to have a clear, well-defined process to follow, which covers each stage.

To ensure the successful delivery of group supervision taster sessions, certain elements must be in place.

Format of the session

Generally, there are two formats through which to deliver taster sessions: Emergent or Themed sessions.

Emergent sessions

In these sessions, participants are asked to bring any topic they wish for discussion and to reflect upon certain questions before the session.

Useful questions are:

- *What aspects of your coaching practice would you like to discuss?* This could invite questions or concerns around their work with specific coachees, their coaching approach or the process they follow when working with clients.
- *What area of your professional development would most benefit from support?* This question brings the focus onto their own development as a coach. Issues are likely to be centred around, although not limited to, aspects of the Coaching Competency Framework (2020)[6] and the Code of Ethics (2020).[7]
- *In the wider context of coaching, what would you most benefit from discussing right now?* This could be any coaching-related issue, such as working within systems and organisations, managing the commercial side of coaching or any other concerns that the participant needs help in resolving.

Once the presenting coach has responded, the supervisor may wish to invite feedback from other participants. It can be useful at this stage to reiterate the rules of effective feedback before doing so – or even to send this information with the pre-session guidelines.

Guides for effective feedback may differ and commonly include:

- Being clear, specific, and concise with your communication
- Basing comments on information gained directly within the session
- Owning the feedback – saying "I noticed . . . ", I saw . . . " or "I heard . . . "
- Considering how the feedback would feel if you were to receive it

Themed sessions

When coaches have not yet experienced supervision, it can sometimes be difficult to know what can be brought to the session and what the "rules" are. This is understandable because, in my experience, individual supervisors have different methods and practices they favour based on their training, knowledge and understanding. Group supervision taster sessions based around a specific theme or topic have been growing in popularity. This format encourages participants to reflect upon one specific topic as a whole group and arguably offers more guidance on what participants might bring and allows for more focused discussion.

When setting up themed sessions, the topics are likely to be based around the Coaching Competency Framework (2020) or the Code of Ethics (2017) of the relevant professional coaching body or may include topics relating to the wider coaching agenda, such as diversity, spirituality or mental health.

By setting themed topics for group supervision taster sessions, participants can select the supervision session that resonates best with them. The added advantage is that the Supervisor has some idea of what might arise in the session, although of course there is no guarantee that there will be no surprises in store!

Supervisor requirements

The group supervision taster session supervisor must be an experienced practitioner, fully versed in the delivery and facilitation of group supervision sessions. It is expected that they will be members of a professional body, adhere to a code of ethics, are in supervision and may be accredited coaching supervisors. An understanding of the primary functions of supervision, plus underpinning theoretical knowledge, and practical experience of using different modalities will be invaluable in the successful implementation of this initiative.

Depending on circumstances, the supervisor must either:

*   Have access to a room where the supervisees can meet knowing that they will not be interrupted, nor overheard by others, as they share their issues
*   Or be comfortable using technology platforms that enable delivery of virtual supervision sessions

Maintaining confidentiality is crucial, so for participants to know that once the session is underway there will be no disturbances, or incidents to interrupt the flow, is important in putting them at ease so that they gain the most from their experience. This is especially important when considering running the session virtually as interruption by a family member, colleague or pet may create a disruption in flow and require management by the supervisor and group members.

Participant requirements

Participants are expected to arrive on time for the session, mindful that the time allocated for the session will be divided equally between all parties present.

Having an open mind, being curious and non-judgmental, and supportive to others in their approach will form part of the ground rules set by the supervisor at the beginning of the session. Participants ensuring that they are able to concentrate and contribute, respect others' views and allow each person time and space to share stories and challenges is all part of making this intervention successful.

Supervisee preparation includes the following:

*   Identifying an aspect of their coaching practice to explore
*   Thinking about what has gone well or what could have gone better
*   Determining if they have become stuck and would like the opportunity to explore further
*   Reflecting on their most recent coaching sessions

They may also bring questions about how to do the following:

*   Contract with clients
*   Articulate their coaching approach

- Meet the coaching competencies of their professional membership body
- Adhere to their professional membership body's code of ethics

They may even have questions around whether they need to invest in further training or development.

Sometimes the questions they bring will be more around commercial practices – fee setting, marketing, branding and so on, so it can be helpful if the supervisor confirms whether these elements are in, or out, of scope for the taster session. These parameters are usually determined by the preference of the individual supervisor.

Practical arrangements

To make sure that the session runs smoothly, it helps to give supervisees clear instructions to beforehand.

Send out an invitation at least two weeks ahead of the scheduled session along with information covering the following:

- Date, time, and duration
- Name and contact details of the supervisor
- Details of fees (if applicable) and invoicing process
- Cancellation policy
- Physical address or dial in details
- What preparation is required from the participants prior to the session
- What the process will be and what to expect
- Evaluation
- Next steps

Be clear about whether you will send reminders prior to the event, and how participants can contact you in the event they are unable to attend. Contracting with participants in this way sets the ground rules for the whole experience

Supervisee preparation

In addition, it may be useful to give the participants some guidelines of practice, such as the following:

- Keep an open mind
- Learn from the experience
- Consider other perspectives
- Notice their own reactions, emotions, and thoughts that arise during the session
- Be as open and honest as they can about their situation and circumstances
- Share any insights that they have gained during similar experiences
- Reflect upon alternative ideas and approaches

- Explore how other approaches may work
- Allow themselves to be challenged
- Implement changes to their coaching approach that are due to insights gained from the session

Giving clear guidance about what is expected of them, whether that be via email, a telephone conversation, or in the form of a set of frequently asked questions, or FAQ's, will help with the smooth running of the event and help ease any anxiety for participants.

Setting up the evaluation process

The evaluation of a successful group supervision taster session through a short questionnaire or survey will give vital feedback to the Supervisor hosting the session and enable the participants to further reflect on the benefits gained through their experience. A follow-up discussion about their learning and insights gained and how they will implement them is a useful way of signposting participants towards the next steps on their coaching journey.

It is important to consider the method of evaluation during the initial set up. Sometimes this is left to the end of the process; however, thinking this through early on will enable organisers to put the necessary documentation and instructions in place.

It could be beneficial to include requirement to complete an evaluation of the session as part of the initial contracting process. Sharing clear guidelines on how the participant may give feedback if they have a poor experience or if they have a complaint would also be worthwhile. Including details such as these is not only considered to be best practice, but also raises the professionalism of the service on offer.

Send out the evaluation requests as soon as possible after the session. Make sure that the questions asked will give useful information that can be fed back into the overall process to support continuous improvement.

Suggestions include:

- Would you recommend these sessions to others? What reason would you give?
- What did you hope to gain from the session – and did you gain it?
- What did you find most helpful about the session?
- What do you think you are most likely to do now regarding your future supervision arrangements?
- What other information or support do you need?

Structure of the group supervision taster session

Each group supervision taster session will have its own unique feel, style and pace evolving from the individuals attending and the issues explored. However, a pre-determined basic structure helps individuals focus on the insights and learning, rather than the process itself.

A typical approach could be:

Arriving and setting the scene

As with any intervention, this is a crucial step to help put everyone at ease so that they can gain the most from the experience. The supervisor should arrive earlier than participants to give themselves time to prepare.

From the beginning, the supervisor will begin to create an atmosphere of trust and openness. This can be done by welcoming the participants, introducing themselves, contracting and outlining the process.

Talking through how the session will evolve gives the participants time to settle, get into the right mindset and be fully present for the session. Being mindful that participants are often encountering supervision for the first time, it can be useful at this stage to reaffirm the purpose of the session and for the supervisor to contract accordingly.

For example:

"The purpose of this group supervision taster session is to enable you to experience group supervision, which will support your learning and development in your own coaching practice. Through participation in this session, you will be able to reflect upon the content and process of the coaching you deliver and gain alternative perspectives and feedback that will enhance your professional development.

This offers you the opportunity to develop and share understanding and skills that relate to your client work and connect with others engaged in this reflective process".

Contracting for the session

Some early contracting is established when the guidance and information is shared ahead of the session, however as the session begins further clarification can be helpful.

> *Be clear about your 'rules of engagement', mutual responsibilities and boundaries.*[8]

Because contracting for the session is imperative, it may help to devise a script to ensure that all key points are covered each time.

Example of opening script:

"Having signed up for this session, you will have received an outline of the running order and preparation guidelines. These are shared to encourage you to be pro-active and gain the most from this experience.

You have been asked to bring a topic to discuss and, in a moment, I will invite you to share your:

- Name
- Location

- Type of coaching you practice
- Current knowledge, understanding or experience of supervision
- Topic for discussion

I will take a note of what comes up under each topic, and I will come back to these points as we progress through the session. I aim to spend 10 minutes with each person's topic, as there are four in the group, and we have one hour together.

Depending on what surfaces, we may need to be flexible. I will take ownership for finishing on time, although I ask each of you to be mindful of time too. If there are recurring themes that would indicate a common interest in a specific topic, I will bring that into the forum too.

Please remember that we expect you to work in the spirit of confidentiality. Should a conflict of interest arise, please voice it so that we can agree how we want to handle it as a group. Regarding confidentiality, I would like to contract with you that what emerges in this session remains confidential within this group. And to let you know that, when I work with my own supervisor, I may review my work as a supervisor on this group supervision session – observing anonymity, of course. Are we all in agreement?"

It is also useful to contract for, and gain agreement about, whether the participants' email addresses will be circulated to the group and to do this at the beginning of the session.

Beginning the session

The supervisor will agree a running order with the group.

People may have a preference to go first or last or somewhere in the middle. If you are running the session virtually, it is sometimes helpful to name the participants in the order they appear on the screen, thus removing the hesitation to "volunteer" to go first. It is useful to remind participants that everyone will get an opportunity to discuss their issue.

Often, the topics brought to the session show a similarity when they are first stated, or it could be that themes arise among the topics that suggest a natural order for the session.

Once the order is established, the presenting coach is encouraged to give more details about their issue and begin their exploration. At an appropriate point, the supervisor will ask them what help they would like from the group. The supervisor's role is then to provide facilitation, allowing other attendees to contribute naturally to the discussion. The skill of the supervisor is in enabling everyone to have a fair share of the allocated time, both to share their own topic and to contribute towards supporting others in the group.

Taster sessions often follow a straightforward format. Mutually establishing the ground rules ensures that participants are both engaged with and part of the process.

Questions such as the following enable participants to determine if they would like to be asked further questions, to gain ideas of how to move the situation forward or to share experiences:

- How would you like the group to be for you?
- What would be most helpful for you?
- How will you know you have received the support you need?

Knowing the participants' desired outcome gives the supervisor the opportunity to shape the session to meet their diverse needs.

Depending on the content and the time still available, the supervisor may offer additional perspectives. If any ethical issues are raised, it is important to ensure the participant is clear about appropriate courses of action.

The supervisor is responsible for the timekeeping of the session. Being able to respectfully move the session on while checking that the coach is ready to do so is something that gets easier with practice! It can help to have stock phrases to hand such as: "So . . . that feels like quite a rich discussion. Are you OK for us to move to the next person now?" or "OK, I'm conscious of time. . . . Have we done enough to move your thinking forward a bit?" or "I'm aware we could spend much more time on this one".

This process is repeated for all the participants.

Summarising the session

The supervisor will continue to deliver the session by working around the group, ensuring that all points raised at the start of the session have been addressed.

Once each participant has had the opportunity to discuss what they brought to supervision and feedback has been given and received, if there is any time left there may be an opportunity to invite any additional questions from the group that have not previously been raised or that have emerged as a result of the discussions.

To close the session, the supervisor summarises the key learning points that have been addressed during the taster session. Inviting the participants to share one final comment before closing the call – such as an insight gained, a learning point or an acknowledgement – is a supportive way of bringing the session to an end.

Follow-up

Reminding participants to give feedback on the taster session and to spend time reflecting on their experience is pivotal for their personal development.

Provided that permission to do this has been gained, either before or during the session, the supervisor may wish to circulate any additional resources that were discussed by themselves or the other participants during the session.

Common issues explored during group supervision taster sessions

The most common issues brought to supervision by those experiencing it for the first time are concerns about how the supervision process itself will work, that they will be chastised for their approach and that they find themselves lacking somehow – yet they also seek to normalise their experiences when working with clients.

New coaches often will have concerns about how they meet the coaching standards and competencies of their professional bodies. The range of issues brought to supervision can generally be structured as the following outline. Although these are drawn from the Coaching Competencies of one professional body, they are also generic enough to apply across the coaching field.

Meeting ethical, legal, and professional guidelines

Frequent concerns arise in understanding how and when to refer a client to another professional. Knowing when a client needs professional assistance outside of the coach's area of expertise, and how to communicate that with the client, is often a source of anxiety. How to comply with the prevailing laws of the country in which the coaching takes place and/or in which the client organisation is operating, comes a close second. Questions tend to focus on General Data Protection Regulations covering data protection and privacy in the European Union and the European Economic Area and rules and legislation and maintaining confidentiality when working with a sponsor and client.

Experienced coaches might bring increased depth and complexity to inquiries around ethical dilemmas. They may also bring concerns about how they increase their range of interventions and tools while being mindful of the systemic impact that these will bring. For more experienced supervisors, supervision may be more about deepening their practice, enhancing their (self) awareness and enhancing their higher-level capabilities.

Establishing the coaching agreement and outcomes

Contracting with a coaching client is key. For novice coaches, this is usually an area of concern. Supervision is the ideal arena to discuss and determine what needs to be included. Supporting the coach to understand their own coaching approach and, more importantly, how they can then articulate it to their client, is a valuable use of supervision as a resource.

Experienced coaches also run into difficulty in contracting. They are often engaged in complex team assignments or senior-level assignments with multiple stakeholders, presents myriad opportunities for something to fall out of alignment.

Managing self and maintaining coaching presence

With so much to think about in regard to setting up the coaching contract, meeting ethical, legal and professional guidelines, successfully employing a coaching model and being in service of the client, it comes as no surprise that this is often high on a new coach's agenda. Offering a themed session around this topic is an excellent way of supporting a coach to build their confidence when working with clients.

Experienced coaches who are new to supervision may be tentative about bringing issues, especially those connected to managing self and maintaining coaching presence. A skilful supervisor will be able to bring these concerns and considerations to the fore, offering more depth for discovery that the whole group may benefit from.

Designing strategies and actions

Understanding the best way to inspire clients, providing support while learning to implement new behaviours and knowing how to leave accountability with one's clients can be a source of angst for coaches. Providing a safe space to discuss ideas and strategies for the coach to implement is a valuable use of the supervision space.

Experienced coaches coming to supervision for the first time may have a comprehensive toolkit of interventions. In this case, they might want to explore new models from recent training or how to reflect more deeply on standard strategies – or they may even be seeking a fresh approach to their work.

Undertaking continuous coach development

Having completed their training, new coaches are often confused about how to continue their personal and professional development. As we know, regular supervision provides a superb framework to support ongoing development, and a taster session around this topic can be useful for participants.

Experienced coaches may seek support from the supervision group to consider where to find their next developmental stretch.

Working within the organisational context

Many coaches will gravitate towards working within the executive arena, and attending a taster session on how to be of best service to senior leaders in a business context is likely to be a useful exploration. Having a good appreciation of setting up a tripartite contract, meeting the needs of additional key stakeholders, understanding the roles and responsibilities of those involved and maintaining confidentiality are key to establishing and delivering a successful intervention within corporate environments.

Progression

The purpose of offering group supervision taster sessions is to enable participants to experience and appreciate the value gained from engaging in coaching supervision. After the group session is an ideal opportunity to reiterate the benefits of ongoing supervision and any current opportunities that are relevant.

Professional membership body requirements

When participants engage in supervision, it is useful for them to know the specific accreditation or credentialing requirements of their professional membership body. These will differ according to the level of membership and/or accreditation or credentialing that members hold or are seeking to hold.

Any accreditation or credentialing application usually requires evidence not only of specific hours of supervision undertaken but that these have taken place over a definitive period of time. Information about the specific requirements can be found on the relevant professional coaching and supervision membership websites. Therefore, it is good practice to maintain a supervision log and update it regularly.

Further resources

For coaches wishing to try out supervision, there is no better resource than consulting a coaching network for advice and guidance. Discovering who provides supervision for peers and asking for recommendations and connections is a useful approach.

Many professional bodies have directories of those who offer supervision, and it is worth speaking to a number of these before choosing your supervisor. Most will offer an exploratory session so that a coach can experience their style and approach and assess whether the style of interventions seems beneficial for them.

Summary

Offering group supervision taster sessions provides a vital component in promoting supervision to the wider coaching population and educating those who have little or no knowledge of the benefits that this can bring. For coach training schools, it introduces their coaching students to the notion of continuous professional development and practice development as part of maintaining standards across coaching; for the supervisor, it may be a way to promote their offering and begin to nurture relationships with new coaches; for the professional body, a chance to influence the growing profession.

Participating in group supervision can be less scary for individuals stepping into new territory, as the camaraderie that this intervention engenders lends itself to reducing apprehension about the experience and making it an enjoyable one. It is not unusual for the taster session to be sprinkled with laughter as lightbulbs of insight flash and blinkers are removed.

By their very nature, these short supervision sessions cannot deliver the deep and meaningful learning and insights that develop over time when undertaking regular and consistent supervision. It takes time to build the trust and type of relationship that permits a human being to lay themselves open to feedback and challenge.

However, this does not mean that participating in taster sessions is without merit. Working with strangers in a safe environment and being open and transparent about perceived shortcomings while remaining receptive to receiving well-considered feedback is a useful addition to any professional development plan, especially if, as intended, it might sow the seeds for ongoing reflective practice.

The described format for group supervision taster sessions supports participants in gaining insights and learning, and most importantly, affords them the opportunity to experience for themselves the power of the supervisory relationship. In much the same way as the coaching intervention, the magic is in the co-creation of a relationship based on mutual trust and support.

Presenting a choice to coaches to either bring their own emergent issues, or to attend a specific themed session, gives the participant agency to choose. Experiencing a space that is held and contained by the supervisor explicitly for the development of participants through acceptance and a non-judgmental approach helps participants distinguish between coaching supervision and other forums which may be more critical to their development.

It is possible that attendees of a taster session will choose to pursue further group coaching with the supervisor. Sometimes it will emerge that the whole group wants to continue together, and it is worth mentioning this possibility when initially contracting with the group, provided this is within the wider contract of engagement.

In the same way that we take coaching models and techniques and adapt them to be of best service to our clients, this format of delivering a taster session is designed to offer a broad standard structure within which supervisors will bring their own personality and style and make it their own.

Notes

1 AC. (2020). The Association for Coaching. www.associationforcoaching.com.
2 EMCC. (2020). The European Mentoring and Coaching Council. www.emccglobal.org/.
3 ICF. (2020). The International Coach Federation. www.coachfederation.org/.
4 AOCS. (2020). The Association of Coaching Supervisors. www.associationofcoaching-supervisors.com.
5 Centre for Coaching in Organizations. (2019). Group Supervision in Organizations. www.seslhd.health.nsw.gov.au/sites/default/files/groups/Improvement_Academy/Group_Supervision_in_organizations_WhitePaperFeb2019.pdf [Accessed: 8 January 2021].
6 Association for Coaching. (2020). AC Coaching Competency Framework, Association for Coaching. https://cdn.ymaws.com/www.associationforcoaching.com/ [Accessed: 8 January 2021].
7 Association for Coaching. (2020). AC Global Code of Ethics for Coaches, Mentors and Supervisors, Association for Coaching. www.associationforcoaching.com/ [Accessed: 8 January 2021].
8 Passmore, J. (2011). *Supervision in Coaching*. London: Kogan Page.

Chapter 13

Fifty-plus years of supervision

Individual, group, peer and community, the development of a distinct profession

Joan Wilmot Shohet

In this chapter, I describe my supervision journey over the past 50-plus years, including my current phase as "midwife" to the Independent Supervisors Network (ISN), a community of supervisors made up of peer supervision groups and peer supervision dyads and based on the principle of peer accountability.

I love my work. I am a supervisor. It is an amazing job. I would describe myself as a phenomenological process and systemic supervisor. Bert Hellinger describes being phenomenological as:

> *[Demanding] great self-discipline . . . the first thing one has to do is to forget everything one has heard on the subject . . . It's like emptying yourself inwardly. Secondly one has to be without intention . . . Then one waits.*
>
> (Hellinger, 2006: p. 21)

This is the process, and he describes it as being

> *Without desire, knowledge and fear.*

Psychoanalyst Wilfred Bion (2018) echoes this direction to go into a session without memory, desire or understanding. Both Hellinger and Bion ask us to be empty and let what needs to happen to come through us. It is as if we spend the first half of our lives, or part of ourselves, accumulating techniques, theories and such; the second part of our lives, or the other part of ourselves, is spent emptying ourselves and waiting.

A memory surfaces of the first time this happened with me. I was completely stuck and didn't know what to do or say. *I* couldn't do anything, and then *I* was out of the way. All *I* did was trust just enough to stay in that not-knowing place, and the work happened perfectly. So, maybe we first experience the place of not knowing when we have to give up trying and surrender because there is no other choice.

> *In the end, learning how to disappear is the best way I've found to make my true self visible to myself and others.*
>
> (Jeff Tweedy, 2020)

DOI: 10.4324/978100314345-14

What I like to do as a supervisor is to create a space that people come into loving the work they do and/or finding the work they love. It is our creativity, our form of self-expression, our method of surrender. It is place where there is no separation between work and play. A place where one can be one's authentic self. We are the music and the space, as in the quote attributed to Claude Debussy (Koomey, 2001): "Music is the space between the notes". Supervision is the space. As Peter Caddy, co-founder of the Findhorn Foundation, said:

Work is love in action (Miller, 2017).

Here is an example. I was travelling on a Southern service train, watching the guard. He was both uniquely himself and at the same time in service to us, the passengers, the train company, the job. He hosted the train. As each person stepped onto the train, he checked their tickets, not only to make sure they had the correct ticket, but also to see if they were in the right carriage to be closer to the exit for their station. At each station he would move – *balletically* is the best word I can use to describe the way he moved – to the doors and acknowledge everyone leaving and boarding. He was joyful. He was his authentic self. The impact on me of seeing someone in their own authority and at the same time in service was an affirmation that life and therefore me as part of life, is simple and perfect just as it is, no separation, no struggle; just at home in one's own skin. In an interview between Hedy Schleifer[1] and Sue Wintgens (Wintgens, 2020), Schleifer said:

You can either be a hostage to your life or a host to it.

He was clearly the latter.

I have been talking about love and work. And this brings me back to my work, my life, my autobiography and to exploring the reasons why I have been so passionate and engaged with supervision all my adult life. As a child growing up in the late 1940s and 1950s in postwar Britain, work was central to everyone around me; without it we could well have become homeless or gone hungry. It was how people defined others and themselves, how they valued themselves and were valued by the outside world.

Early on in my childhood, I recall that the question following, "How are you?" was often, "How's work?" and then, directly to me, "What are you going to do when you grow up?" I never thought about how cultural this was until I started learning Greek about five years ago and discovered their second question was usually, "Are you married?". I realised the values and identity of Greek culture were measured differently from the society and culture in which I had grown up and this contrast helped me become aware of and appreciate both cultures.

So work was what my parents and relatives spent the majority of their lives doing or talking about. Jobs, pay packets (and later, salary), training (at night school) for better work, and then there was housework and homework and, as soon as I was old enough, a Saturday job. How much are we hostage to work, and how much is it a segue to freedom and independence? It is our thinking, our beliefs that are the determining factor, and they can always be enquired into and moved towards health.

In 2010, a BBC TV programme called "Jobless" (BBC, 2010) offered a powerful illustration of the importance of work in our lives and to our well-being. People who had been made redundant were interviewed. The comments from those who had just lost their jobs were striking:

> . . . *Loss of self-value, worth, respect.*
> . . . *Drifting into a huge chasm until you eventually think the place would be better off without you.*
> . . . *The link between jobless and mental health can happen in five weeks, low self-esteem, anxiety, depression and insomnia.*

And a comment from a nine-year-old girl on seeing her parents jobless was particularly striking.

> *You do a job for money and also for other things like self 'esteemt' (sic) and stuff, so I'd like a job when I grow up.*

Work as autobiography

We are always coming from our autobiography – our own autobiography plays out in our work – the career choices we make, the models with which we resonate, the people with whom we work (Keemar, 2020).

Or, as Krishnamurti said, *our conditioning* (Krishnamurti, 1984).

I invite you to look at your life and work from the perspective of your lived autobiography. It is food for the soul.

As I look back to my roots, it would appear from the limited information I have, that I come from a long line of workers/labourers and domestic servants. I quite often joke that I am at heart a cleaner and that supervision is polishing our mirrors and glasses so we can all see what is to be done and how to do it. Only with my stepfather and my own generation and three out of my four adult children has my family moved into salaried professions or freelance careers. Interestingly, one of our four sons works with his hands, following in the footsteps of the maternal grandfather he never met.

Before my mother married, she was a secretary in a factory making aircraft engines, and then she worked as a school secretary for most of the time we were growing up. Only recently did I realise I was brought up by a working mother – it wasn't the norm in the 1950s in Britain. It was a mixture of personal circumstances – my mother was twice widowed in her twenties; the second time, my sister and I both were under two, so she had to work – and social pressures. Her family had moved from Wales to Coventry to find work when she was in her late teens. Coventry was an industrial city where there was work, and workers were needed both during and after the Second World War.

For me, supervision is a place where one has space and time to hold and honour the worker and the work: something that may not have been available to my ancestors; the hero's journey of their ordinary and at the same time extraordinary lives mainly untold, unsung and unrecognised even by themselves. The poet and leadership consultant David Whyte beautifully conveys this in his writing (1994, 2001, 2009).

A supervisee illustrated this many years ago when she introduced her new client to me by recounting the story of his mother when she was pregnant with him and then in his first year of life. It was fraught with accidents, mismanagement, mishaps, misfortune and seemingly negligent practice from professionals – and then she told me, almost in passing, what his work was. He was a Health and Safety Officer! In that moment we could see that he could not have become anything else, and in realising it there in the supervision, something laughed and something breathed.

In recounting the previous story, I have a dawning realisation that maybe there is something in there reminiscent of my own early life which has led me to my work as a supervisor, going much further back. My mother lost her first child in childbirth and nearly died herself as the result of botched work. I am named after my brother, who would have been called John. The story that passed down to me was that after this happened, my father went to the hospital, lifted the doctor up by his collar and said, "Don't you ever do that to a woman again". In the telling of the story, it was somehow conveyed to me that the doctor was humbled, learned from and transformed by the exchange that day. Maybe this was my first experience of radical supervision?

I love meeting people and looking with them at their lives through the lens of their work. The supervision relationship gives me permission to do that. As Judy Ryde, psychotherapist and trainer, said in conversation with me, supervision is like going into Dr Who's Tardis. It can look quite ordinary on the outside, but when you are invited in and enter (both are necessary), it is vast, infinite, beautiful and awesome. It is where our personal and professional development can walk hand in hand.

My supervision journey

I first received supervision in the mid-1960s and started giving supervision five years later, and very soon after, I began training supervisors. Over the years, I have experienced supervision as a student, as a social worker in mental health and therapeutic community settings and for the past 40 years as a freelance supervisor. I have experienced tutorial, clinical, managerial and supportive supervision. The four aspects have enriched each other greatly, and I felt nourished, supported and challenged by all my supervisors and thought supervision was the best thing ever. It was only later that I discovered this had not been the experience for some people. In fact, that was a blind spot of mine. I wonder if some of my own supervisees may have suffered from my exuberant pursuit of what riches might lie below the surface – unaware of the bruising they may have experienced in similar situations.

Looking over my career in supervision reminds me of the work of psychiatrist Ivor Browne (2013), author of Music and Madness. Here he recounts the changes that have taken place in the mental health field over the 20th century. In my supervision journey, we can also see some of the changes that have taken place over the past half century in the field of supervision. Specific training in supervision began, followed by accreditation. There seems to be a trajectory, whatever the work or profession. A need arises, and something comes into form, followed by a request/demand to provide training in it, purportedly to increase quality and value. It then becomes a requirement and finally an institution forms out of it, or another institution takes it over or under its wing. I wonder about the dynamics and unconscious forces that drive this universal process and what, other than the original need, is now driving it or being driven by it. I come back to this at the end of this chapter.

In thinking about the development of supervision as a process and as a profession in its own right and the changes that have occurred in my time as a supervisor, I like Gaie Houston's definition of supervision – the three P's of Plumbing, Poetry and Policing (Houston, 1990) It is useful to wonder in what order those elements arise in the work and how the order may have changed over the years and continues to change. The biggest challenge or discipline is being able to reflect on all of this and to be able to recognise our own subjective lenses. The observer is always part of the field, as much as the observed.

My journey, 1966–1972

I first experienced supervision on my first two placements from my postgraduate social work course in Sheffield. In both, I had weekly one-to-one supervision, and I recall two things. One is the support I received, and the other is how I defended myself by trying to cover all bases ahead of my supervisor. My openness and my defensiveness appear to be key components of my personality, and it was during that year I first began to have a dim awareness of them and give them some attention.

My first paid work was at the age of 23 as a trainee psychiatric social worker in a mental hospital working with hospital patients or their spouses. My supervisor was the head of the social work department, known in those days as the Lady Almoner. I met weekly with her for supervision, and there were regular staff team meetings which were very much along the lines of supervision and involved everyone, including the secretaries. It also involved locking the door, so as not to be disturbed, and sherry. Many years later I met an ex-colleague from those days who told me that the lady almoner was very likely an alcoholic. Nonetheless, I always found the team/group supervision very helpful, either because of, or in spite of, the sherry. I also learnt a valuable lesson from both that job and the patients – or maybe I always saw the world that way, and it was an affirmation – we are all simultaneously amazing and insane. It is a fine line of circumstances and intensity whether we end up as the patient, the therapist or the supervisor.

It was also the 1960s, a time when humanistic psychotherapy, like many other things, was bursting into the field. There was Thomas Szasz (1961) who, in his book

The Myth of Mental Illness and throughout his career, argued that mental illness was "a metaphor for human problems in living" and that the patients were willing to carry the madness for society. There was co-counselling and cooperative enquiry, Ronnie Laing and Joseph Berke, family therapy, birth work, Quaesitor, the growth centre started by David Blagden Marks and a whole host of therapists coming from many different countries and disciplines. They brought new ideas like seeing how the world is inter-connected, how we project and how we create our own reality – or, put another way, the dawning realisation that we were, as De Mello (1990) says,

> *Seeing the world not as it is but as we are.*

Here is a personal story to illustrate that from an early session in therapy. At the age of 28, I had gone into individual and group therapy with a Gestalt/Reichian therapist, Richard Dror.

Richard:	*Joan, everything is 95% projection.*
Joan:	*No way! (Said hotly and indignantly.)*
Two weeks later	
Richard:	*Joan, I was wrong about projection being 95% projection.*
Joan (thinking):	*Of course you were wrong!*
Richard:	*It's 100%.*
Joan:	*What!*

It took me a few years to begin to believe him, and I am still embracing that truth, being humbled and often made uncomfortable by it.

My journey towards supervision continues in Gosport in my role as a mental welfare officer. Based in the Town Hall alongside other local government officers, there was no clinical, or even management supervision. The clients and books were my supervision, in particular Searles (1979) and Mattinson (1975) and in addition informal peer supervision with my two colleagues and my first husband, David Wilmot. Learning from my clients and my peers was invaluable. I was young, innocently curious, and naïve, but, maybe as a consequence, open. I think what that gave me was a lack of "othering" and a lack of fear. I had a complex caseload, with responsibility for emergency mental health admissions and assessment of risk and danger to either the client or others. It was heart-opening and humbling work and a space where I was rarely judgmental, not as I was/am in my personal life. In fact, that is the core of supervision for me, as epitomised by Rumi (1207–1273). It truly is "the place beyond wrongdoing and rightdoing, I'll meet you there".

Amidst the profound nature of the work, I learnt the delicate art of giving and receiving; the balance of "give and take" that orders life, love and relationships. Much later, I saw this reflected in the family constellation work of Hellinger (1998). However, at the time I was offered cups of tea at each home visit and accepted them all. I remember once drinking 13 cups of tea one day. I don't even like tea, but that wasn't the point.

Sometime after we left, I went back to Gosport and revisited some of my ex-clients – "it didn't work". I was no longer in the role, so the container of the contract couldn't work. Also, I had just completed a year's training in social work and had not integrated my learning, so I was coming more from my head than my heart or belly. I was no longer in that "empty" place that Bert Hellinger talks about at the beginning of this chapter, but I was filled with theory and techniques that I was keen to use and a desire to be helpful instead of "waiting".

My other local authority social work followed on from my two years in Gosport. I joined the newly formed Social Services in Kingston upon Thames in which the children and families, mental health services and welfare were all amalgamated under the 1970 Local Authority Social Services Act. It was an exciting time, and I thrived on the work. There was inevitably more administration and bureaucracy because of the increased size and complexity, but also opportunities for being part of creating it and inevitably also being subject to it. I learnt about systems and organisational dynamics, the power of story and how to interrupt story. To begin to see how the same dynamics turn up whatever the situation and the beginnings of the life-long lesson of not taking everything so personally. I had weekly supervision, and now, 40 years on, I am going back to weekly sessions. Having another or others at your back, side and in your face – what a gift!

Richmond Fellowship therapeutic community, 1972 – 1980

After a year's Certificate of Qualification in Social Work training at Croydon College and giving birth to my first son, I went to work for the Richmond Fellowship in a residential therapeutic community. I was literally a working mother, as my son came to work with me from the start. This is where I experienced work and personal and public life merged together – there was no real separation, although they each had their own boundaries, and it was important for me to be very conscious of those boundaries. They were the learning edges for all of us. Each aspect of the lived experience informed, and at times challenged, the other. The maintenance of the house and garden, its cleaning and the provision of meals were equally as therapeutic to the residents and staff as the therapy groups, individual therapy and weekly community meetings.

The house was also the senior staff training house. It was where, as a core staff team of four, we developed our own inhouse supervision and a supervision training programme for senior staff from other houses who would attend three-month placements at the house.

This is where I lived parallel process and projective identification: seeing, feeling and beginning to understand how we are dreamed up and dream each other up, co-creating our interactions with each other. Experiencing small- and large-group dynamics, looking at the community systemically and how to take it personally and not personally at the same time and learning ways to explore the coded language we all use to simultaneously connect with and hide from each other. The dance of fear and love, the dance of intimacy and withdrawal.

Only after considerable immersion did I/we come to have more of a cognitive understanding of what was going on and could we, as a team, make some combined sense of it. In those felt insights, the shifts could happen in the individual and/or the community. We would come to discover that if we embraced whatever arose in one of us, especially if we paid attention to sensations and didn't take them personally, we were able to recognise the possibility that we were also picking up some of the unconscious dynamics at play. We became more able to enter into "the knowing field", a term taken from constellation work by Barbara Morgan (2017), and in doing so we could navigate the ruptures and transform through them.

In-house supervision was weekly, both one-to-one and group. The groups each had their own distinct purpose, so there were case discussions, business, reflective pre- and post-groups for the groups we ran for the residents, learning meetings and feelings meetings, to name a few. As I write this, I see how the weekly supervision structure held us in transformative work for the clients, the staff and the community that would not otherwise have been possible – the three-fold mutual healing process between client, practitioner and supervisor as described by Gertrud Mander in *Supervising Psychotherapy* (2002).

In this community, I learnt about boundaries and at the same time how to be inclusive. Instead of trying to create the "perfect environment", we found that what was, was the perfect environment for the therapeutic work. We coined the phrases "everything is data" and "everything, but everything is grist for the mill" and "unclear contracting" – phrases that I still use today in my supervision training groups. As a team we encountered numerous "lightbulb moments" when assumptions suddenly became visible that had inevitably been made at the beginning of a contract but had been invisible and could not be understood until we encountered them later.

We learnt how tricky the voice in our head is and how convincing it can be, even though it clearly isn't true. We learnt how aggressive self-protection and defensiveness can be – fiercely protecting ourselves as if our lives depended on it. If I decide I have to defend against you, I am making you an enemy. No wonder you don't like it and want to attack me in return. We learnt how infectious fear can be and how infectious love can be. We learnt skills and understandings not only for our profession but also for our lives and our relationships.

Freelance psychotherapist, supervisor and trainer supervisor

In 1980, I set up in private practice as a psychotherapist. Peter Hawkins, Robin Shohet and I had begun teaching group dynamics, team development and supervision whilst at the Richmond Fellowship. We established the CSTD during our final few months there. We were being commissioned by outside agencies to run supervision and team development courses and from these, with Judy Ryde, we developed the supervision and supervision training courses that we run to this day.

Besides seeding changes in mental health provision, with the emptying of the mental hospitals and the birthing of community health provision such as the Richmond Fellowship and the therapeutic community, the humanistic movement in psychotherapy that emerged in the late 1950s and early 1960s was also affecting change in other areas too, such as education (Rumi et al., 2004). Shortly after leaving the Richmond Fellowship Peter Hawkins and I joined the Institute for the Development of Human Potential (IDHP, 2001), which grew out of the Human Potential research movement at Surrey University and was an organisation that ran two-year part-time courses in group facilitation, started in 1976 by David Blagden Marks, John Heron, Tom Feldberg, Frank Lake and Kate Hopkinson.

Its values and principles were very much in keeping with the Zeitgeist of the time – self-direction, self-actualisation, the peer principle, the strength of community, self and peer assessment and the belief in human potential. I was part of the IDHP for more than 10 years. Once the course that Peter Hawkins and I facilitated was validated by the committee, like everyone else, we became full members of the committee. It was the most flattened hierarchy I have ever experienced and, at the same time, required me to step into my authority.

Two major learnings from my journey with IDHP and which confirmed my previous work as a supervisor are encapsulated in the following African proverbs:

> *It takes a village to raise a child.*
> *If you want to go fast, go alone; if you want to go far, go together.*

It describes a community model of holding: the supervisor holds the practitioner, who is in turn held by the tribe. With any individual, group organisation or system, the question is, how do you take responsibility, develop and be accountable to your patients, clients, customers, employers and hold and be held yourself? What structures can serve and both mirror and model the society in which it exists?

The emergence of the Independent Supervisors Network (ISN)[2]

In the counselling and psychotherapy world in the late 1970s and 1980s, the British Association for Counselling and Psychotherapy and the UK Council for Psychotherapy were growing, stepping into and taking on those roles and responsibilities and becoming accrediting bodies. In 1991 and 1992, two conferences were held on the dynamics of accreditation. These conferences were a response to concerns about the professionalisation of the psychological therapies into bodies that included in their remit the registering, licensing and training and decision-making of who could or could not be counsellors and psychotherapists. The Independent Practitioners Network was one of the outcomes of those two conferences.

As mentioned earlier, this seems to be a stage of development for many organisms, organisations and professions. What drives it? Is it first and foremost size? Is it a need to be recognised by the "outside world", to be seen and take one's rightful place? Is it a fear of being taken over? Is it a fear of loss of integrity from both inside and outside? Is it a need to belong? I would imagine it is all of these and more.

With regard to supervision as a profession, we seem to be at a similar point. It can be seen as and can become a separate profession and can set up its own network with ISN as that body, and if it doesn't, it will probably be taken over by another body or bodies, most likely the psychotherapy and counselling bodies.

Everything has emerged from what went before and then becomes distinct from it. The child comes from the parents and then, over time, develops its own identity, leaves the family and sets up its own family. So it is with supervision – it has elements and features of counselling and psychotherapy, and supervision is an integral part of that practice, as is the child with its family of origin, and over time it grows into its own self. The most significant difference and development is in the capacity it has developed to hold people in their work. Supervision is a process, a relationship; a verb, not a noun. The words "supervision" and "supervisor" are both a challenge. They need to be explained, described, embodied, experienced. Here are few I have heard over the years – a "time to think", "work facilitation", "work discussion group", "therapy for work", "reflective practice", "spiritual practice", "holistic medicine" and "shamanic practice".

As supervision is both process and relationship, it needs a body and a structure that reflects this, and a network of peers can offer this. Parallel process is at the core of supervision and integral to it. Supervision works when the supervisor, the supervisee and the supervision both mirror and model the processes of all that is involved.

The idea of the ISN was first discussed in 2016. Looking back over my own journey of supervision, the birthing of ISN seems part of my own journey and that of the supervision profession. Therefore, it is simultaneously personal and not personal – something I learnt as I was catapulted into this world by caesarean section but only came to understand much later, during birth regression work.

The ISN is currently a small but growing network of peer groups and dyads who from time to time meet up with another group or dyad. There are also yearly conferences. Right now, it is poised on a threshold – in a liminal space, a space where we have left something behind, yet we are not yet fully in something else. Life feels rather like that at the moment too.

This challenge of being poised between individualism and community is reflected in ISN's having two names – Independent and Interdependent. It is reflected in our western society either or/, us and them, separation, 'othering', difference, me against the world, blame, justice, power, helplessness. I could go on. So how to hold the 'and/and', the interdependence. There is an ancient African word Ubunto which I am told translates to "I am because you are". The poem 'Please call me by my true names' (Thich Nhat Hanh, 2005) speaks all of this too.

For me supervision is where I can practice and live this. A space in which I can hold and be held in relationship to what is important to us both individually and collectively. The tenets of slowing, down, enquiry and parallel process in its ability to both mirror what is there and model new possibilities; and how focusing on the macrocosm of what the supervisee brings, opens up to the microcosm of each moment in our lives, makes all this possible. The joy of being self and other (IDHP, 2001).

A good time to ask questions and enquire, which is the very core of supervision. So here are some:

Is supervision a distinct profession?
Is it a resource for any work or profession?
If so, how can it become a visible resource, a process for all work and workers –
. teachers, plumbers, builders, shopkeepers? The list is endless.
Do supervisors and supervision need their own institution?
If so, what form most represents its essential values and processes?
Can it be modelled on an Open Tribe[3] (Goss, 2014)?
What structures would enable it to provide support and challenge for the
supervision tribe?

And here are some possible aspirations for ISN:

How can it develop and encompass the personal, professional and spiritual devel-
opment of the profession and its members?
How can it create a place and space where accountability, relationship and
mutual learning can be engaged with?
Change always starts at the edge so how can it go to the edge and step onto the
path that is not yet there?

As a way of engaging with that edge and in the joyful spirit of enquiry that supervision is, I want to conclude with a poem by Hafiz.

> *Pulling out the chair beneath your mind*
> *And watching you fall upon God*
> *What else is there for Hafiz to do*
> *That is any fun in this world?*

Substitute your own name for Hafiz and your own beliefs, values, whatever God is for you – and see what you fall upon. What else is there for us to do that is any fun in this world?

Notes

1 Clinical psychologist and couples and relationship therapy expert Hedy Schleifer (www. hedyschleifer.com).
2 Independent Supervisors Network (ISN) began in 2016 and is also known as Interdependent Supervisors Network.
3 Open Tribe is the concept of balance between two compelling human imperatives: one towards connectedness and belonging and the other towards exploration and adventure.

References

Bion, W. R. (2018). *Elements of Psychoanalysis*. London: Routledge.

Browne, I. (2013). *Music and Madness*. Cork, Ireland: Atrium.

De Mello, A. (1990). *Awareness*. New York: Penguin Random House Company.

Goss, S. (2014). *Open Tribe*. Chadwell Heath: Lawrence Wishart Publishing.

Hafiz 14th Century Poet.

Hellinger, B. (1998). *Love's Hidden Symmetry: What Makes Love Work in Relationships*. Phoenix, USA: Zeig, Tucker & Theisen Inc.

Hellinger, B. (2006). *No Waves Without the Ocean* (pp. 21–24). Heidelberg: Carl-Auer Verlag.

Houston, G. (1990). *Supervision and Counselling*. London: Rochester Foundation.

IDHP. (2001, June–July). *Self & Society*, 29(2). www.idhp.org

IPN. www.ipnetwork.org.uk.

ISN. www.independendentsupervisorsnetwork.com.

Keemar, K. (2020). Presentation at ISN Conference Supervision as Autobiography. 3 July.

Koomey, J. G. (2001). *Turning Numbers into Knowledge: Mastering the Art of Problem Solving* (p. 96). El Dorado Hills, USA: Analytic Press.

Krishnamurti, J. (1984). *Dialogue 1 Brockwood Park, England – 05 October 1984*. https://jkrishnamurti.org/content/what-do-we-mean-conditioning [Accessed: August 2021].

Ladinsky, D., & Hafiz, S. (2006). *I Heard God Laughing: Poems of Hope and of Joy*. London: Penguin.

Mander, G. (2002). *Supervising Psychotherapy* (pp. 48–49). London: Sage.

Mattinson, J. (1975). *The Reflection Process in Casework Supervision*. London: Tavistock Institute of Marital Studies.

Miller, T. (2017). *Go to the Brink and Look Over: Peter Caddy's Inspiration*. https://www.findhorn.org/blog/petercaddyinspiration/ [Accessed August 2021].

Morgan, B. (2017). *Coming Home: A First Step Into the World of Family Constellations*. Bath, UK: Knowing Field Press.

Richmond Fellowship. www.richmondfellowship.org.uk.

Rumi, J., Barks, C., Moyne, J. (2004). A Great Wagon. In *Selected Poems*. London: Penguin Classics.

Ryde, J. In Conversation with Judy Ryde. *Psychotherapist and Trainer*. www.cstdbath.co.uk.

Searles, H. (1979). *Countertransference and Related Subjects*. New York: International University Press.

Szasz, T. (1961). *The Myth of Mental Illness*. New York: Harper.

Thich Nhat Hanh. (2005). *Cali Me by My True Names: The Collected Poems*. Berkeley, USA: Parallax Press.

Tweedy, J. (2020). Jeff Tweedy on Song Writing. *The Guardian*, 25 November 2020.

Whyte, D. The Heart Aroused: Poetry and the Preservation of the Soul in Corporate America (1994); Crossing the Unknown Sea: Work as a Pilgrimage of Identity (2001); The Three Marriages: Reimagining Work, Self and Relationship (2009)

Wintgens, S. (2020). Kairos Encounter Centre. https://suewintgens.co.uk/video-resources/. Interview with Hedy Schleifer.

Woods, B. (Director). (2010). *Jobless* [Film]. True Vision TV. truevisiontv.com

Index

Note: Page numbers in *italics* indicate a figure and page numbers in **bold** indicate a table. Page numbers followed by "n" indicate a note.